THE DYNAMICS OF INSTITUTIONAL CHANGE

The Dynamics of Institutional Change

Local Government Reorganization
in Western Democracies

edited by
Bruno Dente and Francesco Kjellberg

SAGE Modern Politics Series Volume 19
Sponsored by the European Consortium for
Political Research/ECPR

Ⓢ SAGE Publications
London · Newbury Park · Beverly Hills · New Delhi

Chapter 1 and editorial material
© B. Dente and F. Kjellberg 1988
Chapter 2 © D.E. Ashford 1988
Chapter 3 © F. Kjellberg 1988
Chapter 4 © M. Kiviniemi 1988
Chapter 5 © L.J. Sharpe 1988
Chapter 6 © Yves Mény 1988
Chapter 7 © T.J. Anton 1988
Chapter 8 © B. Dente 1988

First published 1988

SAGE Publications Ltd
28 Banner Street
London EC1Y 8QE

SAGE Publications Inc
2111 West Hillcrest Street
Newbury Park, California 91320

SAGE Publications India Pvt Ltd
C–236 Defence Colony
New Delhi 110 024

SAGE Publications Inc
275 South Beverly Drive
Beverly Hills, California 90212

British Library Cataloguing in Publication Data

The Dynamics of institutional change:
    local government reorganization in
    western democracies. — (Sage modern
    politics series; 19).
    1. Local government   2. Comparative
    government
    I. Dente, Bruno   II. Kjellberg, Francesco
    352′.000473   JS67

ISBN 0–8039–8043–4

Library of Congress catalog card number 87–062786

Printed in Great Britain by J.W. Arrowsmith Ltd, Bristol

Contents

Preface

Joint ventures in research have normally a long period of incubation. This volume is no exception to the rule. It all started at the meeting of the European Consortium for Political Research in Salzburg in 1984, where we organized one of the sessions with the ambitious title 'Towards a Theory of Local Government Reorganization'. We had both previously made some attempts to tackle the subject. We now wanted to try out some of our ideas about the complexity of institutional transformations at the local level, and to entice our colleagues to join us in this enterprise.

We felt at that time that amazingly little had been done to unravel this ubiquitous feature of contemporary political development. There were, certainly, a number of informative and well-phrased descriptions of reorganizations in single countries. But comparative studies and systematic attempts to understand this almost universal phenomenon, were hard to come by; let alone any theorizing about the topic. We were faced with a glaring discrepancy between a multitude of empirical facts, in many cases elegantly couched, and a conspicuous lack of analytical frameworks and theoretical perspectives. It seemed worthwhile to try to fill the gap.

The major part of this volume has its origin at the ECPR meeting in Salzburg. To widen the comparative scope and to broaden the gamut of theoretical perspectives, we later invited other colleagues to participate in this venture. Having now reached an end (of sorts), we would like to thank the contributors for all their patience and persistence. Hopefully, the enterprise has sensitized us all to the need of pursuing the subject further.

We would also like to acknowledge the benevolent support by the Sage editors and not least the useful comments by the anonymous referee. It helped us to avoid quite a few pitfalls.

Most Western countries (and a number of other countries) have for years been involved in reorganizing their local government system. Too little seems to be known in each country about what the others are doing, and why they are doing it. This volume may offer some clues. But first and foremost, it aims to place the general phenomenon of institutional transformations on the research agenda.

Bruno Dente   Francesco Kjellberg
Milan   Oslo

1

Introduction

Bruno Dente and Francesco Kjellberg

The problem stated

Few government reforms have been as widespread as the reforms at the sub-national level that have taken place in the last two or three decades. Anyone looking for a Western country that has not experienced some local government reorganization in one form or the other, would soon become discouraged. There have, of course, been other important institutional reforms in many countries during this period, but hardly any have been as ubiquitous as the reforms of the sub-national units and of the relations between the various levels of government.

However, this common trend has its counterpart in the great variation of its forms in different contexts. In some countries the reorganization has mainly consisted of redrawing the administrative boundaries of the territorial units, with or without a reshaping of their organizational structure. In other countries the emphasis has been much more on a redistribution of tasks among the various levels, most frequently combined with attempts at reshaping the financial relations between them. The impression of variety is compounded by the fact that in some cases the reorganization has had a comprehensive character, its various elements being considered, decided and implemented in a fairly integrated fashion, while in other cases the process has been one of piecemeal change, each reform being enacted independently. Furthermore, this general trend towards reorganization does not preclude striking differences in the politicization of the process: in some situations we have been confronted with a lively political debate on the reform proposals, with ideological principles pitched against one another, while in other instances the discussion, if any, has been quite subdued and the reforms seemingly uncontroversial.

Trying to come to grips with these administrative events raises two sets of questions. The first addresses their near-universality. Why have so many developed societies experienced some kind of basic reorganization (or attempts at reforms) of local and regional government? What has been the basic motivator behind the ubiquitous pattern of institutional change? The second set of questions refers to the variability of the reforms. Why have they taken place at different stages and why has their substantive content varied in different countries? And why has the political debate on the reorganization been more intense in some cases than in others?

There has been no lack in recent years of detailed descriptions of such reforms in single countries, but few attempts have been made to compare them systematically, in order to uncover the underlying factors that have generated and moulded the reorganizational process. While edging forward our knowledge of the varieties of reform, the contributions assembled, for instance, by Rowat (1980), Gunlicks (1981) and Zehetner (1983) have also sensitized us to the analytical problems in comparing the various experiences. Indeed, a reading of them makes it clear that the seemingly simple questions raised above call for complex answers. They depend on a differentiation between categories of reform and between the various factors that might be at play in the reshaping of sub-national units of government.

The short answer to the question, why so much reorganization, is that it is intimately linked to recent developments in the public sphere; it is a reflection of what we used to term the welfare state, but now more aptly tend to term the interventionist state. Such a view, in all its generality, has lately gained wide currency. It is indeed obvious that local government reorganization would hardly have taken place without the dramatic expansion of the public sector in most advanced democracies since the Second World War. From this point of view local government reorganization may be looked upon as an 'institutional afterthought' (Ashford, 1982). It appears everywhere as an attempt to solve the tension between the organizational requirements the expansion has given rise to and existing institutional arrangements. However, it is also evident that the ways in which the widening of the public sphere has taken place, the specific character it has had at various stages, and not least the ideological elements supporting local government, have had an impact on the types of reform, on their sequence in time and on the conflicts they have engendered.

These are some of the issues dealt with in this volume. By bringing together analyses of the reorganizational experiences in different countries, the book confronts the questions of comparative study of institutional change and of analytical perspectives on the dynamics behind such changes.

Local government reorganization and the new institutionalism

Political science has recently experienced what almost amounts to a paradigmatic shift — a recurrent phenomenon in the discipline. There has indeed been an increasing interest in the state as an institutional entity. Attempts 'to bring the state back' are legion, and the trend has even acquired its own label: new institutionalism (March and Olsen, 1984). The winds of change have come from many quarters. The trend has involved scholars with divergent orientations, ranging from neo-marxist political economy to public choice theories (Evans, Ruschemeyer and Stockpol, 1985; Ostrom, 1977). What it all amounts to is a renewed concern with the role of institutional variables, that is, the structure and functions of public agencies in shaping political phenomena. Such a concern was never completely extinct, and certainly not in local government studies, but its resurrection has given these studies a sharper analytical edge.

Like other approaches in political science, the new institutionalism has its limitations. The most apparent one is the difficulty of pursuing systematic cross-national research on the basis of institutional aspects. When the focus is on central government, as it largely has been, the new institutionalism might easily fail to produce fruitful and convincing results, due to lack of comparability. Central government institutions seem to differ so much from one country to another as almost to preclude any theoretically fruitful comparison. This barrier is compounded by the fact that most institutions at this level are fairly stable. If they change at all, they do so at such a slow pace as to blur the issue of the dynamics behind the change. The organizational structure and the functional scope will often be regarded as constant, or changing very slowly, and the question of how and why institutions alter will, therefore, hardly be raised in a significant way.

If not completely solved, the empirical problems of institutional change are attenuated when the new institutionalism is brought to bear on analyses at the sub-national level. The barriers are more easily surmounted at this level for a number of reasons: some of the basic institutional traits are common to most developed countries; the number of cases are infinitely larger; and — as already pointed out — there has been, at this level, a high incidence of fundamental reforms and rapid changes. The new institutionalism seems, therefore, a highly promising avenue in this case. Moreover, at the present juncture local government studies are in need of such a general approach which might enlarge their theoretical perimeter.

There is no doubt about the present boom in this field: an impressive number of books, articles, conference papers and dissertations pour out every year. If it ever appeared to be in a stagnant disciplinary backwater, the field is definitely not so any more. Nevertheless, local government studies may now be in danger of becoming the victims of their own success. Comparing, for instance, the numerous recent contributions with earlier more sparse scholarly production, one is struck by the difference in general significance of the more recent studies. The methodological and analytical standards may not be lower, but the questions raised now seem more strictly circumscribed to local government per se.

It is an unavoidable trend in any intellectual venture to generate a growing specialization, thus secluding its field of study from outside interventions. However, taking as a measuring rod, for instance, the discussions raised by Dahl's work on decision-making processes in New Haven (Dahl, 1962), the marginal value for the advancement of political science of recent local government research seems rather low. There are notable exceptions: one example would be the study by Putnam and his colleagues on Italian regional governments which has revived the interest in institutional performance (Putnam et al., 1983). But in general, there seems to be a growing insulation of recent local government studies from the mainstream of political science. Increasingly, theories and methods created outside the field are applied to local politics and administration, while the reverse seldom occurs.

The fortune of local government studies is presumably connected with the apparent facility for doing systematic comparative empirical research in this field. The data are often easily available, the main actors are readily accessible and a sufficient number of units of analysis assured at reasonable research costs. These advantages are not to be lightly dismissed. However, important as they are, they were not the main reasons why local politics and government attracted interest in the past. It was rather the particular position of local government at the crossroad between society, politics and administration, that raised so many questions. From Selznick to Dahl and Lowi, the 'classical' local studies enquired into the complex relationships between organization and environment, interests and politics, policies and political institutions (Selznick, 1949; Dahl, 1962; Lowi, 1964).

Raising the question of local institutional change, and moulding it in comparative perspective, might be a promising way of rescuing local government studies from their success and stimulating new ventures in a traditional field of research. We do know a good deal about the various aspects of local politics and administration, probably much more than at the national level, but we are suffering from a lack of general notions in this field. Concentrating on local government reform might be a way of reintroducing such notions, linking local government studies to the main streams in political science, thus widening their theoretical scope.

Some theoretical perspectives

Given the aims of this volume, it may be useful to take a quick look at the ways in which local government reorganization has been conceived and interpreted. There is no copious literature on the subject, few attempts having been made to isolate the main factors behind local reforms. In addition, they have been flawed by some confusion as to their level of analysis, as they generally move rather freely between a behavioural, an ideological and a structural level, without clarifying what are to be perceived as necessary and sufficient conditions for the reorganization process.

A case in point is Brand's comparison of the amalgamation reforms in Britain and Sweden (Brand, 1976), one of the first systematic attempts of this kind. Addressing the boundary reforms in the two countries and emphasizing their connection with other reforms ('like the change in educational system — and many other major public institutions'), Brand points in particular to the impediments to these reforms: 'Change in the structure of society involves an alteration of the symbols of the society' (1976: 43). And he goes on to argue that breaking through this resistance requires the development of a powerful group which regards such a large non-incremental change as necessary. This role was taken up by the planning profession in Britain and by the Social Democratic party in Sweden, reflecting the party's belief that social benefits should be applied equally throughout the country. Thus, even having as its starting point the expansion of the public sphere, Brand's discussion develops largely into an exercise in behavioural analysis, with a smattering of ideology thrown into it. It revolves around the question of who are the actors in the process, the promoters, the instigators and the opponents of the reform.

The importance of Brand's comparative study is that it articulates a general perspective, which has imbued a variety of contributions in local government studies. Indeed, most of the debate on centralization/decentralization trends in academic quarters as well as in administrative environs, is moulded in it. The driving forces are conceptualized as actors — bureaucrats, expert groups, political parties and organizations — motivated by a benign or a malign ideology, depending on an author's own value premises. The main concern is the decision-makers and their overt objectives, as exemplified by one of the most accurate descriptions of local reform in

England and Wales, namely the account by Wood (1976). Emphasizing the different stands by the Labour Party and the Conservatives, and the absence of a generally accepted solution to the problem of the 'best' structure for local government, Bruce Wood highlights the circumstances where eventually 'a Government initiative was possible' (1976: 177). Despite the differences in scope between this study and the work by Bourjol (1975) on French local government reforms, the basic perspectives are strikingly similar. In his detailed historical account Bourjol is, at least partly, concerned with the fortunes of the various political forces in framing and implementing the reforms in France. In the same vein, even if much more analytically oriented, Rhodes has presented a number of highly valuable contributions, making use of organizational theory and focusing on the strategies pursued by the actors in reform processes (Rhodes, 1980).

The merit of such micro-level analysis and of the behavioural approach is evident. It is extremely useful in coming to grips with the intricate political processes that might unfold within a given structural framework. But its limitations are also apparent. The perspective might shed light on how reorganization comes about, but it does not reveal much about why the reforms get started in the first place. If one wants to understand the changing character of the framework itself — why certain kinds of reforms are being considered rather than others and why they at some point become items on the political agenda — one has to pursue a more explicit structural analysis. A prerequisite for understanding the variations in the reform process over time is therefore an explanation of the pressure for change ingrained in different situations, that is to say, the structural conditions exploited or opposed by the various actors.

Some major steps have lately been taken in this direction by applying a neo-marxist approach — or a perspective influenced by this theoretical stance. Following Poulantzas (1968), O'Connor (1973) and other theorists, a number of scholars of a marxist leaning have been concerned with a redefinition of the state and the political system as something more complex than the marxian 'committee for managing the common affairs of the bourgeoisie'. The way out of this seeming theoretical impasse has been the notion of relative autonomy of the state from the economic structures and the 'social formations' of capitalist societies (Gough, 1979). This notion builds on a conception of the state as reflecting two basic and often contradictory functions: accumulation and legitimation. More specifically the contradiction will be reflected, according to O'Connor, in the tension between three distinct tasks: (1) social investment — projects and services that increase the productivity of labour; (2) social consumption — projects and services that lower the reproduction costs of labour power; (3) social expenses — projects and services which are required to maintain social harmony, that is, to fulfil the state's legitimization function. Part of the argument is also that the development of the welfare state has both expanded and made more complex the last task, and intensified the inherent tensions among all three of them.

The focus of these theoretical attempts has admittedly been the national government. Indeed, in some instances the local level as a separate entity has been obliterated altogether. Introducing the notion of 'local state', Cockburn (1977), indeed, defined the entire problem of intergovernmental relations, and *ipso facto* the whole set of reorganizational attempts, out of the analysis. Nevertheless, in a somewhat diluted form the approach has made its inroad in studies of local government transformations. Rejecting the doctrinaire stances of the neo-marxist school, Saunders, for example, defines the basic functions of the different levels of government in terms highly reminiscent of neo-marxist conceptions. While central government will have as its basic function social investment, local government will have social consumption as its functional prerogative. To this correspond, according to Saunders, different ideological principles and modes of interest articulation, creating a set of contradictions between the two levels (Saunders, 1981). Even if the contact with the reorganizational realities is somewhat sketchy, Saunders' model has usefully contributed to a more structural analysis.

Another more explicit attempt to consider local government reforms from such a structural viewpoint, has been made by Dearlove (1979). In spite of his polemics with neo-marxist scholars, he discloses a quite similar approach in his analysis of the reorganization of British local government. He explicitly defines 'the problem of local government' as an 'aspect of an overall problem of the public sector in a capitalist economy' (1979: 244). Almost paraphrasing O'Connor, he concludes by emphasizing that 'the problem of local government is but a facet of the general problem which requires the capitalist state to fulfil the two basic and often mutually contradictory functions of accumulation and legitimization' (1979: 256). The contemporary reorganization in Britain — as elsewhere, we must assume — reflects in this view the tension between capitalism and democracy, resolving it in a particular direction.

The neo-marxist approach exhibits some very strong points. Defining social consumption or collective consumption (Castells, 1976) as the distinctive functional trait of local government might serve well as theoretical underpinning for the analysis of the reform process. Not least, it opens up a discussion of the development of new kinds of legitimacy and of the role played by institutional changes in this.

However, what this approach wins in perspective by recognizing the links between local government and the surrounding social and economic relations, it loses in specification by its high level of abstraction, compared to a more pedestrian behavioural approach.

The way out of this seeming impasse is to connect the reorganizational pattern more clearly to the major stages in the development of the contemporary state in Western societies. Whether we term it welfare state or interventionist state, the important fact is that it accounts for around 50 percent of GDP in the various countries, in some cases even more. First came the expansion of the social service basket. A substantial increase in social welfare, education and health care took place, generally involving local authorities. This trend was bound to create tensions in relation to the existing institutional arrangements. The emphasis on larger and more efficient local units can be seen as an emanation of it. But also the second phase in the development of the welfare state necessarily had an impact on the role to be played by local government. More articulated regional and labour market policies led to an intertwining of central and local government. This phase also implied a substantial enlargement of public activity, as well as penetration into new areas, creating a need for more integrated policies at the various levels.

This approach has been successfully utilized by Ashford (1982). Contrasting Britain and France, in a detailed analysis he relates the expanding activities of the sub-national system to national policy-making. Central to this are 'the complexity of the welfare state and the mutual dependence that increasingly characterizes central–local relationships' (1982: 27). As will be seen, such a perspective is pervasive in the present volume. Several contributions focus on the connection between the welfare state development and the transformations of local government. This emphasis on the significance of local government reform for the development of the welfare state establishes a possible link between the behavioural aspects of local reform and the structural features enabling and constraining them, and fills, at least potentially, the lamented gap between macro and micro perspectives.

One reorganization or several reforms?

Any attempt to link a theoretical perspective with empirical data faces several analytical problems. The first in order of time is the need to ascertain whether the object of the enquiry is a single entity, or whether under the same label a number of different phenomena are revealed.

Since Linnaeus, the first requirements of any scientific venture is to provide sound classifications. It is therefore somewhat surprising that the different components of local government reform have seldom been spelled out. This might partly be due to the disproportionate interest shown by scholars in recent years towards the centralization/ decentralization issue. If everything concerning sub-national units is interesting only in so far as it alters the balance of power between centre and periphery, it has been argued, then all types of reform and change can be put on a single continuum. Accordingly, there is no need for further specification. The argument is hardly convincing. Even from this perspective one has at least to distinguish between the reforms which enhance local discretion and those which restrict it.

However, the problem is much more complex. Having learned that centre–periphery power relations hardly constitutes a zero sum game, since common goals exist, third parties intervene, and the environment is far from stable, there is an apparent need to classify local government reorganization along dimensions different from their external effects or their intended goals. In other words, exactly because we know by now that local government is more complicated than was once believed (and, one might add, much more important within the different polities), any attempt to study its institutional transformations must start with providing a categorization of their various forms and types.

A first necessary step, as noted by Kiviniemi in Chapter 4, is to differentiate between reforms and changes. The first term evokes a conscious attempt by a specific actor or set of actors to transform local reality, while the second term refers mainly to unanticipated consequences of decisions and actions with a different goal. The relevance of this distinction is obvious. Not every transformation of the institutional framework is the direct result of a political or administrative decision; many micro-decisions may, for instance, result in one major unforeseen institutional change.

Next is the need to establish a taxonomy of the reforms, since any description aiming to go beyond mere generalities will necessarily have to deal with various facets of reorganization. The increasing saliency of fiscal reforms, or more broadly the reshuffling of the grant system in most countries, has prompted an awareness of the variety of reorganization. But the different forms have seldom been considered together. A juxtaposition of fiscal and territorial reorganization hardly does justice to the complexity of the phenomenon, collapsing a multitude of reforms into two broad types. It would be an oversimplification to identify, for instance, territorial reorganization entirely with the redrawing of boundaries of the local government units at the district level (amalgamation), leaving out its possible functional alternatives like intermunicipal co-operation or reorganization at the intermediate level. Likewise, one needs to look at fiscal reorganization as only one of a whole array of attempts to reshape the division of functions between the various levels of government and the content of local government activity.

The reorganization pie could be divided in a number of ways. The value of a taxonomy depends entirely on its purpose, and the chapters which follow make reference, implicitly or explicitly, to different categorizations. However, a framework that seems to capture the outstanding features of local government reorganization can be constructed on the bases of two dimensions (Kjellberg, 1983). Firstly, the reforms might be differentiated according to whether they pertain to the relationship between the different levels, or whether they mainly concern the internal administration of local authorities. We might call this the scope of the transformation. It brings to our attention the fact that a direct impact on intergovernmental relations is only one of several goals of attempts at reorganization. Quite a few reforms are indeed solely aimed at internal changes, although they might eventually have an indirect impact on intergovernmental relations. It is analytically important to keep the two separate, as the ideologies behind them and the political processes they might engender are likely to differ.

Secondly, the reforms may be subdivided according to whether they aim at (1) changing the organizational structure; (2) reshaping the type of decisions by local authorities; or (3) reorganizing the flow of financial resources. The second dimension might thus be termed the substantive content of the reforms. Who does what, how and with whose money, are each distinguishable issues and are likely to be dealt with differently in various situations.

Even if somewhat blurred at the edges, these distinctions offer a starting point for a more specific categorization. Seen jointly and expressing them typologically, the two dimensions — scope and content — point to six categories of reforms (Figure 1).

Some specification is in order, before considering the six categories that result from this exercise. Empirically, the actual reforms in a given country will be a blending of two or more such categories. Seldom, if ever, will they appear as single enactments. This is, of course, the same as saying that the figure indicates analytical categories and not empirical entities. Another *caveat* concerns the association of the intergovernmental reforms with national legislation and the adjustments of the internal aspects with local decisions. This may come readily to mind, but is actually misleading. In many countries the internal organization of local units is indeed regulated by central government. Nevertheless, important changes have been initiated and enacted by individual local authorities, national government

Scope

		Adjustment of intergovernmental relations	Adjustment of internal local aspects
	Changes in organization	(1) Structural reforms	(4) Organizational reforms
Content	Changes in decisional aspects	(2) Functional and procedural reforms	(5) Decision-making reforms
	Changes in financial resources	(3) Intergovernmental financial reforms	(6) Local financial reforms

Figure 1   *Types of local government reform*

eventually legislating to confirm an established practice. Urban decentralization is a case in point, having spontaneously developed, for instance, in Italy as in Scandinavia (Kjellberg, 1979; Dente and Regonini, 1980). Again, this specification also indicates the analytical character of the scheme, underscoring that the type of reforms are at the outset to be differentiated from the way in which they are launched and enforced.

Let us then attempt to clarify the six categories with some illustrations. Starting with the reforms that pertain to the adjustment of intergovernmental relations, the first type might be termed structural reforms, as they concern territorial division and organization. All changes in the number of local units are included in it. Such transformations might occur by introducing new levels of government. A pertinent example would be the regionalization which has taken place in France, Italy, Belgium and Spain in the last decades; or the innovations at the county level and the establishment of special urban or metropolitan districts experienced in many countries. Another instance of structural reforms would be the redrawing of boundaries and the amalgamations of existing local units, the territorial reforms in Great Britain, Germany and Scandinavia being the most notable cases. Finally, the category also encompasses changes in the sphere of intermunicipal co-operation, whether established by mandatory requirements, induced by financial incentives or simply resulting from voluntary agreements by local units. More often than not the reorganization process seems to have started with structural reforms, later to be followed by different types. Accordingly, they have often been regarded as *the* local government reorganization, in spite of the fact that other types might have had at least as much impact on modern local government.

Our second category, functional reforms, incorporates the decisional aspects and encompasses three varieties. First, there is the recasting of tasks between central government and local authorities. Much of this might take place in a piecemeal and incremental way through particular programmes and legislation in specific sectors. However, from time to time a major reshuffling is likely to occur, either in connection with structural reform, as in Denmark and Great Britain, or without any apparent reference to it, as in Italy and Norway: older tasks are redefined and new ones usually added on the basis of administrative and political considerations of what the appropriate responsibilities of different levels should be. Often related to this are changes in procedural aspects, the second variety of our functional category. They concern the authority of supervision and control by central government. Particularly in later years, such reforms or reform proposals have been squarely placed on the political agenda, as witness the recent abolition of the venerated prefectoral *tutelle* in France and Italy and trimming of the prefectoral prerogatives in Norway. Finally, functional reforms may affect the very framework within which decisional powers are exercised. The introduction of policy-planning systems is a case in point, drawing the limits of discretionary powers of both central departments and local agencies. Such transformations in the architecture of decision-making often appears linked with the establishment of new levels of government, like regions, but is also likely to take place in other contexts.

The third and last category directly impinging on intergovernmental relations, includes the financial reforms. Often linked with the functional reforms and apparently originating in 'the fiscal crisis of the State' (O'Connor, 1973), financial reforms have attracted much attention in the field of local government studies. Given the impact that central grants generally have on the resources of local authorities, any transformation of the amounts transferred, and of the allocational rules, is bound to influence the extent of local autonomy. The shift from discretionary to more objective criteria in allocating the funds, as well as the change from specific to general grants — notably in Denmark and Norway, but visible in other countries as well — are obvious examples. Moreover, the financial relations between centre and localities are also shaped by modifications of the local taxation system, transferring some taxes from the centre to the periphery and vice versa. Whether they are connected with the redistribution of tasks or not, financial reforms — impinging on the grant system or on taxation, or both — will have a far-reaching impact on the extent and content of local activity, and thereby on the degree of direction from the centre.

With the fourth category we leave intergovernmental relations and move specifically into the ambit of local authorities themselves. What we term organizational reforms refer to the relationship between administrative and political organs, as well as to the links between citizens and local decision-making bodies. Pertinent examples are the reshaping of local and regional administrative structures, the introduction of new forms of city management, the redefinition of the role of the mayor and, not least, the creation of decentralized municipal units or neighbourhood councils. Such reforms seem to differ from other types by being initiated by the localities rather than by central government. They appear, more often than not, as local adjustments to changes brought about by other reforms.

The decision-making reforms which comprise the fifth category in our taxonomy are in fact likely to appear in tandem with organizational reforms. Still, they are sufficiently different to be kept analytically apart. Their clearest manifestation is the introduction — particularly prominent in recent years — of more synoptic decision-making in the localities in areas such as long-term budgeting and corporate planning. But they also include attempts to give more room to popular participation by establishing better information channels, local referenda and the like.

The sixth and last category in our scheme concerns autonomous action by the local authorities in modifying the financing of local services. The range of these reforms is admittedly more limited, but there are instances of autonomous local taxation within the limits set by national legislation, as in the case of rate-capping in Britain. Moreover, the category covers the grey zone between taxation and users' charges, which in many instances has become increasingly important. To everybody's surprise it was discovered recently, for instance, in Norway, that the municipalities had very different policies in setting fees and charges. Balancing on the borderline between changes and reforms, actions in this case seem clearly relevant for understanding what reorganization is about.

Again, these six categories are definitely not mutually exclusive. On the contrary, they are linked in many ways and tend empirically to come in clusters. Still, there are some striking variations between countries not only in the specific content of the different reforms, but also in the way in which they combine and in their sequence in time. Denmark, for instance, experienced in a relatively short period of time in the early 1970s a global reorganization which included all six categories of reforms. At the other end of the spectrum is Sweden which appears to be a typical case of unidimensional reorganization:

it concentrated almost exclusively on structural reforms, notably a consolidation of the municipalities. Between these two extremes we find cases with partial and prolonged reorganizations, as in Great Britain and some of the German *Länder*, where structural reforms were introduced jointly with functional and/or fiscal and internal organization reforms.

There seems also to be some basic patterns. Apparently, there is an either/or situation concerning the varieties of structural reform, the redrawing of municipal boundaries or the creation of new intermediate tiers. Countries with a penchant for amalgamations have shunned regionalization and vice versa. In contrast, the introduction of intergovernmental policy-planning systems seems in general to have favoured the establishment locally of synoptic decision-making and, almost as a corollary, internal organization reforms.

Such variations in reorganization patterns are hardly fortuitous. They reflect the national policies toward local government, the strategies pursued in bringing the institution more in tune with the prerequisites of the contemporary state. Decomposing the elements which go into what is perceived as a single phenomenon makes it possible to visualize their different configurations. And reconceptualizing local government reforms as specific policies might throw some light on the general issue of institutional change. By connecting the different types of reform with the specific processes surrounding them — the actors involved, their rationales, and their mutual interaction — we might take a first step in tackling the more general problem of institutional transformation.

The content of this volume

Not all the issues raised so far can be satisfactorily dealt with in a collection of essays. The contributions gathered in this volume nevertheless provide some insight in the complexity of institutional change at the local level. They certainly confirm the widespread feeling that local government is far from being a stable setting. Reforms, changes, or both, have occurred in all the countries discussed. The fact that they differ widely in comprehensiveness, ranging from small adjustments to overall reorganizations, is overshadowed by the fact that several micro-changes can bring about a macro-transformation, as suggested by Kiviniemi.

However, the similarities end here. There are countries, in fact, where important changes have occurred without any specific or conscious attempt to reform the system, as Anton shows is the case in the United States. On the other hand, the never-ending story of French local reform, seems to have produced only minor changes in the way in which the system works, as Yves Mény points out. In spite of the emphasis in this book on transformations — intended or enacted — one should not forget the permanence of some fundamental features, not only in France. As Dente indicates in his analysis of reforms on the basis of different legitimizing ideologies, the role of the most traditional ones — legal and the clientelistic legitimacy — is not to be lightly dismissed. Moreover, as Ashford notes, intergovernmental relations tend to change far more slowly than national policy priorities and objectives. Accordingly, it is not surprising that major differences in the local government system of the various countries are still apparent after the long period of reforms that has affected them all.

However, transformations have occurred in virtually all aspects of local government. Why this has taken place was the first question raised in our introduction. A tentative answer has already been given: the transformations of local authorities are clearly related to the increased functional scope of contemporary states, the rise — and the possible fall — of the welfare state. As will be seen, this way of reasoning is by far the most common theme in the following chapters. For most of them it not only provides a plausible explanation, but it also links the institutional transformations with the structural changes which, in their turn, form the basis of the welfare state itself. For instance, the reforms of local government finance in the United States, as noted by Anton, seem clearly connected with the rise of welfare policies. Nevertheless, the link between public expansion and local government reorganization should not be interpreted in a simplistic or mechanical way. First, as Douglas Ashford reminds us, local leaders were in many cases initially suspicious about the rise of the welfare state, as being enacted through central policies. Second, even in countries like France, where the changes at the local level seem minimal, social services have expanded widely. And finally, as Sharpe points out, many welfare state policies affecting the stabilization of the business cycle, such as labour market policy or industrial policy, have mostly, if not solely, been implemented at the central level.

A more promising way of establishing a link between the welfare state and local government is to specify the character of public expansion and the types of local reform. Such an attempt is made by both Kiviniemi and Kjellberg. Kiviniemi distinguishes between the rise of the welfare state, with its stress on planning, and the segmentation phase, in which negotiation and implementation of discrete local experiments appear to be the main strategy. Kjellberg goes further, trying to identify which local reforms are in accordance with the three different phases into which he divides the development of the welfare state since 1945. Thus, structural reorganization is related to the first phase characterized by the overall aim of providing direct benefits to the citizens. The rise of regional planning, and of synoptic decision-making, with its related emphasis on the intermediate level of government, characterizes the second phase, mainly concerned with control over the business cycle and full-employment economic policies. Finally, financial reforms appear in Kjellberg's discussion as related to the third phase, the one in which financial steering and control is introduced as a way of influencing the level of aggregate demand.

Convincing as these attempts may be, their authors are fully aware that the picture might be more complex. Other factors have to be taken into consideration. Sharpe, for instance, suggests that urbanization trends and constitutional/administrative traditions (expressed by the contrast between Napoleonic and non-Napoleonic states) are determinants in this respect. According to Anton, one powerful factor behind the transformation is the very existence of many authorities, 'bumping into one another'.

What also emerges in nearly all the chapters is the relevance of values in generating and shaping the changes. Anton takes up a common theme in the literature, in suggesting that the various transformations have originated precisely in the conflict between the values of participation and efficiency. Dente, for his part, shows how various types of legitimacy have different operating ideologies, setting the stage for the debate about necessary reforms. In Kjellberg's perspective 'the prevailing ideology surrounding the institution' is one of relevant sets of variables explaining reform trends. And most of the discussion in Sharpe's contribution is a critique of the dominant ideology of local government reorganization in the 1970s in England and Wales.

The emphasis on values and ideologies brings to the fore what seems to be a profound ambiguity at the base of local government itself. Kjellberg expresses the point by contrasting the autonomous model and the integration model of local government, while Sharpe poses the question of whether reorganization should give priority to the role of local authorities as 'reflectors of subjective communities' or as providers of services. More generally Kiviniemi sketches the evolution of local authorities in the development of the Finnish state, pointing out their different roles in the four periods he identifies. And at a more abstract level Dente tries to delimit the different meanings of local government within various types of legitimacy. The use of ideal types makes it difficult to reach straightforward conclusions at the empirical level. Nevertheless, Dente's exercise clarifies the diverse rationales for having political/administrative bodies at the local level.

Clearly, the socially shared significance of local government, the main values surrounding the institution, and the functional expansion of the contemporary state, are three interlocked structural factors. If the goal is to develop a general theory of local government transformation, they all have to be carefully investigated. Hopefully, this volume will contribute to this end. But there are other elements, of a more behavioural nature, which also have to be taken into consideration. Reforms are attempts by specific actors to modify the way in which public affairs are conducted. Like all such endeavours they are shaped by more concrete and mundane factors than structural transformations of governmental action and ideological changes. For instance, mistakes can be made, as noted by Sharpe, who argues persuasively that the British reorganization of the 1970s was unable to reach its own goals. This is a useful warning against an excessively Hegelian approach, bound to label as rational self-interest what is in fact the result of cognitive limits or wrong analyses.

This is not to say that actors with rational self-interests do not exist in the world of local reorganization. The different essays provide us with copious evidence that they exist. The role in the process of national politicians interested in symbolic politics is brought out by Mény. Likewise, the national administrators interested in reducing the complexities of intergovernmental relations, are seen by Sharpe as the only winners of the reorganization game. And Ashford warns us of the determinant role played by the 'reserve army' of social workers in getting local reforms on the political agenda.

Obviously, the reorganizational process is made up of various actors, each of them intervening with their own goals, objectives, and strategies. Different constraints and opportunities are at work, as shown by Sharpe in discussing the relevance of the non-executant tradition in British administration and of the lack of constitutional rule in opening the way to sweeping reforms. But such considerations, putting the accent on behavioural and process-related aspects of reorganization, are familiar and do not seem to need further elaboration. What we felt needed particular emphasis, by way of introduction, is the connection between local reforms and the general transformations of Western polities over the last decades. The essays in this book highlight how institutional transformations, at whatever level they take place and however comprehensive they might be, are part and parcel of the changing character of state and society. Institutional changes have a significance well beyond their importance in administrative or financial terms. They have a far-reaching impact on the political system. In order to understand what is happening to the government and politics of Western societies, as well as to experiment with new approaches to the very old problem of the dynamics of institutional change, a closer look at the sub-national level is essential.

References

Ashford, D.E. (1982) *British Dogmatism and French Pragmatism: Central–local Policy-making in the Welfare State.* London: George Allen & Unwin.

Bourjol, M. (1975) *La Réforme municipale.* Paris: Berger-Levrault.

Brand, J. (1976) 'Reforming Local Government: Sweden and England Compared', in R. Rose (ed.), *The Dynamics of Public Policy.* London: Sage.

Castells, M. (1976) *The Urban Question.* London: Edward Arnold.

Cockburn, C. (1977) *The Local State.* London: Pluto.

Dahl, R.A. (1962) *Who Governs?* New Haven, CT: Yale University Press.

Dearlove, J. (1979) *The Reorganization of British Local Government.* Cambridge: Cambridge University Press.

Dente, B. and Regonini, G. (1980) 'Urban Policy and Political Legitimation', *International Political Science Review* 1(2): 187–202.

Evans, P., Ruschemeyer, D. and Stockpol, T. (1985) *Bringing the State Back In.* Cambridge: Cambridge University Press.

Gough, I. (1979) *The Political Economy of the Welfare State.* London: Macmillan.

Gunlicks, A.B. (ed.) (1981) *Local Government Reform and Reorganization: an International Perspective.* Port Washington: Associated Faculty Press.

Kjellberg, F. (1979) 'A Comparative View of Municipal Decentralization: Neighbourhood Democracy in Oslo and Bologna', in L.J. Sharpe (ed.), *Decentralist Trends in Western Democracies.* London: Sage.

Kjellberg, F. (1983) 'Die Reformen der Kommunalen Gebietskörperschaften und Regionen in Dänemark, Norwegen und Schweden', in F. Zehetner (ed.), *Reformen der Kommunen und Regionen in Europa.* Vienna/Munich: Jugend und Volk Verlag.

Lowi, T.J. (1964) *At the Pleasure of the Mayor.* New York: Free Press.

March, J.G. and Olsen, J.P. (1984) 'The New Institutionalism: Organizational Factors in Political Life', *American Political Science Review* 78(3): 734–49.

O'Connor, J. (1973) *The Fiscal Crisis of the State.* New York: St Martin's Press.

Ostrom, V. (1977) 'Some Problems in Doing Political Theory: a Response to Golembiewski's "Critique"', *American Political Science Review* 71(4): 1508–25.

Poulantzas, N. (1968) *La Pouvoir politique et classes sociales de l'état capitaliste.* Paris: Maspero.

Putnam, R.D., Leonardi, R. and Nanetti, R.Y. (1983) 'Explaining Institutional Success: the Case of Italian Regional Government', *American Political Science Review* 77(1): 55–74.

Rhodes, R.A.W. (1980) 'Developed Countries', in D.C. Rowat (ed.), *International Handbook on Local Government Reorganization.* London: Aldwych Press.

Rowat, D.C. (ed.) (1980) *International Handbook on Local Government Reorganization.* London: Aldwych Press.

Saunders, P. (1981) *Social Theory and the Urban Question.* London: Hutchinson.

Selznick, P. (1949) *TVA and the Grass Roots.* Berkeley, CA: California University Press.

Wood, B. (1976) *The Process of Local Government Reform 1966–74.* London: George Allen & Unwin.

Zehetner, F. (ed.) (1983) *Reformen der Kommunen und Regionen in Europa.* Vienna/Munich: Jugend und Volk Verlag.

2

Decentralizing Welfare States: Social Policies and Intergovernmental Politics

Douglas E. Ashford

Although economic pressures have monopolized the welfare state debate in recent years, the changing intergovernmental framework of social service provision may be more interesting in both a practical and a theoretical sense. To a greater degree than may have been recognized at the time, the many reorganizations of local government systems over the 1960s and 1970s were a response to increasing demands for local social services. Such demands arose in part because the nationalized welfare state programme of the 1950s, largely pensions, disability and sickness protection, were not appropriate to the new array of social needs that emerged as states accepted major new social responsibilities. New social issues such as drug addiction, child abuse, single parentage and the mentally handicapped were not easily organized at the national level, nor were such needs evenly distributed among subordinate units of government. As a result, the advance of the welfare state was accompanied by important intergovernmental adjustments.

Although the democratic states varied significantly in how rapidly and in what order they chose to recognize national social needs (Flora and Heidenheimer, 1981; Ashford, 1986), there were, and remain, independent political and administrative constraints, operating at both national and local levels, that affected how social services might be organized and whose political interests might be enhanced or hurt by various intergovernmental combinations. Thus, the intergovernmental solutions, as well as the national governmental structures, that were used to build welfare states were only partially a product of social needs. The independent political, institutional and even constitutional effects on intergovernmental structures are often visible decades and even centuries later. Put differently, in most countries the intergovernmental network was initially a deterrent to rapid nationalization of social policies; the USA is perhaps the most dramatic illustration, with unemployment benefits still being heavily influenced by state-level policies (Harpham, 1986). For this reason, local governments often incurred the wrath of national-level social reformers, most notably perhaps in Britain, where Lloyd George, Aneurin Bevan and Richard Crossman were agreed that the complexities of local government and local politics should not stand in the way of achieving immediate social reforms.

More often than not, national policy-makers regarded the centre–local network of political and administrative linkages as an unfortunate, if not antagonistic, obstacle to achieving national social reforms. This situation was perhaps most pronounced in Britain, where the local authorities inherited the onus of the Poor Laws and the workhouse and so were positively identified with everything that Edwardian politicians, and more than a few top administrators, found objectionable in British social policy. Not only did the British Local Government Board inherit the most distasteful of Victorian social policies (Lambert, 1962), but at the turn of the century the Board was administered by a former radical union leader, John Burns, who became a staunch defender of the Poor Laws (Brown, 1977). The problem was compounded by the intense poverty resulting from severe unemployment between the wars. The successor to the Local Government Board, the Ministry of Health, finally managed to divest local authorities of Poor Law responsibilities with the Local Government Act 1929, although the local-level Poor Law machinery continued to operate until the National Assistance Act 1948 completely nationalized poverty assistance. As we shall see, the new complexities of relieving poverty are once again drawing local governments into the morass that for so long made them the detested partners of national social reform.

For the moment, all that is needed is to see that the intergovernmental network acted as a kind of political Wagner's law on the nationalization of social policy. The nineteenth-century network was not designed primarily to meet social needs, nor were the predominantly conservative leaders of nineteenth-century local governments eager to advance social reforms, even when their colleagues in capital cities thought reforms were needed. There were of course exceptions, such as the Speenhamland effort of 1795 to compensate the poor with a living wage (soon overruled by Parliament), but by and large, dispersed and localized authority produced conservative social policies.

National leaders of the last century were probably justified in their suspicion that local leaders were unreliable and unenthusiastic allies of social change. The interesting change in recent years is the great growth of local social services. With this growth, large public unions, new client groups and huge non-profit organizations have become active defenders of social reform at the local levels of governments. Whether this 'reserve army' of social workers, professionals and volunteers will become permanent local and intergovernmental actors remains to be seen, but localized welfare is a major structural change in the intergovernmental network of most modern welfare states.

The shifting balance of national and local social policy-makers

For nearly a century, national policy-makers have been in the process of centralizing social policy — its control, accountability and resources. The balance of political forces was not always as disproportionate as it is today. In Britain in 1910, local social service expenditure was twice that of national government (Peacock and Wiseman, 1967: 106–7). However much such diverse people as the Webbs, Lloyd George and Sir Robert Morant regarded local authorities as profligate and unaccountable, they looked with envy on the funds being dispersed by British local authorities (Allen, 1934). Historians differ over when national government decided that local government was an expendable resource for purposes of social policy, but the trend was certainly clear as early as 1870, when Gladstone ignored Sir George Goschen's masterful study of how urban local authorities lacked a tax base to meet their needs while the wealthy rural counties were levying ridiculously low taxes (Ashford, 1982a). Mrs Thatcher is only the most recent of many British ministers with little respect for local government.

Less noticed, perhaps, many of the early social reforms in Britain called on local governments to do more without providing additional resources. The custom of imposing new responsibilities on local authorities and then providing national funds to pay for these services has had a long history. The Poor Law Amendment Act 1834 was the basis for some of the first grants to local agencies, when Poor Law Unions organized education and medical care for pauper children. Britain's first and ineffective unemployment relief programme of 1905 worked through local public works boards. But from roughly 1900 onwards, few social reformers saw local governments as a reliable vehicle of policy implementation. Beveridge's labour exchanges of 1909 were clearly not compatible with local government areas. The early health reformers were deeply distrustful of the inherited Poor Law and public health hospitals of local authorities. Momentum for nationalized health was built on a medical consensus that localities had inferior facilities and were likely to meddle with medical fees if given substantial influence (Newsholme, 1925). For obvious reasons, the immense needs for unemployment relief in interwar Britain could not be handled through local authorities, even though the overworked Local Assistance Boards provided assistance for the long-term unemployed from 1929 until the formation of the National Assistance Board in 1935. Even so, bit by bit, localities were excluded from social policy implementation, and the final complete nationalization of the major British social programmes after the war was only a sequel to a trend that had begun fifty years before.

In the more slowly advancing French welfare state, the departments and communes never developed the local social responsibilities that British localities had acquired from early Victorian times. None the less, the republican creed placed important social responsibilities on all units of government, and well into the twentieth century the departments and communes remained the main agents of social policy. The first great republican debate over social reform in the 1880s was about the creation of local *bureaux d'assistance publique* to supplement the more aristocratic and religious local *bureaux de bienfaisance* (Ashford, 1986; Weiss, 1983). Both the first public assistance law of 1905 and the first pension law of 1908 were organized around departmental funds and committees. Although never assigned the heavy social responsibilities of British local authorities, under the influence of regional differences and party fragmentation the French social security system could not avoid centre–local tensions. The most dramatic case is family allowances, which developed from both republican and liberal Catholic sentiments. The 1932 family allowance law was locally administered, and even the best efforts of the postwar nationalizers of French social insurance failed to merge the family funds in a *caisse unique* in the face of well entrenched local family assistance agencies (Ceccaldi, 1951).

There are even stronger structural constraints on the nationalization of social policies in federal systems. The conflicts between levels of government can be traced over many years. The German system of medical insurance, for example, is an intricate and ponderous organization of local funds and agencies dating from Bismarck's sickness insurance of 1883 (Stone, 1980; Andic and Veverka, 1964). As in other countries, the intense inflationary pressures of the 1920s produced strong national pressures to overcome excesses and differences of localized poverty assistance (Leibfried, 1986). Though now effectively nationalized, the German social security system is still based on a federal structure. Not surprisingly, in the USA the transformation was even slower. From 1902 until 1927, nearly 80 percent of all public assistance was provided by local governments. By 1940, under the impulse of New Deal programmes, the federal share doubled but remained under 20 percent. After falling to negligible levels after the war, the Johnson and Nixon administrations pushed the federal share up to 30 percent (Ashford, 1984). More remarkable, perhaps, the rapid expansion of national assistance such as food stamps and Aid for Dependent Children under the Republican presidency of Richard Nixon, when local public assistance spending declined to 25 percent of the total, was in part justified by the fiscal stress of local government (Derthick, 1975). Unlike Britain over a century before, increased national assistance was intended to preserve a strong federal structure.

The historical balance between local influence and national social policy suggests that, well before the nationalization of major social programmes in the postwar period, intergovernmental linkages affected how localities might subsequently implement localized social policies. In general, the rapid development of national welfare programmes and dependence on national revenues diminished interest in joint ventures. The British localities, for example, developed extensive social responsibilities in the Victorian period, but the intricate system of functionally organized local boards, each with its own tax rate, under separate national ministries until roughly 1888, cloaked the fiscal contribution of localities and facilitated the growth of national inspection. British localities accepted heavy social responsibilities relatively early in their development, but got little recognition for their effort (Ashford, 1982a). As national ministries launched new localized programmes, Westminster paid the bill in exchange for powers of inspection and the right to set standards. As a case of intergovernmental influence over social services, Britain may be the exception that proves the rule, because strong national powers have not prevented large variations among localities in service provision (Rhodes, 1981). Whether differential service provision is a function of local differences or intergovernmental networks is unclear, but even a strongly centralized system cannot prevent significant local service variations.

The British case contrasts sharply with that of France, where concessions to national policies are frequently accompanied by substantial concessions to local interests (Ashford, 1982a), and with the USA, where efforts to curtail the generous local social programmes of the 1960s and 1970s were delayed by local politics for some years. To be sure, Reagan's Omnibus Reconciliation Act 1981 shifted about $10 billion in federal programmes to the states, but this was only a fraction of the programme the President hoped to unload on to local resources, and many of the transferred programmes are still surrounded by special protective clauses (General Accounting Office, 1982). The President has wisely subdued his once extreme rhetoric about state and local government waste and inefficiency. Some of the major social programmes brought under block grants — for example, the Community Mental Health Centers (CMHCs) — do not appear to have been damaged by devolution to the states (Rich, 1982).

National social programmes with local impact must take intergovernmental politics seriously because intergovernmental networks change more slowly than national policy priorities and objectives. Where local government systems are easily overruled, as in Britain, taking social responsibility does not appear to gain national respect for local actors or local preferences. Despite the relatively slow growth of the French welfare state, programmes with strong local support, such as child allowances, were accepted between the wars and successfully defended by local organizations in 1945. If *aide sociale* was transferred to the French departments only in 1984, it may well have been because French mayors do not sign blank cheques, rather than because of local ignorance or even a rejection of larger social problems. Proposals to devolve large segments of Whitehall on to British localities, along with a suitable transfer of resources, have been debated on and off for generations, but the French actually decided to make such a move. The USA, in contrast, still grapples with the same intergovernmental tensions that limited the early formation of the American welfare state. Even Reagan's enormous popularity did not permit him to use his 'New Federalism' to override local needs and preferences.

Shifting social policy to local levels

Comparisons of the gradual reappearance of localized social services would be easier if they were accomplished in similar ways. To be sure, the problems were often the same, such as the realization that thousands of mentally ill people were quite possibly unnecessarily institutionalized, or that under-achieving children often lived in poor neighbourhoods with inferior schools. In Anglo-Saxon countries it was not unusual to have large pressure groups mobilize public opinion and legislators, as in the case of the British Child Poverty Action Group (CPAG) or Shelter (a British public housing pressure group). But across countries, the political similarities are more deceptive than simple social need. The French Association for Family Allowances has a strong organization that has been subsidized by government since the 1890s. Moreover, unlike many children's services in Britain and the USA, the modern national funding agency (the Caisse Nationale des Allocations Familiales, CNAF) provides numerous auxiliary services through volunteer organizations and schools. The surpluses of family allowance funds have made it the target of other deficit-ridden social services, in particular medical care, but the CNAF is a semi-autonomous organization with its own publications, hundreds of local chapters and links to parent and school organizations throughout France. Unlike the British CPAG, the CNAF lives within government as much as outside it. In terms of the shifting balance of power between national and local agencies in provision of social benefits and social protection, the political and administrative differences are very great indeed.

The early political possibilities for shifting social services to lower levels of government were constrained in two ways. First, there were very different institutional assumptions behind the nationalization of social security systems in the late 1940s and 1950s. As might be expected, the US social security administration, and the entire ideology of self-help associated with the 1935 Social Security Act, represented national insurance as an extension of individual choice and personal savings (Derthick, 1979). Citizens, government and Congress agreed that social security was simply another form of individual prudence. The more controversial aspect of national insurance — unemployment protection — remained state-administered. Hence, national insurance was never a barrier to expanding local services once the President and the Congress decided to fund new programmes. At least one such service, Aid for Dependent Children (ADC, formerly AFDC), received indirect recognition in the 1935 Act but remained dormant for roughly thirty years until President Johnson's Great Society plans vastly amplified family assistance. In part to cultivate support for his negative income tax proposals, and thereby simplify federal programmes for the poor, President Nixon heaped additional funds on the food stamp programme (to get farm votes) and thereby nationalized another major programme for the poor (while failing to get tax reform) (Nathan, 1975; Lynn and Whitman, 1981). These programmes were seen as major sources of revenue relief for local government, and their passage in Congress was possible because of various intergovernmental and federal coalitions of interest.

In a loosely joined and politically localized system, the profusion of local social services in the 1970s soon produced what Derthick (1975) called 'uncontrollable spending'. At rates of growth that would soon outdistance national income, local, state and non-profit agencies were flooded with new funds for social services. Neither the federal bureaucracy nor the national social security system was inclined or able to resist this transformation. But in more tightly organized and more nationally politicized welfare systems, the resurgence of local social services posed very different political and administrative problems. To be sure, over the 1970s the most visible area of localized social services, the 'personal social services' of the British local government system, was the fastest growing element in the British social protection system (Social Services Committee, 1982). Even under Thatcher, the 116 social service departments of local government managed to add over 10,000 social service employees during the period of stiff hiring and budgetary controls from 1979 to 1984 (Walsh, 1985: 102; Webb and Wistow, 1982a). Over that period, total local government employment dropped by more than 3 percent while local social service employment increased by 13 percent.

But unlike the US social security system, which was constructed with reverence for federal and local politics, the British Beveridge Plan of 1945–6 was, much like the 1911 National Insurance Act, passed with little regard for local government. To be sure, in 1911 the House of Lords was alarmed that a small increase in land taxes might lead to higher local taxes; but for nearly a century Britain has been enacting major national social reforms with little more than a nod towards the independent concerns of local government. The Reconstruction Committee of 1918 had before it an elaborate plan for local government reform, but the MacClean Report, like most other major social reforms of the period, was pushed aside as Lloyd George tried to erect a new national coalition with the Conservatives (Johnson, 1968; Morgan and Morgan, 1980). Throughout the early 1940s, the awkward shape and size of local governments troubled wartime planners of health nationalization, who saw in them a recognized obstacle to the best organization of health care; but ministers regularly brushed the issue aside. Those who raised objections, like Morrison, endangered their parliamentary careers (Donoughue and Jones, 1973). As the stream of laws depriving local government of its functions in the areas of policing, transport, water provision, etc., appeared throughout the 1950s and 1960s, local government was seldom considered a partner of national government. Thus, it is hardly surprising that, once national policy-makers began in the late 1960s to realize that they badly needed local skills and local assistance in order to respond to many new social ills, the intergovernmental structure worked sporadically and often ineffectively.

The British experiments in weeding out the inconsistencies between national and local social policies were fitful and uncertain. Perhaps the first was the Community Development Programme (CDP), modelled on the US Community Action Program (CAP) and a modest response to growing inner-city tensions and neglect in the late 1960s (McKay and Cox, 1979). There followed the reorganization of local social services under the Seebohm Committee (1968), another demonstration of Whitehall's ineptitude: launched at roughly the same time as the Royal Commission on Local Government but with different objectives (namely, the unification of local social service within the orbit of a nationally directed social service expansion), Seebohm threatened not only to make hash of the tediously worked out local functions and boundaries of the Royal Commission, but also to steal the political thunder of a giant ministry run by an ambitious and clever man, Richard Crossman (Thomas, 1973). The result was that Seebohm was asked to delay while local government reform caught up. Another influential minister, Judith Hart, saw her reform pushed through Parliament on the day before Wilson dissolved his government in 1970, while the intricate local reform slipped into Tory hands in the following government. The Local Authority Social Services Act 1970 cannot be fully analysed here, but suffice to say that the merger of diverse specialities of local social workers was more an act of national determination, masterminded by the major Labour Party adviser on national social security, Richard Titmuss, than a collective effort to bring national and local government into harmony around shared social goals (Mays et al., 1983; Cooper, 1983).

As these illustrations suggest, intergovernmental networks vary in their capacity to build programmes around mutual national and local interests. British ministerial desires can be arbitrarily imposed on new programmes in ways that would be easily vetoed by powerful local officials in France or the USA. In most countries, ministerial empires and national party politics occasionally give way to productive collaboration across levels of government. If intergovernmental compromise is difficult, either local authorities are whiplashed by successive governments arbitrarily changing policies, or they turn to confrontation, as illustrated by Peter Shore's modest plan to aid inner cities in 1974. Shore's plan drew fire from a no less ambitious minister than Shirley Williams, whose Department of Education saw the move as a threat to comprehensive (integrated) education and a potential loss through dispersion of scarce resources for education. Local governments disliked the idea because they had just digested a major reform. A decade later, a frustrated Conservative government would desperately revive inner-city pogrammes as massive racial and youth riots shook Britain. The problem is not that national or local officials in Britain are unable to identify common social interests, but that the intergovernmental network is an unwieldy and unwelcome device to assist centre–local policy-making.

All this is not to say that serious obstacles to the formulation and implementation of social policy are not to be found in the intergovernmental networks of other countries, but only to show that British difficulties in generating shared responsibility and shared objectives for new local social programmes are not confined to social programmes alone. Intergovernmental negotiation in Britain produces neither the local political rewards of American federalism nor the local administrative rewards of the French intergovernmental bargaining. France has never depended heavily on the *collectivités locales* for social service provision; but, as we have seen, neither did the social security system totally ignore local involvement in social services. An elaborate array of elected social security advisory councils at the national and departmental levels helped link social policy to the intergovernmental networks. French social security elections became part of the intense and continual electoral mobilization of the French people (Laroque, 1953). The French social security was never as politically isolated from local or state government as the American system (at least until the 1970s), nor was it as administratively centralized as the British system.

The critical political link between French social security and intergovernmental politics developed through labour unions, who took, and continue to take, social security elections seriously because control of the various social security administrative councils allows them to allocate important auxiliary funds. Until 1960 the major political struggle within French social security was for control of the employees' union, the Fédération Nationale des Organismes de la Sécurité Sociale (FNOSS). FNOSS acquired political prominence because for many years the Communist Party used the union to control the training, promotion and pay of social security employees (Catrice-Lory, 1982). Much as in the local government *réseau*, the territorial committees, as well as the national committees of the social security funds, became part of an elaborate political game to see how the social rewards and privileges of FNOSS would be distributed. Organized along occupational lines, French social security used the centre–local network to allow occupational groups to reject Communist control of the social security jobs and auxiliary benefits.

Thus, the growing need to delegate social services to local levels over the 1970s and 1980s must be assessed within the different contexts linking social security to intergovernmental networks. In the USA, new social policies rarely escaped federal politics. Programmes and grants were soon immersed in the familiar struggle between cities and states for the direction of new programmes. The localized structure of US politics and administration predominated in the political struggle, while the old social security bureaucracy was virtually unnoticeable in the competition for new local social services. In Britain, the pressure for new local social services was easily mired in ministerial and political rivalries at the national level, often reviving the Victorian struggle between urban and rural local authorities. From the 1960s onwards, the growth of social services could not be separated from the desperate and unsuccessful attempts to increase local resources, while the nationalized system of benefits could easily procrastinate and obstruct efforts to shift services to local levels. The intergovernmental network in Britain eluded responsibility, as did national policy-makers. New programmes moved forward slowly, often with reversals that confused local government.

Different patterns can be seen in other countries. In Germany, the main effort seems to have been the co-ordination of the already highly dispersed structure of social benefits and assistance with client needs (Grunow and Hegner, 1980). In the more centralized administrative state of France, the struggle was curiously politicized — not because politicians wished it so, but because the future of social security and local social services influenced labour union rewards and direct benefits for union members. Like many policy choices in France (Ashford, 1982b), the transformation of social policy was easily nationalized by mobilizing local actors through the territorial network. If the departments and communes were passive actors in this contest, it was not because they did not see rewards, but because the social security system did not yet provide incentives and opportunities to influence their behaviour. As we shall see, once national politics provided such an opportunity in 1981, local governments were eager to accept a major role in the French welfare state.

The local social bureaucracy: the welfare state reserve army

In speaking of the 'reserve army' of localized social services, the intention is to identify those actors who are likely to play a key role in the expansion and control of local social services in the future. The huge nationalized social security agencies can of course exercise influence, particularly where national social security employees are concentrated in large single processing centres such as Britain's national social security complex in Newcastle, with 30,000 employees. But for the most part, national employees of the welfare state are relatively well paid and, in a period of economic dislocation, enjoy the additional reward of job security. Indeed, it is interesting that in Britain and the USA the generous benefits of government employees have become a target for economies in national-level social spending. The potential influence of the local 'reserve army' depends, of course, on the overall administrative structure of each country, but it seems likely that the number of locally employed social service workers will continue to grow. As this takes place, we can anticipate more effective union organization, better mobilization of clients, and more effective intervention in local political decision-making.

In the USA, the social work professions roughly doubled between

1940 and 1970 to nearly 200,000 persons (Richan, 1981: 55). The immense expansion of ADC benefits provided a platform for the steady growth of local children's services, as did ancillary programmes in education such as Operation Headstart. When ADC (then AFDC) was renewed in 1967, President Johnson was annoyed that thirty states had not fully implemented the programme and that about 12 million children of poor families were ineligible. The 1967 law stipulated that communities must hire more social workers to see that all needy families receive benefits under the programme (Milnor, 1983). In the case of ADC as well as programmes for drug addiction, mental health, and educational assistance for mentally handicapped children, laws expanding local social services provided federal funds for administrative costs and often some funding for training new officials and social workers. Thus, under federalist rules programmatic change nearly always carries with it funds for organizational and administrative expansion.

There are no wholly reliable figures for social workers in France, but a recent estimate of social workers specified 5000 attached to the Direction of Social Affairs, Ministry of Social Security (personal communication, 1983) with at least twice that number thought to be organized through hospitals (non-profit agencies), labour training programmes (a public corporation) and schools (a ministry). Although the Socialist government made a small increase in the Ministry of Social Security budget for 1985, the ministerial budget most directly linked to local social activities, 'interventions sociales', was reduced by 4.6 percent to about Fr 11.5 billion (National Assembly, 1984: 23). Nearly half of this budget goes to the *collectivités locales* as part of the national contribution to *aide sociale*, which roughly corresponds to public assistance in other welfare states. Under the Decentralization Law 1982, plans were made to transfer *aide sociale* and parts of public housing to the departments.

While social workers often find themselves fragmented within the various intergovernmental networks, they have been an almost continual source of national concern in Britain. The Local Authority Social Services Act 1970 was in many respects a nationally enforced effort to unify social workers, and to compel local authorities to unify social services. Whitehall directly attacked professional and clinical differences among social workers that less centralized governments had been reluctant to undertake, but in doing so it again overrode local preferences and practices. The approximately 25,000 social workers in Britain (DHSS, 1981) were encouraged to form a new national organization, the British Association of Social Workers, to ease national designs. The transformation is noteworthy not only as a repetition of a familiar Whitehall tactic to construct consensus around new policies, but as a manoeuvre in administrative politics that few modern democratic governments could attempt, much less bring off successfully.

As in most countries, social workers are highly differentiated. For organizational purposes, their influence is to a large extent determined by how they fit into the intergovernmental structure. The British case was the most highly centralized in this respect because, even by 1945, two of the three main groups providing local social services were under strong national direction. The first, child care officials and social workers, were the charges of the Home Office, whose powers originated with the Child Care Act 1948 but could be traced back through the long history of Home Office responsibility for orphans, foster children and delinquents. The second link was once removed: under the National Assistance Act 1948, the local authorities retained responsibility for residential care of the elderly poor, but their housing costs were to be met through supplementary benefits provided by national assistance. The third element was the highly trained social workers dealing with psychiatric and mental health attached to the National Health Service (NHS), who often disapproved of the less professional mental health workers in local government services. As the array of ministerial interests, not to mention those of attentive sideliners such as the Department of Education, suggests, building a local coalition among these agencies was virtually impossible, much to the detriment of local government.

For the present, all that can be shown is how the highly centralized power struggle could at best provide only a temporary solution to the growing complexities of providing local social services. In 1970, few foresaw the important changes that would take place in the provision of local social services over the next decade. By 1980, the local government arm of service provision, the personal social services, would be spending £1.2 billion or about 20 percent of all local government expenditure (Goldberg and Hatch, 1981: 4). No sooner had local social service provision been unified in 1970 than new proposals began to appear to adjust these services to new needs, new professional standards and aims and, eventually, new fiscal limitations (Central Policy Review Staff, 1975; Nissel et al., 1980). As in many British reforms, the departure of 1970 seemed better designed to permit ministers and Whitehall to claim a victory than to encourage those implementing the policies and, were those possible, the beneficiaries of the policies, to shape social services to their needs. Only one such example can be provided here, the case of mental health; but among new legislation adding to local social responsibilities were the Health Services Act 1968; the Children and Young

Persons Act 1969, the Chronically Sick and Disabled Persons Act 1970 and the Children's Act 1975.

Mental health is a particularly good example for indicating the internal weakness of centre–local policy-making in Britain because it involves three major actors: the Treasury, the NHS (and indirectly the Department of Health and Social Services or DHSS) and local government. As in the USA, there was general agreement in the early 1970s that the mentally ill and mentally handicapped urgently needed attention (Walker, 1982). The goal was set out by White Papers from both Conservative (DHSS, 1971) and Labour (DHSS, 1975) governments. The declaration of intent was followed with the Jay Committee on nursing needs for improved mental health care (Jay Committee, 1979). The complexities of implementing a policy linking three major agents of social care were partly exposed by the Joint Working Group on Personal Social Services which reported in May 1980 (DHSS, 1980). The earlier White Papers stressed what local authorities hoped national government would provide in the form of residential care for the elderly, care for delinquent and mentally handicapped children and domiciliary care for a variety of services that local authorities are required by law to provide. As labour cut into local grants, the Working Group was appointed by the Joint Consultative Council on Local Finance in 1977 to clarify local problems of providing assistance for low-income persons, especially from the main public assistance agency, the Supplementary Benefits Commission (SBC — since abolished by Thatcher). The report contained ample evidence that local authorities were poorly compensated by the NHS for providing de-institutionalized health care and were mired in procedural disputes with the SBC in obtaining payments for basic services for the poor.

To understand the financial plight of local government as Whitehall set out to reform mental health, it is necessary to review the progress of 'joint finance', a governmental scheme designed in the mid-1970s to enable local authorities to share NHS funds when providing local mental health services. Well before Thatcher, the growth rates for local funding of personal social services fell from nearly 20 percent (1973/4) to under 3 percent (1976/7) (Webb and Wistow, 1982a). Joint finance seems a typical Whitehall improvisation to assure all interested parties that each enjoyed the best of all political worlds, while satisfying no one at the local level. Labour Party forecasts of joint finance for 1981/2 were over £68 million. The Conservative consultative paper on mental health and local service provision of 1981, *Care in Action* (DHSS, 1981: 5), anticipated only £51 million for 1980/1 and £58 million for the following fiscal year. The actual amount paid to local authorities for mental health care provision in 1980/1 was £41 million and for the following year £49 million (Association of Metropolitan Authorities, 1984a: 23). Given that local social service spending was over £1 billion by 1980, the steady erosion of local mental health funds suggests that Whitehall exercises a degree of control over British social spending that would amaze Stockman's Bureau of the Budget. To be able to extract roughly £20 million of announced, if not approved, funding for a programme so small as local mental health services suggests a form of central control over social spending that few, if any, welfare states have been able to achieve.

The problem was that no sooner did Britain decide on a new allocation of social services, and hopefully an understanding between the NHS and local government, than the fiscal crisis of 1974 had set in. While both Labour and Conservative parties were prepared to offer more for local social services, as testified in the Jay Report, the Goodman Report on charitable assistance and the Wolfenden Report on volunteer services, the means of aligning these good intentions with the activities of the NHS and local government seemed to slip between the cracks of policy-making (Webb and Wistow, 1982a; Booth, 1981). Like Peter Shore's effort to resurrect a small number of Labour district councils, Barbara Castle's joint finance proposals of 1976 seems a token effort to reassure Labour councils that Treasury cuts in direct grants might be replaced with NHS funds. In a period of austerity, the idea was equally appealing to a hard-pressed Tory minister a few years later when the Secretary of State for Social Security, Peter Jenkins, also supported the principle of joint finance (Glennerster, 1982).

The Conservative proposal was no more reassuring than the promises of Barbara Castle. The difference was of course that Castle was making promises as an election approached, while Jenkins was making promises at the dawn of a new government. His paper made clear that any relief for local health needs would be subject to a 'tapering' agreement, whereby the local authorities would eventually become totally responsible for the cost of any transferred services; that there were no guaranteed funds for personal social services; and that the localities could not expect similar concessions, however illusory, for education or housing (DHSS, 1981: 5). Elsewhere the document made clear that localities could not expect that the strictly controlled cash benefits might be replaced by benefits in kind which might give local social service departments more discretion over service delivery (DHSS, 1981: 16). Coupled with firm cost controls to restrict NHS expenditures, it is unlikely that any local director of social services was sanguine over the future of local social services as the Thatcher government swung into action.

Compared with intergovernmental negotiations in other major democracies, it is difficult to see how the British arrangements for improving mental health served anyone's interests, except perhaps the rhetorical needs of DHSS secretaries of state working under severe Treasury constraints. After a decade of negotiation, review and study, a workable solution seems no nearer, and in 1984 it was decided to have another review of joint finance. Similar to removal of local authority tax powers under the Thatcher government, not only were the localities left disgruntled and uncertain, but in fact, few funds were made available from the NHS. Even where local authorities made agreements with the NHS to improve mental health care, as in Warwickshire, the DHSS could reject local solutions.

The problems facing the British local social services are by no means unique to Britain, but it seems virtually impossible to extract a mutually agreeable and reasonably effective policy solution from the British intergovernmental network. However, with many of the same economic constraints, the French transferred social programmes involving over $1 billion to the departments, and the USA persuaded the states to take over the administration of the entire national system of community mental health centres (Rich, 1982).

The rigidities of intergovernmental decision-making in the case of joint financing of mental health programmes might be dismissed as a special case were it not that other intricate policy questions requiring mutual adjustment among levels of government and across jurisdictional boundaries have commonly caused difficulties in Britain. Other countries seem more prepared to make concessions to the 'reserve army' of professionals, officials and volunteers who provide increasing amounts of specialized social services in the advanced welfare states. There is every reason to think that the overlapping interests of national and local social services will grow. The British scheme of housing benefit, for example, links local authorities to the Ministry of Housing and the DHSS through social security funds used to subsidize housing for the poor. Quite apart from the unworkability of the Housing Benefit scheme, another poorly designed intergovernmental policy, the local authorities are now directly involved in calculating need for supplementary support (Association of Metropolitan Authorities, 1984b: 25). They are also involved with the calculation and administration of Educational Maintenance Allowances (EMAs), special grants for disabled and poor children. Supplementary benefits for the long-term unemployed, the aged and the disabled increasingly involve local authorities in the massive system of cash benefits for the poor (Leach, 1981; Beltram, 1984). There is little reason to think that the delicate problems of co-ordinating intergovernmental social policies will disappear in the foreseeable future. As in Britain, where local authorities are arbitrarily excluded from such decisions, adjustments will be slow and difficult.

Concluding remarks

The purpose of this chapter has been to show that the growth of local social services, while an intriguing sequel to the nationalization of social needs a generation ago, is not likely to be politically neutral or administratively simple. First, local governments in all the democracies have experienced enormous changes in their social service activities over the past century, and this experience, in particular the readiness of national government to share resources with lower-level governments, has affected local capabilities and local expectations in lasting ways. Second, the creation of national social security systems in the postwar era provided another opportunity to forge working relationships with local governments. For both political and administrative reasons, governments responded very differently, not only because the justification of national insurance itself posed different political problems, but also because nationalization of social security had different intergovernmental implications for each democracy. Third, although the role of localities in social service provision has steadily grown over the past decade, governments differ in the extent to which they involve local politics, local capabilities and local preferences in finding mutually satisfactory solutions to the intergovernmental dimensions of social services.

Not surprisingly, the ability to use local government constructively in solving new social problems is heavily grounded in the readiness and ingenuity to use local government for other purposes in years gone by. Where, for either partisan or administrative reasons, social programmes are highly centralized, the possibilities of reaching mutually acceptable agreements for expanding local social services seem diminished. The unknown factor in this transition may be the 'reserve army', that is, the growing organization of social workers, auxiliary workers in social service unions, the social service pressure groups with their strong local foundations and the expanding numbers of volunteer workers in local social services. Unlike the uniform needs that were easily attached to national bureaucracies in the postwar period, the local welfare state needs more differentiated and more specialized care. One way or another, the new local social services will be localized and their labour-intensive nature will gradually generate a 'reserve army' of concerned, informed and trained persons. Just as pensioners and the poor learned to mobilize and to protect their claims in the emergent welfare states, so also the 'reserve army' may learn to use the intergovernmental network to establish its claims in another transformation of welfare states.

References

Allen, Bernard H. (1934) *Sir Robert Morant: a Great Public Servant*. London: Macmillan.

Andic, Stephan and Veverka, Jindrich (1964) 'The Growth of Government Expenditures in Germany since Unification', *Finanzarchiv* 23(2): 169–278.

Ashford, Douglas E. (1982a) *British Dogmatism and French Pragmatism: Centre–Local Policymaking in the Welfare State*. London and Boston: George Allen & Unwin.

Ashford, Douglas E. (1982b) *Policy and Politics in France: Living with Uncertainty*. Philadelphia: Temple University Press.

Ashford, Douglas E. (1984) 'Structural Comparison of Social Policy and Intergovernmental Politics', *Policy and Politics* 21(4): 369–89.

Ashford, Douglas E. (1986) *The Emergence of Welfare States*. Oxford and New York: Basil Blackwell.

Association of Metropolitan Authorities (1984a) *Community Care: Helping Adult Mentally Ill and Mentally Handicapped People*. London: AMA.

Association of Metropolitan Authorities (1984b) *Local Authorities and the Social Security System*. London: AMA.

Beltram, Geoffrey (1984) *Testing the Safety Net*, Occasional Papers in Social Administration no. 74. London: Bedford Square Press.

Booth, Timothy (1981) 'Collaboration between the Health and Social Services: a Case Study of Joint Care Planning', *Policy and Politics* 9(1): 23–49; (2) 205–26.

Brown, Kenneth (1977) *John Burns*. London: Royal Historical Society.

Catrice-Lorey, Antoinette (1982) *Dynamique interne de la sécurité sociale*. Paris: Economica.

Ceccaldi, Dominique (1951) *Histoire des prestations familiales en France*. Paris: Association Nationale des Allocations Familiales.

Central Policy Review Staff (1975) *A Joint Framework for Social Policies*. London: HMSO.

Cooper, Joan (1983) *The Creation of the British Personal Social Services, 1962–74*. London: Heinemann.

Department of Health and Social Security (1981) 'Care in the Community: a Consultative Document on Moving Resources for Care in England', July, mimeo.

Derthick, Martha (1975) *Uncontrollable Spending for Social Service Grants*. Washington: Brookings Institution.

Derthick, Martha (1979) *Policymaking for Social Security*. Washington: Brookings Institution.

DHSS (1971) *Better Services for the Mentally Handicapped*, Cmnd. 4683. London: HMSO.

DHSS (1975) *Better Services for the Mentally Ill*, Cmnd. 6233. London: HMSO.

DHSS (1980) 'Report of the Joint Working Group on Personal Social Services Charging Policies', May, mimeo.

DHSS (1981) *Care in Action: a Handbook of Policies and Priorities for the Health and Personal Social Services in England*. London: HMSO.

Donoughue, Bernard and Jones, George (1973) *Herbert Morrison: Portrait of a Politician*. London: Weidenfeld & Nicolson.

Flora, Peter and Heidenheimer, Arnold (eds) (1981) *The Development of Welfare States in Europe and America*. New Brunswick, NJ, and London: Transaction Books.

General Accounting Office (1982) *A Summary and Comparison of the Legislative Provisions of the Block Grants Created by the 1981 Omnibus Budget Reconciliation Act*. Washington, DC: GAO.

Glennerster, Howard (1982) 'Social Planning: a Local Study.' Department of Social Administration, London School of Economics, mimeo.

Goldberg, E. Matilda and Hatch, Stephen (1981) *A New Look at the Personal Social Services*. London: Policy Studies Institute.

Grunow, Dieter and Hegner, Friedhart (1980) *Welfare or Bureaucracy? Problems of Matching Social Services to Clients' Needs*. Königstein: Verlag Anton Hain; Cambridge: Oelgeschlager, Gunn and Hain.

Harpham, Edward (1986) 'Federalism, Keynesianism, and the Transformation of the Unemployment System in the United States', in D. Ashford and E.W. Kelley (eds), *Nationalizing Social Security*. Greenwich, CT: JAI Press.

Jay Committee (1979) *Mental Handicap Nursing and Care*. London: HMSO.

Johnson, Paul Barton (1968) *Land Fit for Heroes: the Planning of British Reconstruction*. Chicago: University of Chicago Press.

Lambert, Royston (1962) 'Central and Local Relations in mid-Victorian England: the Local Government Act Office, 1858–1871', *Victorian Studies*, 6: 122–39.

Laroque, Pierre (1953) 'Problèmes posés par les élections sociales', *Revue Française de Science Politique* 3(2): 22–30.

Leach, S.N. (1981) 'Relationships between Supplementary Benefits Offices and Social Service Departments', *Policy and Politics* 9(3): 349–71.

Leibfried, Stephan (1986) 'Welfare Guidelines: Regulating Weimar's Poor', in D. Ashford and E.W. Kelley (eds), *Nationalizing Social Security*. Greenwich, CT: JAI Press.

Lynn, Laurence E., Jr and Whitman, David D.F. (1981) *President as Policymaker: Jimmy Carter and Welfare Reform*. Philadelphia: Temple University Press.

McKay, David H. and Cox, Andrew (1979) *The Politics of Urban Change*. London: Croom Helm.

Mays, John, Forder, Anthony and Keidan, Olive (eds) (1983) *Penelope Hall's Social Services of England and Wales*, 10th edn. London: Routledge & Kegan Paul.

Milnor, Andrew (1983) 'AFDC with Special Reference to New York and Pennsylvania', mimeo.

Morgan, Kenneth and Morgan, Jane (1980) *Portrait of a Progressive: the Political Career of Christopher, Viscount Addison*. Oxford: Clarendon Press.

Nathan, Richard (1975) *The Plot that Failed: Nixon and the Administrative Presidency*. New York: John Wiley.

National Assembly (1984) *Rapport de la Commission des Finances*, Annexe 4, 'Affaires sociales et solidarité nationale', Première session ordinaire de 1984–1985, 10 October. Paris: Imprimeries Réunies.

Newsholme, Sir Arthur (1925) *The Ministry of Health*. London: Putnam.

Nissel, Muriel, et al. (1980) *The Welfare State — Diversity and Decentralisation*. London: Policy Studies Institute.

Peacock, Alan and Wiseman, J. (1967) *The Growth of Public Expenditure in the United Kingdom*, 2nd edn. London: George Allen & Unwin.

Rhodes, R.A.W. (1981) *Control and Power in Central–Local Government Relationships*. London: Gower Press.

Rich, Robert F. (1982) 'Mental Health Policy-Making at the State and Federal Levels:

Challenges for the 1980s'. Carnegie Mellon University, Pittsburgh, mimeo.

Richan, Willard C. (1981) *Social Service Politics in the United States and Britain*. Philadelphia: Temple University Press.

Seebohm Committee (Committee on Local Authority and Allied Personal Social Services) (1968) *Report*, Cmnd. 3703. London: HMSO.

Social Services Committee (1982) *Public Expenditure on the Social Services*, White Paper, Second Report, House of Commons Paper 306–I and 306–II, 1981–2 Session. London: HMSO.

Stone, Deborah (1980) *The Limits of Professional Power: National Health Care in the Federal Republic of Germany*. Chicago: University of Chicago Press.

Thomas, N.M. (1973) 'The Seebohm Committee on Personal Social Services', in R. Chapman (ed.), *The Role of Commissions in Policymaking*, pp. 143–7. London: George Allen & Unwin.

Walker, Alan (ed.) (1982) *Community Care: the Family, the State and Social Policy*. Oxford: Basil Blackwell and Martin Robertson.

Walsh, Kieron (1985) 'Workforce', in S. Ranson, G. Jones and K. Walsh (eds), *Between Centre and Locality*, pp. 100–18. London: George Allen & Unwin.

Webb, Adrian and Wistow, Gerald (1982a) 'The Personal Social Services', in A. Walker (ed.), *Public Expenditure and Social Policy*, pp. 135–64. London: Heinemann.

Webb, Adrian and Wistow, Gerald (1982b) *Whither the Welfare State? Policy and the Implementation in the Personal Social Services, 1979–80*. London: RIPA.

Weiss, John (1983) 'Origins of the French Welfare State: Poor Relief in the Third Republic, 1871–1914', *French Historical Studies*, Spring: 47–78.

3

Local Government and the Welfare State: Reorganization in Scandinavia

Francesco Kjellberg

Introduction

Local government in Scandinavia today is a different institution from what it was at the end of the Second World War. Now, having the responsibility for 50–60 percent of the total public outlays, which amounts to more than 50 percent of GDP, it has become by far the most important implementing agency of welfare state programmes. In the last four decades, the entire system of local government in all three countries — Denmark, Norway and Sweden — also experienced a wholesale refurbishment, leaving few of its original features untouched and involving the entire local government structure, its functions, and its finances. Some of the changes were quite visible and highly dramatic. By the 1970s, only 10 percent of the number of Swedish communes that existed in the 1940s remained; the corresponding figure was slightly higher in Denmark, about 20 percent. In the 1980s a large part of the special grants were abolished in favour of a general grant in both Denmark and Norway, paving the way for new relations between central government and local authorities. In addition, all three countries experienced, to greater or lesser extent, a tendency towards regionalization in the guise of a strengthening of the intermediate level of government.

Why did all this occur? And how did it come about? In order to answer these questions we need to attempt to develop a theory of local government reorganization. The Scandinavian experience may have been more comprehensive, but it is hardly unique. It is an example, more or less particular, of a more general phenomenon that has occurred in most of Western Europe. An answer often given to these questions, therefore, is that the trend reflects the expansion of the public sector. In this chapter we will essay to go beyond such generalities, analysing the Scandinavian experience, in particular the structural and functional reforms, in terms of various stages in the development of the welfare state and the changing ideological perspectives surrounding the institution. We will look at the changes that have taken place as a result of the interplay between types of reform, requirements of the public sphere and ideological premises. Accordingly, before describing the reorganization pattern in the three countries, we will first look at the variations in the ideological elements, and will later cover briefly what appear to be the main phases in the development of the public sphere.

Two basic perspectives on the role of local government

Mackenzie (1961) made the point succinctly years ago: there is no theory of local government. The institution of local government embodies a variety of values, autonomy, participation and efficiency, which on many occasions have been shown to be uneasy bedfellows (Sharpe, 1970; Ylvisaker, 1959). Nevertheless, it is possible to distinguish between two main perspectives on the role of local government in a modern context, which to an increasing extent have been competing with each other as the ideological justification for the reorganizational process of the last two or three decades. One we may term the *autonomous* model of local authorities and the other, the *integration* model of central–local relations.

The autonomous model
The first perspective is more easily circumscribed, since it basically reflects the traditional view of the relationship between central and local government. Its essence is a definition of the two spheres of government as relatively separated, with the local authorities' actions, unimpeded, as far as possible, by the central organs. Irrespective of the magnitude of the municipal sphere, from this perspective the role of the state is only to monitor the activities of local authorities, without intruding into their domain. This perspective has a close affinity to a liberal ideology and is based on the assumption that a fairly clear demarcation is possible between the appropriate tasks of the local units and the functions of the state. The traditional structure of local government was indeed tailored to the prevailing laissez-faire values in the nineteenth century, being based on a conception of the municipal sphere as restricted and clearly delimited in relation to other governmental spheres.

In its purest form, such a perspective is a residue of the past. But in a more diluted form, it was still a powerful element of the ideology surrounding local government institutions in most developed countries in the period after the Second World War. In the Scandinavian countries, at least, it was particularly evident in the conception of the non-socialist parties. The platform of the Norwegian Conservative

Party in 1949, for instance, emphasized that 'the party wants to restore municipal self-government and it strongly opposes the centralization trend that is now under way. Clear boundaries have to be drawn between the functional domain of the state and the domain of the local authorities' (quoted in Sørvang et al., 1981: 15). And the Norwegian Liberal Party voiced a similar concern in its programme in 1947:

> Municipal self-government is in serious danger. Central authorities are intervening more and more in the autonomy and functions of the local authorities, in the economic, in the social as well as in the cultural field. The Liberal Party will actively oppose the undermining of the municipal self-government. (Quoted in Sørvang et al., 1981: 23)

This is far from being a prerogative of Scandinavian conservatism. It has been argued, for instance, that 'the hope that the territorial, functional, political and economic boundary in the modern Welfare State can be permanently fixed . . . is a romantic idea deeply rooted in British history and culture' (Ashford, 1982: 4). Not all British local government experts will agree with this. Still, the perennial British 'local government in crisis' syndrome seems very much akin to such a view. The insistence that levels of government be kept distinct, founded as it seems to be in liberal dogmas about the proper conduct of government, might have pleased John Stuart Mill.

Nevertheless, the transference of the ideological baggage of the nineteenth century to the middle of the twentieth was bound to create administrative tensions. The discrepancy between the autonomous model and the realities, which had been visible as early as the 1930s, became glaring after the Second World War. Local and national government then started to operate in tandem, forming almost a single, intermeshed system of making and delivering policies. The continuance of these ideas in the era of the welfare state would have placed severe restrictions on what could be done with local government (Ashford, 1982: 4). It had therefore increasingly to compete with another perspective, which was more in tune with the administrative and political realities.

The integration model
The second perspective defines the appropriate relation between the two spheres quite differently. It accentuates their integration, perceiving the functional divisions between central and local government in a flexible and pragmatic way; they have to be adjusted to the needs of particular circumstances. As much as the first perspective is related to a liberal ideology, the integration perspective has an affinity to an interventionist ideology. Accordingly, its clearest manifesta-

tions are to be found either on the leftist side of the political spectrum or in a *dirigiste* political culture like France. A typical example of its leftist manifestation is the following statement by the Social Democratic representatives in a government commission in Sweden in the 1970s:

> The distinctive feature of modern local authorities is that they no longer only administer functions of exclusive concern to the citizens of the municipalities, but that they participate in the entire reform process in the society. In this process they have been conferred increasingly more functions. (SOU 1975: 41: 471)

The perspective was also apparent in the programme of the Norwegian Labour Party at the first local elections after the Second World War, which stated:

> In our time the municipal activities are a most important part of national policy. The local authorities are becoming to an increasing extent channels through which the state policies are implemented. The Norwegian Labour Party looks at local government in a quite different way from the non-socialist parties. In all sectors of public activity the state and the municipalities are becoming more and more interconnected. (Quoted in Sørvang et al., 1981: 11)

It is tempting but deceiving to identify the two perspectives with, respectively, a decentralist and a centralist strand. The monitoring of the local authorities, inherent in the autonomous model, might easily develop into stringent control, as the activities of the local authorities expand in conjunction with the widening of the public sphere. On the other hand, close integration between central and local authorities cannot be identified unambiguously with a high degree of central steering. The role of informal structures with their intricate pattern of influence runs counter to such an interpretation (Tarrow, 1977; Thoenig, 1978; Scharpf, 1978).

A recent contribution by Thrasher (1982) may help to clarify this point. Discussing various conceptions of central–local relations, Thrasher juxtaposes two models: (1) the 'principal-agency model', according to which local government is to be supervised from the centre; and (2) the 'partnership model', which perceives (and recommends) the relationship to be characterized by mutual dependency and co-operation. This bears some resemblance to the distinction introduced above between the autonomous and the integration models. But the two pairs of concepts are not completely overlapping. Taken together, they rather indicate a two-dimensional ideological space, as illustrated in Figure 1.

Theoretically, both the autonomous and the integration models have a potential for central supervision as well as mutual partnership.

Model of the relationship

		Principal agency	Partnership
Government levels	Separate	1	3
	Intertwined	2	4

Figure 1 *Models of central–local relations*

And there is no reason to believe that this ambiguity will be dissipated in the ideological debate about local government institutions.

An additional point has to be made in this connection. The autonomous and the integration perspectives are not to be identified with the non-socialist and the socialist parties, respectively. While becoming more prominent in different parts of the political spectrum soon after the Second World War, both perspectives were increasingly to be found in both camps. Indeed, a most important feature is the tension between these two main strands, not only between the political parties but also within the parties.

It is their particular blend in the various circumstances that moulds the reorganizational process, i.e. the type of reforms that have been envisaged and the way in which they have been implemented.

From welfare state to interventionist state

There is hardly any disagreement about the role played by the welfare state as a primary motor for the reshuffling of local government in developed countries. The general argument is that the welfare state, through the enormous expansion of the public sector, has increased the reliance on lower-level decisions and policy guidance, resulting in a multiplication of decision-making bodies at all levels (Ashford, 1982: 16). The question, however, remains: what are the specific features of the welfare state that have led to such fundamental changes at the sub-national level? And furthermore: does the concept of welfare state have such a clear content as unambiguously to cover the entire development of the public sphere after 1945?

The short answer to this is no. The longer answer is that we have to distinguish between three distinct phases in the development, differing in their specific structural requirements on the sub-national level. The notion of the welfare state becomes unnecessarily diluted if it is stretched to cover all three of them.

The first phase might be identified as the one in which the emphasis is on social consumption services, i.e. the provision of direct benefits to the citizens, in the attempt to equalize the social conditions in society. It corresponds to the classical version of the welfare state, which, as articulated by Marshall, Titmuss and other advocates, was basically aimed at granting social rights to all. As pointed out by Flora and Heidenheimer (1981), the welfare state might be interpreted as an answer to increasing demands for social–economic equality, or as the institutionalization of social rights related to the development of civil and political rights. Defined in this way, the roots of the welfare state in most countries are to be found in the nineteenth century. But it came to full bloom in the years after the Second World War, when the term itself was introduced in political parlance. It now entailed a substantial increase in the national minima for social security, education and health care, all of which in many countries had been, if not the exclusive prerogative, at least one of the main responsibilities of local authorities. Such issues had traditionally been part of the 'low politics', to be kept separate from the 'high politics' at the national level (Rose, 1984). They had now moved to the centre-stage of the political system.

Accordingly, as the social service basket widened dramatically in tune with the institutionalization of the welfare state, two seemingly conflicting trends appeared at the sub-national level. On the one hand, local government greatly expanded its scope, becoming the main vehicle for the implementation of national programmes in the social and educational sphere. The political system as a whole became increasingly dependent on the local organization of nationally determined policies (Ashford, 1982). Thus, the importance of the local authorities was clearly augmented, as was their potential leeway in the execution of policies in various fields. But at the same time, the development of the welfare state also implied that social services should be standardized and routinized so as to minimize local variations. This second trend hit local government in a different manner: adhering to national objectives and standards implied a curtailment of its independent impact. Hence, the responsibility placed on local government by the institutionalization of social rights created an urge for rational and efficient administration. It was the administrative capability for social service delivery, the *Verwaltungskraft* of the West German reforms, that was now in the forefront. Combined, as it often was, with the still predominant autonomous model of local government, it tended towards a restructuring of local government units, particularly at the district level.

The emancipation of local government thus had to go through an administrative uplift. Several paths were seemingly open; intermunicipal co-operation and the establishment of special purpose units were two possible solutions to the administrative strains created by the mounting involvement of local government in nationally determined policies. But the earlier the trend was set in motion, and the more involved local authorities had traditionally been in social service delivery, the more likely it was that reorganization at this stage would take the shape of amalgamation. The merger of communes and districts implied an efficient pooling of the administrative resources needed for the implementation of broad social programmes, simultaneously retaining at least the illusion of local self-government.

This first phase of the welfare state did not raise so much the question of new functions for local government as the issue of new structures to handle the expansion of old functions. The second phase was to be somewhat different in this respect. The welfare state, concomitant with the enlargement and efficient administration of the social service basket, describes one part of the development of the public sphere, even if, admittedly, a most important part. The distributional goal was also pursued indirectly through various programmes aimed at reducing more generally social and economic imbalances in society. One may interpret this trend in a neo-Marxist vein as 'social expenses, i.e., projects and services which are required to maintain social harmony' (Gough, 1979: 51; O'Connor, 1973). Or one may see it as a response to broad political pressures. But whatever the open or disclosed motives behind such a trend, it is hardly disputable that social distribution issues now became intertwined with policies of resource allocation. In other words, as the welfare state evolved, public services not only expanded but also changed their aims and character. Hence, the second phase of the development of the public sphere might be identified with the 'Keynesian revolution', the conscious pursuit of full employment through control of the business cycle.

This is normally identified with trends at the national level of government. Actually, it also had far-reaching implications for the sub-national system. At the national level, it was manifested in the emphasis on macroeconomic planning, something that Andrew Shonfield, writing in the 1960s, made into the key-element in what he perceived to be the reason for the success of modern capitalism. We may easily follow Shonfield's argument that the outstanding feature of the public sphere in this phase of the development was a vast increase in the influence of public authorities on the management of the economic and long-range national planning. A variety of techniques and institutions were developed to meet the demand for coherence in economic decisions, which has a significant impact on national production or public welfare (Shonfield, 1965: 67).

What is left out in Shonfield's magisterial work is the repercussions this trend had at the local and intermediate levels of government. At least two features inherent in this phase of the development of the welfare state in fact impinged on local government, creating the background for new reorganization attempts. One was a more articulated regional and labour market policy, which involved local authorities in a wider spectrum of public programmes and led to a closer interlocking of activity between centre and localities. This made for both structural and functional reforms, particularly at the intermediate level. The other was the continuous expansion of public activity and its penetration into new areas, leading to a need for more comprehensive and integrated policies at the various levels and between levels of government. And this also called for new reforms in the shape of planning devices.

Introduced under different rubrics, synoptic decision-making therefore became a prominent trait at the sub-national level, adding to the intricate web of intergovernmental relations (Kjellberg and Offerdal, 1984). While the emphasis in the first phase had been on efficient administration of the expanded social services, the second phase of the welfare state concerned a different aspect: the integration of policies and programmes within localities and regions, as well as across levels of government. But again, it would be outlandish to conceive one single solution.

As the problem of co-ordination within government grew, planning techniques and institutions were universally put on the reorganization agenda. However, whether or not they were actually implemented, and the way in which they were framed, is a reflection of the tension this trend fostered in relation to the dominant ideological perspective. While the structural reforms at the district level could be accommodated with the autonomous model, the functional and decision-making reforms were bound to create strains in relation to it. To be carried through, they had to be supported by the integration model.

Finally, a somewhat different emphasis is to be found in the third phase of the development. The focus here is much more on financial steering of public activity. In its various forms the financial reforms are obvious attempts to come to grips with what has been perceived as a governmental 'overload' (Rose and Peters, 1978; Rose, 1980). The increasing complexity of public activity, its penetration in the private sphere and its widening share of the national product accentuated more and more the need for steering public finance and the economy in society. In the interventionist state that now took shape, the distributional aspects became tied not only to the issues of resource allocation, but also to the goal of economic stabilization, that is, to the control of aggregate demand and consumer spending (Ashford, 1980).

In this phase, it became increasingly evident that the sub-national units were a prime motor for the expansion of public activity. Both in France and in Britain, local current expenditures increased in the 1960s at an annual rate of about 13 percent, which was 3 percent faster than the growth of the national expenditure in both countries. The same pattern can be detected in Scandinavia, as well as a number of other countries. Obviously, if one wanted to regulate the ebb and flow of public finance in this situation, local government was one of the most likely instruments. There is a logical and indeed a clear empirical connection between a conscious effort to steer the economy and functional reorganization, particularly in the form of financial reforms.

To recapitulate the development of the public sphere in the postwar period cannot be perceived as a uniform and uni-dimensional trend, and it may not be easily summarized in terms of the welfare state. Its various phases are characterized by different aspects and, correspondingly, different pressures on the sub-national system and the intergovernmental relations. One such phase relates to the social services, where the expansion requires efficient delivery systems in the localities. Another relates to situations in which the emphasis is on co-ordination and more rational formulation of the multiplying public programmes; this tends to raise the issue of an extended planning system in the localities and to bring into focus the intermediate level. Finally, a third phase can be identified in which the very magnitude of the public sector, and the concomitant demand for a more active economic steering, leads to a reconsideration of the financial intertwining between central and local government.

In some situations these different phases manifest themselves in a clear secular trend. In other cases they appear simultaneously, and as clearly interconnected. Indeed, the second and third phases seem to go together in most contexts, both being closely linked with the formulation and implementation of the encompassing programmes and policies that characterize the advanced interventionist state. By differentiating between various phases in the welfare state development, I am not suggesting a neat and tidy sequence of reorganizational forms; they may be superimposed on each other, making the empirical world more messy than we would like it to be. This distinction may help us, however, to understand why particular forms have occurred at all. The three phases indicate different structural settings, which, together with the ideological elements in a particular situation, have generated the reorganization process and delimited the options. They define the political arenas in which the actors play out their interests.

**Empirical illustrations: reorganization in the
Scandinavian countries**

With this analytical scheme as a background, we will now consider
the main features of the reorganization in Denmark, Norway and
Sweden. The three countries cover the whole range of local government reforms, and at the same time are almost prototypes of the
modern welfare state. Accordingly, they are useful cases for tracing
the nexus between the various reforms, the different phases in the
development of the public sphere and the ideological elements surrounding local government. However, in spite of their many similarities, there is a pronounced difference between Norway and Sweden
on the one hand, and Denmark on the other, in their reorganizational
pattern. While in both Norway and Sweden the reorganization
appears as a prolonged process stretching over several decades, the
Danish case is an example of a swift break with the past. It is
therefore appropriate to consider them separately, raising the question of whether the two patterns may not reflect different structural
premises. First, we will consider the Swedish and Norwegian cases,
both countries being the earliest starters in a West European context.
Then we will examine the Danish case, as Denmark was among the
late-comers on this score.

*Sweden and Norway: towards an integrational
model*
The connection between the widening of the social service basket and
the structural reform at the district level is strikingly evident in the
Swedish amalgamation reform. The 90 percent reduction in the
number of communes in Sweden after the Second World War, from
about 2500 to about 280, came in two waves, the first as early as the
1940s, the second in the 1960s. The structural reform of the 1940s in
particular reflected the need to 'bring about a more rational municipal division', in tune with the new functions of the localities (SOU,
1945: 38: 7). The connection is clearly apparent in the appointment of
the Municipal Amalgamation Commission in 1943, which was due to
the work of an earlier commission dealing with reforms of the social
sector, the majority of which had recommended the establishment of
special-purpose units for social services ('social service communes'),
as a way of making the administration of social benefits in the
localities more efficient. The minority, however, wanted to attain the
same goal through a complete revision of the municipal structure
(SOU, 1945: 38: 9). It was, therefore, a concrete issue rooted in the
early phase of the welfare state development that brought up the
question of a reapportionment of the Swedish municipalities. The

directive of the Municipal Amalgamation Commission made the
point very clearly. The Commission was to consider

> the changes in the society and the many new tasks that had been conferred
> to the local authorities, requiring a more rational municipal division.
> Accordingly, the new apportionment of the communes should give spe-
> cial consideration to the development in the social sector and to their
> adaptation to the school districts. (SOU, 1945: 38: 14)

However, the direct connection between the reapportionment of
communes and the most typical programmes of the welfare state is
only part of the amalgamation story. The structural requirements for
a more efficient and rational administration were forged by the still
predominant ideology at that time: the autonomous model of local
government. Even within the Social Democratic Party, the municipal
sphere was as yet perceived as a separate and relatively independent
sphere of governmental action. Indeed, the restructuring of the
municipal boundaries and the abolishment of the smaller units was
viewed as the only way to maximize both local efficiency in the social
and educational sector and local autonomy. Neither special-purpose
units, nor the transfer of functions from local authorities to other
levels, nor an increase of financial support to the smaller districts was
perceived as a viable solution. The problem confronting local government as a consequence of 'the extensive reforms to be expected in
both the social welfare and the educational sector' (SOU, 1945: 38:
187) required more functional administrative units. Accordingly, the
Commission suggested a reapportionment that would do away with
more than 50 percent of the municipalities. The proposal was
adopted without more ado by the government and passed in Parliament with hardly any opposition. There was at that time complete
consensus on the need to achieve the twin goals underlying the
reform: administrative efficiency and local autonomy.

The Norwegian case is almost a blueprint of the Swedish amalgamation reform. The reapportionment of the Norwegian municipal structure was not as drastic as the Swedish one, but the underlying logic
was strikingly similar. The territorial reorganization at the district
level was seen quite explicitly as a step in the construction of the
welfare state.

As early as in 1946, the Norwegian Labour government appointed
a Municipal Amalgamation Commission composed of members of
Parliament and civil servants. The terms of reference were indicative
of the Labour Party's basic orientation towards reorganization at that
time. The commission was 'to propose a revision of municipal boundaries with the objective of introducing amendments that [would] be

more in accordance with the changed conditions for the localities and which from an administrative and economic standpoint [would] place the municipalities in a better position to undertake their task' (Kommunalinndelingskom, 1952: 11).

The Commission followed this directive very closely, proclaiming administrative efficiency to be the main goal to be achieved by a structural reform. It stated unequivocally that central government had 'the right to expect municipal administration to be as effective as possible. Antiquated administrative structures, which [might] inhibit the development of the welfare state, should not be maintained' (1952: 25). At the same time, however, it was evident in the report that the autonomous model had a strong influence on the definition of local government. In fact, the basic perspective imbuing the work of the Commission was a blend of the traditional view of local government as a distinct and separate sphere of activity and the need to provide the localities with the administrative resources to carry out the many functions imposed — or in the process of being imposed — on them through the expansion of the public sphere. The Commission stated that 'each municipality [had] to develop into a community which exists autonomously within the boundaries prescribed by the law' (1952: 26). But it also argued that it was imperative to establish economically viable units. In order to attain the last objective without relinquishing the first, there was only one solution: to create larger municipalities, which might combine 'local competence and complete economic responsibility'. Hence, the aim of the amalgamation was to establish local units that, 'while retaining the principle of self-government, would favour the development of local economy; breed stability in municipal finances; provide a fair geographical distribution of tax burdens; and allow for a qualitative development of the administrative apparatus and a more efficient public management' (1952: 26).

It is further indicative of the connection between the structural reform in Norway and the basic welfare state programmes that the report explicitly linked the redefinition of the municipal boundaries with a major school reform. According to the guidelines for the implementation of the mergers, particular consideration was to be given to the planned introduction of comprehensive schools.

Thus, both the Norwegian and the Swedish amalgamation reforms seem almost perfect illustrations of the functional relation between a specific phase in the development of the welfare state and a particular type of reorganization, that is, structural reforms at the district level. The combination of an early start in the widening of the social service basket and a well entrenched role of the localities in the administration of social services in the two countries may have made the adoption and implementation of such a reform easier than in other contexts. But the relation is hardly unique.

The last element to be noted in the two cases is that the integrational perspective did not at that time represent a threat to the liberal notion of local government as an autonomous sphere of action. Hence, in both countries the political tension in connection with this reorganization was fairly mild, with the non-socialist parties, particularly in Norway, arguing for intermunicipal co-operation and voluntary amalgamation as an alternative. The next stage of the reorganization process was to be somewhat different.

In the 1960s, both Norway and Sweden experienced a new wave of reforms, quite different in nature from the earlier amalgamations. To be sure, Sweden now introduced a new reapportionment of the communes. But the very scale of this territorial reorganization, reducing the number of communes from about 1000 to about 280, and its incontestable connection with the introduction of a more extensive planning system in the localities, makes it appropriate to consider the reform as part of a regionalization trend.

The problem of the local government was again put on the political agenda in Sweden at the end of the 1950s. The Labour government then appointed a committee of experts to advise it on restructuring the municipal boundaries, which were perceived as not being in tune with the new planning functions of the local authorities. This was the modest beginning of what was to become perhaps the most 'scientific' structural reform in Western Europe. The committee, which included a generous representation of professional planners, i.e. cultural geographers, did not let the grass grow under its feet. It soon published the report, *Principles for a New Municipal Division* (SOU, 1961: 9), its main feature being a blend of two different perspectives. One was the culture geographers' emphasis on 'growth centres', defined as the crucial elements for a balanced economic and occupational development and therefore, implicitly, for the extension of planning in public activity. The other was the Social Democratic perception of the local authorities as integrated parts of public administration.

The strong influence of the professional planners was palpable in the whole report, but it was particularly striking in the committee's definition of the basic guidelines for a reapportionment: 'From an areal point of view, society can be perceived as made up of cells or regions, which are combined in different systems' (SOU, 1961: 9: 135). The goal was, again, to achieve a match between administrative divisions and the 'spontaneous regions' created by the urbanization process and the technical and economic changes. Concurrently, the committee stressed the need for significantly larger municipal units, in view of the development of public activity. It strongly emphasized, for instance, that public planning and labour market policy called for a centre with a hinterland of about 10,000 inhabitants. The older administrative units would not do. What was needed was a regrouping of the former communes into what was now termed 'commune blocks'. Swedish scholars are indeed unanimous in suggesting that it was the urge to plan all public services that created the need for this reform (Brandgärde, 1974; Widberg, 1979).

While restructuring according to the proposal was to evolve on the basis of intermunicipal co-operation, the committee made no bones about what the final goal should be: this was the demolition of the municipal structure as it had existed since local government was introduced in Sweden in the middle of the nineteenth century. The Social Democratic government, entirely concurring in the committee's recommendation, quickly presented a bill on municipal apportionment and the establishment of 'commune blocks'. This bill led to one of the most heated political debates in connection with any reorganization reform in Western Europe. The non-socialist parties were adamantly against the reform, arguing that reapportionment of such a magnitude should, in any case, be considered only after an evaluation of the division of tasks between the different levels of government.

Thus, two contrasting views on the local government institution confronted each other. On the one hand, there was the Social Democratic vision of the communes as integrated elements in the total public activity, emphasizing particularly their role in planning. On the other hand, there was the non-socialist, more liberal, definition of local self-government, conceiving of the municipalities as partly autonomous units and stressing the need for a clear distinction between various levels of public administration. It was the first view that won the day, but this was simply a reflection of the fact that the Social Democrats had the majority in Parliament. The Swedish municipal structure would indeed have been different if the Social Democratic Party had not had such a predominance then in Swedish political life.

The role of sub-national units in public planning, and basically the same political constellations, were evident also in connection with the later reforms at the county level in Sweden (SOU, 1974: 84; SOU, 1978: 35), indicating that what was at stake was the changing character of public activity and the growing interventionism of the welfare state.

The regionalization trend in Norway is not as dramatic as in Sweden, but it offers a good illustration of the same tendencies. Unlike the Swedish reform, it left the municipal boundaries untouched. But it included some important innovations at the district level and a considerable strengthening of the political and administrative organs at the intermediate level.

In the mid-1960s, a new planning system for local authorities was introduced in Norway. Structure planning and detailed zoning planning were made mandatory for all Norwegian municipalities. Even more indicative of the basic changes taking place was the fact that the very concept of planning was extended, from a narrow concern with spatial allocation of private and public activities to a broader consideration of social and economic development in local communities. All local government activities that directly or indirectly impinged on land use had now to be considered by the planning authorities. Structure planning was to cover most areas of policy-making with the purpose of co-ordinating and integrating the various activities into a comprehensive policy for the localities (Hansen, 1980: 170–1; Mydske, 1978). The underlying logic of the reform was therefore very much the same as in the Swedish commune block reform.

This similarity with Sweden was even more evident in the introduction of regional planning, which was to encompass two or more municipalities within a county. In contrast with municipal planning, regional planning in Norway was not made mandatory and its implementation was to be the sole responsibility of the municipalities within a region. The point, however, is that the regional councils to be established in such cases were highly reminiscent of the Swedish co-ordination councils, the anterooms of the commune blocks.

As it happens, this Norwegian reform proved to be less than successful. A few such councils were actually installed, with some counties being subdivided into regional districts, but not much came out of the experiment. The strong determination of the Swedish Social Democrats in sweeping away the old structure to give space to the planning requirements of the welfare state was lacking in the Norwegian case. The integration perspective on local government apparently had not achieved quite the same predominance here.

Another avenue was pursued in the reorganization process at this stage in Norway, namely, the strengthening of the intermediate level by a reshaping of the counties. After a protracted consideration of the issue, a complete reshuffling finally took place in the early 1970s. The county councils that had been composed of representatives of the municipal councils were now to be directly elected. They also got an administrative apparatus, independent of the state's deconcentrated administration, thus acquiring a more solid political basis. And most important, through an amendment of the planning act in 1972, the county councils were given a crucial role in the planning system. They were made responsible for strategic planning (county planning), which was to be based on the same concept as structural planning, i.e. on a global concern with both private and public activities within the counties, which were also to have an indicative function in relation to the structural plans of the municipalities.

Whether or not all this actually succeeded may not concern us in this context. The point is that the introduction of a planning system and the regionalization of local government, even if legitimized with reference to the accommodating concept of 'decentralization', was clearly in tune with the requirements of the second phase in the development of the welfare state in Norway as well as in Sweden: a more interventionist stance, and a greater emphasis on co-ordination of public programmes.

This part of the reorganization process in Norway, however, was closely intertwined with another strand, namely, the functional and financial reforms. The division of tasks between the various levels had been discussed throughout most of the period, and one might detect in this case a continuous tension between the two models of local government. On the one hand, in their attempt to clarify the competences of the local authorities, some of the commissions appointed tended to rely — at least in theory — on the autonomous model, i.e. to perceive central and local government as separate spheres. This view was particularly accentuated by the Main Commission for Local Government Reforms, appointed in the early 1970s, which made the 'principle of responsibility' into the basic tenet for such a reorganization. According to this principle, 'the political organ that [had] the responsibility for a task should also have the responsibility for its financing. The state, the counties and the municipalities should each be responsible for the financial coverage of their own respective tasks' (NOU, 1974: 53: 33).

On the other hand, the expansion of the public sphere clearly followed the logic of the integrated model, with central and local government becoming increasingly intertwined in terms of functions as well as finances. The result was that in the 1970s there existed as many as 180 special grants to local authorities, covering a variety of programmes. As the Main Commission saw it, this highly complex and confusing system had to be revised and brought in tune with a clearer division of tasks, also envisaged by the Commission. Accordingly, it proposed the abolishment of almost all specific grants and the introduction of a general grant system.

Interestingly enough, the Labour government was less than enthusiastic about this recommendation. In a White Paper in 1975, the Department of Municipal Affairs stated that it was doubtful about the wisdom of such a drastic reform of the grant system. It argued that there were limitations as to how clear a distinction could be drawn between the spheres of activity at different levels of government; there were a number of instances where the state, the counties and the municipalities each had vested interests and joint responsibility. Therefore, if the divided financial responsibility was to be abandoned, it would be necessary to enact sufficient legal instruments to ensure that the government's main political objectives would be followed (St. meld. nr. 31, 1974–5: 17). Evidently, the central government, or more specifically some of the more important departments, were reluctant at this point to do away with the 'golden whip' as a steering mechanism.

Even if there was hardly any political debate on the issue, the pressure for a trimming of the intricate grant system steadily increased and was articulated in terms of administrative efficiency and decentralization. Not surprisingly, therefore, the same commission a few years later reiterated the proposal for a revision of the grant system for the counties (NOU, 1979: 44) and for the municipalities (NOU, 1982: 15). According to the Commission, the abolition of the special grants and the introduction of a block grant would result in more simplified financial relations between the state and the localities; in a greater sense of responsibility and greater autonomy in both the counties and the municipalities; and, most important from our point of view, in a better overview of public finances (NOU, 1979: 44: 68).

The last argument brought the proposal close to the main concern of central government and in particular of the Department of Finance: the escalation of public expenditure and the need to contain this expansion, of which the localities had become a crucial factor. A revision of the grant system, and *ipso facto* of the entire financial basis of the localities, was consequently in accord with the last phase in the development of the public sphere. A more efficient financial steering had become the paramount objective of central government so as to counteract the continuous increase in public expenditure, which was no longer on a par with the economic resources. In fact, the government was now to follow up the proposal, even in a somewhat diluted form, by introducing not one general grant, but four block grants as a substitute to the many specific grants (St. meld. nr. 26, 1983–4).

The Swedish case is somewhat different on this score. While financial reforms also were put on the agenda, they raised far less political attention. The drastic changes introduced with the territorial reorganization, and the enlargement of the planning system in the localities, did seem to cover the need for a general steering of local government activity. The strength of the integration model, imbuing the earlier reforms, may have made a revision of the financial relations less crucial. Nevertheless, there are elements in the Swedish situation in later years that point in the same direction as in Norway. The containment of the municipal expenditure became an issue in the 1970s in Sweden as well. Thus, the question was raised of introducing a legal maximum rate for local taxation. Furthermore, an arrangement for limiting local spending was implemented, by way of yearly agreements between central government and the unions of local authorities (Wallin, 1978). And these short-term agreements may also herald a more permanent change in the financial relationships between centre and localities in Sweden, in tune with the steering requirements of the interventionist state.

Denmark: a deviant case?

Compared with the other Scandinavian countries, the Danish local government reorganization at the end of the 1960s and the early 1970s appears particularly comprehensive. In all three countries the reforms were of a radical nature, and some aspects of the restructuring were carried to even greater lengths in Norway and Sweden. Nevertheless, the reorganization as a whole in Denmark implied a more decisive and swift break with the past. A major characteristic of the Danish reorganization process was that its various categories — structural, functional, financial, decision-making and internal reforms — were evaluated, discussed and even implemented in a fairly co-ordinated fashion. While the normal pattern has been a piecemeal reform process, the integration of its various aspects is the distinctive feature of the Danish reorganization. From its very inception, it comprised four different elements: an amalgamation reform, an administrative reform, a reshaping of the financial relations, and a redefinition of the functional division between centre and localities. No wonder that it has been considered 'one of the most important Danish reforms in this century, aiming at a thorough restructuring of the public sector' (Bentzon, 1975: 31).

In addition to its comprehensive and integrated character, the Danish reorganization is distinguished by two other features. The first is its pronounced political attribute. The technical and professional components appear rather modest, and the political element is far more predominant than is generally the case in other countries. The second feature is the party-political consensus surrounding most of the reforms, a consensus that was attained through a series of negotiations including all interested parties. This was particularly evident in the amalgamation reform, which, as in the two other countries, was the centrepiece in the reorganization.

In the middle of the 1960s, Denmark was still untouched by the amalgamation wave that had swept the rest of Scandinavia. It was made up of 1388 communes, out of which only 86 were urban communes. Upon completion of the structural reform in 1974, only 275 municipalities were left, and the distinction between urban and rural units had been abolished. Hence, in a few years the number of local units had been reduced by 80 percent, a record beaten only by Sweden in Western Europe. The restructuring of the Danish counties was no less drastic, their number diminishing from 25 in 1965 to 14 by 1970. On this score Denmark indeed deviates markedly from both Norway and Sweden, where, in spite of various proposals for a reduction of county authorities, such a reform has never been implemented.

This staggering restructuring of local government occurred without notable political discord. How could a comprehensive reform of this magnitude be planned and executed in such a seemingly harmonious way? The answer is essentially to be found in the deliberate association of the structural reform with a financial reshuffling and a more extensive decentralization trend — in terms of tasks and functions — than in the other countries. And it was made easier by a protracted negotiation process, which took place in working out the proposals for new municipal boundaries

As in other countries, the very beginning of the reorganization process was associated with the growth of the public sector and its impact on the relation between central and local authorities. However, to this must be added the accelerated urbanization occurring in Denmark after 1945, which as early as the 1950s had definitely outdated the traditional municipal structure. The distinction between urban municipalities and rural communes came increasingly to be questioned, and there was a growing concern with the problems of the urban areas around the cities. The main point of contention was that the incorporation within the jurisdiction of the urban authorities of their surrounding areas would reduce the importance of the counties, as they included only the rural communes. As long as the urban municipalities remained outside the counties, it was impossible to reach an agreement on a revision of municipal boundaries (Bentzon, 1975: 34). This was the background for the appointment of a commission in 1958, with representatives from the Ministry of the Interior, the political parties and the municipal organizations. Its term of reference concerned primarily the various municipal laws. The Commission was to consider whether one single law could embrace all aspects of the local government structure, and only as a last point was it asked to examine the question of more appropriate municipal boundaries.

Nevertheless, the Commission quickly concentrated on the last issue, starting with an evaluation of the impact of demographic and structural changes on the assumptions behind the different types of local authorities. It seemed evident to the Commission that larger, more rational units had to be created, in spite of the widespread opposition towards such a reform (Betænkning, 1966: 6). Information about the actual municipal structure, defined as antiquated and obsolete, would make it possible to create a climate of opinion for an extensive reorganization. Hence, the Commission authorized a number of surveys and reports on the existing structure, and on the basis of a broad documentation concluded that three trends in particular had made the municipal structure inadequate, creating a need for an amalgamation. First, industrialization and urbanization had blurred the distinction between rural and urban communes, making them socially and economically more and more alike. Second, because of the expansion of the cities into neighbouring communities, urban agglomerations were divided into several administrative units, with obvious detrimental effects for planning, taxation and the co-ordination of services. The Commission was, in other words, concerned with the problem of externalities and with the principle of fiscal equivalence (Olson, 1969). And third, the growth of the public sector had created demands upon local administration, which the rural and economically stagnant municipalities were unable to meet.

Unlike the Norwegian and Swedish cases, it was clearly the urbanization trend, rather than the complexities of the welfare state, that sparked off the Danish structural reform. There are two possible interpretations for this. One is that Danish society, as early as the 1950s and 1960s, was more urbanized than the other Scandinavian countries. The incongruities between municipal structure and socioeconomic realities might simply have been too glaring to be bypassed. The other possible interpretation is that a strong liberalistic tradition in Danish society and politics, noted by a variety of scholars, might have pushed the requirements of a developing welfare state more into the background. Together, these interpretations might explain both why the Danish structural reform came later than in the two other Scandinavian countries, and why there was hardly any mentioning of the integration perspective.

The Commission presented its conclusions in 1966. The report envisaged a new local government structure as well as a new law governing local administration. These proposals were the result of a series of debates, information campaigns and compromises, giving them a solid political basis. In fact, the Commission was rather unique in its efforts to stimulate public debate on the questions to be evaluated: its secretariat functioned as consultant to many locally sponsored investigations into the problem, and the Commission was far more open to discussions with the various parties concerned than is normally the case. It was praised in the subsequent debate in Parliament for its 'unconventional approach . . . keeping the general public informed whilst evaluating the matter. . . .' (Folketinget, 1966–7: 6036–7).

The compromise entailed two issues: (1) what became known as the principle of 'one urban community, one municipality' and (2) the incorporation of urban municipalities into the counties. The principle that an urban agglomeration should as far as possible constitute one municipality had been a most contentious issue, coming close to drawing the Commission to an impasse. The squeezing of the tax basis of the towns, arising from an increasing migration to the suburbs, clearly required a redrawing of their boundaries. At the same time, this would lead to a significant reduction of the tax income of the counties, as long as the towns were not incorporated in them. Hence, it was only through the linking of the two issues that an agreement could be reached.

One other reason for the broad consensus on the boundary reform was the flexible standards laid down by the Commission for the consolidation of the municipalities. No exception was to be made on the principle of 'one urban community, one municipal unit'. But nowhere in the report was there any example or preference as to the optimum size of the municipal units to be attained (Folketinget, 1966–7: col. 6038). The very absence of explicit and detailed guidelines seems to have been instrumental in establishing the political platform necessary for the reform. Finally, the Commission quite clearly defined the structural reform as closely associated with a revision of tasks and functions between local, regional and central levels. Together, the two types of reform would strengthen local self-government and increase decentralization; or, as succinctly summarized in the report,

> The implementation of the amalgamation reform requires a rearrangement of functions and responsibilities between central and local authorities. . . . The explicit intention with this reform proposal has been to create the basis for a rational division of functions within public administration, such that the concept of democracy as expressed in the institution of local government can be more firmly entrenched.

This point was reiterated and accentuated in the parliamentary debate that was to follow.

After a debate with hardly a note of discord, a law 'concerning the revision of local administrative boundaries' was passed unanimously in 1967. It authorized the Ministry of Interior to implement such a revision with the following objectives: (1) the establishment of new counties to include both urban and rural communes; (2) a redrawing of the boundaries in such a way that areas integrated in terms of population and occupational structure would form one municipality; (3) the creation of larger municipal units better able to meet their economic contingencies. The bill also stated that the first and second parts of the reform were compulsory, while the third was to be achieved through voluntary co-operation by the smaller communes. However, the whole reform was to be carried through by April 1970. The end result after this three-year period, as already noted, was 14 counties and 278 municipalities.

At the same time, a new law regulating local government administration was introduced. In addition to abolishing the distinction between rural and urban communes, it included a variety of administrative changes. Most important were the introduction of a new steering body — a financial committee — in the municipalities, the upgrading of mayor into a full-time position, and relieving the prefect of its leading role in the counties. In summary, the new law implied a significant strengthening of the political, elected bodies, particularly in the counties.

What happened in Denmark at this stage was therefore something different from the structural reforms in Norway and Sweden. What had been a *conditio sine qua non* in Denmark for a successful outcome of the restructuring, namely, the combination of various types of reforms, was absent in the other Scandinavian countries. On the other hand, the integration perspective, which loomed large in Sweden and was quite prominent in Norway, is hardly to be found in the Danish case. The dominant ideology pointed in a different direction, towards the autonomous model of local government. The goal was not only to create larger units to act as efficient implementing agencies for welfare state programmes, but also to delimit the local domain as a separate sphere of activity. This was baptized 'communalization'. Thus, in addition to the more accentuated urbanization trend, which gave the structural reform a somewhat different content, it was a liberal ideology that moulded the process.

However, the broad political agreement on decentralization did not resolve the classical contradiction inherent in the concept of local self-government, i.e. the tension between, on the one hand, the wish to widen the autonomous sphere of local government and, on the other, the wish to assure that such autonomy would not create glaring differences in the public services delivered in the localities. This dilemma had to be faced in reshaping the financial relations, and it led to a temporary shattering of the party-political consensus on reorganization.

The implementation of the amalgamation reform had hardly started in 1968 when a report was presented on the financial relations between central and local government (Betænkning, 1968). It was the result of a commission appointed in 1963 by the government, on recommendation of its Economic Secretariat, to 'examine the entire set of grants so as to reduce its disadvantages and simplify the system'. The background was that state transfers to local authorities amounted at this point to 40 percent of its total expenditure, about half of the municipal expenses being financed by central government.

Three questions were to be considered: (1) whether such a relatively high central support led to inconsiderate use of public finances by local authorities; (2) whether state financing of such a large share of municipal budgets in the long run would threaten the very principle of local self-government; and (3) whether an expanding system composed of a variety of grants might not become a hindrance for efficient financial policy. The initial objective was to achieve a better control over finances in view of the expanding public sector; as stated in the report,

> The requirements of financial policy have become unavoidably more demanding; it is urgent to examine closely the public sector and to consider how public tasks might be executed at minor costs. This had necessarily to include the grant system, many transfers to local authorities having been established under different conditions than today. (Betænkning, 1968: 11)

It was a clear attempt to hold back the integration between the various spheres of government, which had developed in a piecemeal fashion, strengthening the control at the macro-level.

The emphasis on the grant system was further accentuated in conjunction with the proposal of the structural reform in 1966. The main objective now became the critical examination of the whole set of transfers, thus contributing to a wholesale reorganization. The need for that was quite manifest. The Danish grant system included then more than a hundred specific grants; about 90 percent of them concerned only four areas: education, health, pensions and highways. It was a patchwork arrangement, the system having developed as in other countries in an *ad hoc* and unco-ordinated way over a long period of time. To systematize this staggering variety, the Commission introduced two analytical distinctions: one between automatic and non-automatic government support, and the other between situations where such support might apply. Automatic support was defined as that where central government contributed a definitive amount, provided that certain stated conditions were complied with; non-automatic support was defined as contributions to which local authorities had no stated right, being subject to specific approval by the central organs under specified conditions.

The crucial element in this distinction was the degree of discretion by central administration. The second differentiation was between those situations where government grants were earmarked to specific kinds and levels of activity by local authorities, and those where the transfers took the form of general contributions. A cross-tabulation of the two dimensions indicates the four different types of transfers shown in Figure 2 (Betænkning, 1968: 14).

	Automatic support	Non-automatic support
Specific support	(1) Reimbursement	(2) Special grants
General support	(3) General grants	(4) Contributions

Figure 2   *Characteristics of the Danish grant system*

It appeared that the first category, reimbursements, made up the lion's share of the transfers; the second category, special grants, constituted only limited amounts, while the third and fourth categories, general grants and contributions, hardly featured in the system. The commission argued that the reimbursements could be replaced by a combination of four financial arrangements: (1) an inter-municipal subsidy system; (2) a central tax equalization arrangement; (3) an introduction of general grants according to objective criteria; and (4) a rearrangement of the taxation system, increasing the share of local taxes. It did not forget to mention that any such reform would have to be considered together with the structural reforms. Given that all members of society should have equal access to public benefits, and should share the same burdens, the commission agreed that it would be ill-advised to abolish the former system as long as many local authorities lacked a sufficient economic basis. Equity could hardly be achieved if general grants were introduced instead of reimbursements under the existing structure. However, a reorganization would make it possible to introduce general grants based on objective criteria, supplemented to some extent by tax equalization support (Betænkning, 1968: 76–7). Again, the argument was thus in tune with the predominant decentralization ideology, akin to the autonomous model of local government.

The non-socialist government quickly followed along this path, adopting the alternative of general grants based on objective criteria. In proposing a bill on 'general grants to the local authorities', together with amendments in a number of laws regulating local government activity, it argued along the same lines as the commission:

> The existing transfers are neither relevant to, nor can they be adjusted to, the rapid changes of modern society. The many reimbursements result in a separation between the decision-making bodies and the financing

organs, with the possible consequence of public expenditures increasing more and being differently composed than desired. . . . The new local government structure gives a good basis for revising the underlying principle for the transfers and for a rearrangement of functions between central and local government. (Folketinget, 1968–9: II, App. A, col. 3373)

Various objectives were to be achieved by such a reform. A major goal was to establish a better accordance between jurisdiction and economic responsibility; a second objective was to achieve a better balance between affluent and poorer localities; finally, the new financial arrangement was meant to ensure a rationalization of the transfer system, and thereby of public administration as a whole.

As it appeared, the general consensus on the reform was somewhat fragile. The proposals were met with considerable opposition in Parliament by the leftist parties. Indeed, for the first and only time in the Danish reorganizational process, the debate took form of a confrontation between the two basic views of local government in the contemporary state: the autonomous model and the integration model.

There was no doubt about the opposition of the Socialist People's Party to the bill; its representatives marched out of the assembly, declaring that they would not even take part in the vote (Folketinget, 1968–9: col. 7315). And while the Social Democratic group stayed on, its parliamentary leader made no bones about its critical opinion:

These proposals are indefensible, so indefensible that they are probably without precedent in our Parliament. On several occasions we have cautioned against them. We know that these laws will not have the equalizing effect on local authorities which such a reform should have. . . . Their treatment in parliament has also been indefensible, superficial and by no means adequate.

He concluded by saying that the bill, if adopted, would result in a deterioration of social welfare as well as of the educational system in the localities (Folketinget, 1968–9: col. 7317).

Given the non-socialist majority in Parliament, the bill was passed with a good margin. However, the opposition by the Social Democrats affected to some extent the subsequent reform process. Even if several minor reforms followed immediately, the debate became increasingly dominated by the equity issue: which type of objective criteria would result in a fair and equitable effect, and what weight was to be attached to each of them in determining the amount to be transferred to each county and municipality? Several revisions followed, a Social Democratic government introducing in the late 1970s a new system based on 'expenditure needs' in communes and counties. The obvious difficulty of defining such needs contributed to a prolonged discussion of the pros and cons of the various arrangements. In fact, it was not before 1985 that the specific automatic grants were entirely abolished and a general grant system introduced (Indenrigsministeriet, 1985).

The last stage of the Danish reorganization might give the impression that both views on the role of local government in the contemporary state were prominent in the process. To some extent, the integration perspective does appear in the debate. Given the general prerequisites of the welfare state — the need for steering and for co-ordinating a steadily expanding public activity — it would have been surprising if this had not been the case. Nevertheless, the most significant aspect of the Danish reorganization is the impact of the autonomous model. In spite of the planning reforms that were introduced concurrently with the structural and financial reforms and have been interpreted as a strengthening of central steering (Madsen, 1980; Bruun, 1981), the end result appears different than in the two other Scandinavian countries. The Danish reorganization not only implied the creation of larger local authorities and a redefinition of the financial relations, as in Norway; it also represented, comparatively speaking, a clearer demarcation of the local sphere of activity, more in tune with a liberal concept of local government than with an integration perspective. Denmark appears, on this score, a deviant case.

Concluding remarks

Local government reorganization is part and parcel of the development of the contemporary state. The expansion of the public sector and its mounting complexity have implied an increasing pressure on the institutional arrangements at the local and regional level. The traditional structures with their roots in the liberal state, delimited in scope and non-interventionist in its ideology, could hardly bear the brunt of the *étatisation* in developed societies after 1945 (Chodak, 1983). The sub-national units had to play a new role in the public apparatus that now came into shape. However, the contention in this chapter has been that there is not one pattern of reforms, but a variety of patterns, reflecting different time sequences in the development of the welfare state and the emergence of new ideological perspectives on local government. I have argued that there is a close link between (1) the type of reforms that are considered and implemented, (2) the expansion and changing character of the public sphere, and (3) the prevailing ideology surrounding the institution.

The Norwegian and Swedish cases fit nicely into this perspective. In both countries a clear sequence can be discerned in the reorganization pattern, corresponding to the various stages in the development of the public sphere. For each new step in its expansion, new administrative and political requirements created the premises for different types of reforms. An amalgamation of communes early in the period was followed by a regionalization closely connected with the introduction of synoptic decision-making at the sub-national level, and later by an increasing concern with the financial relations between central and local government. A general shift in the basic conception of local government towards an integration model moulded these reforms, even if reminiscences of the autonomous models also could be detected in the later stage of the process. The interplay of public sphere, the prevailing ideology and the types of reforms implemented at various stages are clearly evident in the process in these two countries.

Not quite so in the Danish case. For one thing, the reorganization process in Denmark commenced at a later stage. The consolidation of Norwegian communes was nearly completed, and Sweden had embarked on a second round of amalgamations, before a similar reform was put on the political agenda in Denmark. Once the process got up momentum, however, it took a more comprehensive turn, involving structural and functional as well as decisional aspects of local government. The various reforms were also more closely combined in the process than was the case in the two other countries. But the most conspicuous aspect, compared with Norway and Sweden, is the exiguity of the integration perspective and the predominance of the autonomous model. The need for decentralization and a clearer demarcation of local activity — what was termed the communalization of the public sphere — was taken far more in earnest. The difference is puzzling and not easily accounted for.

Let us first see what may not explain it. A prerequisite for a consolidation of local units to occur is the role previously played by the municipalities in administering social services. One might assume that, if traditionally such services have been dispensed by central government through its deconcentrated agencies, a restructuring of local government is unlikely to take place. There will simply not be enough momentum for such reforms to break through the normal barriers against institutional changes. The welfare stage may bypass local government entirely, postponing its reorganization to a later stage. Another *sine qua non* for structural reforms to occur is the existence of a national legislation (or state legislation in federal systems) regulating local government. Local charters or home rule, as found in the USA, will work effectively against the consolidation of local units. With such a legal instrument in their hands, the interests vested in the existing institutions will be able to fend off any attempt to redefine local self-government. A voluntary amalgamation is indeed almost a contradiction in terms. The absence of these conditions may thus give the structural reforms a different mode and may even abort the organization trend.

However, they were present in all three Scandinavian countries, and cannot explain the deviant pattern in Denmark. The particular character of this case is therefore to be found in two additional traits that originally were not considered in our model. First, there is the role of the trend towards urbanization. Denmark was clearly a more urbanized society in the 1950s and 1960s than the two other countries, and the problems inherent in larger urban agglomerations were far more pressing. The principle of 'one urban community — one municipal unit' reflected the urgency to internalize the externalities created by the urbanization process, rather than the need to make local authorities into more efficient instruments for the implementation of welfare state policies. Unlike in Norway and Sweden, the urban question loomed large in the first stage of the Danish reorganization process, moulding its later stages as well. The requirements of a more active public sphere were secondary to this.

Second, and partly related to the first trait, is the seemingly stronger liberal tradition in Danish politics. A number of authors have pointed to the far more restricted interventionist element in the development of the public sphere in this country (Esping-Andersen, 1985; Steen, 1986). At least compared with the two other countries, the extent of macroeconomic planning has been modest, labour market policy has been rudimentary, and there has hardly been any industrial policy, just to take a few examples. The wideness of the social service basket might entitle the contemporary Danish state to be called a welfare state, but it is certainly of a different kind than the interventionist state that developed in Norway and Sweden. The strength of the autonomous model of local government is in tune with this basic character.

There is no need to take refuge in a cultural interpretation. The fact that the Danish Social Democrats never got the same hegemony as their Norwegian and Swedish cousins carries us a long way towards an explanation. As Brand pointed out in his comparative study of local government reform in England and Sweden (Brand, 1976), the dynamics of change are intimately connected with the perceptions of certain influential groups. He noticed that in Sweden it was the Social Democratic Party that was interested in the change and moreover had the power to carry it through. The character of the Danish contemporary state, and the moulding of the reorganization according to an autonomous model, might simply be the function of the relative weakness of a strategic actor, the Social Democratic Party.

A comparison of our three cases shows indeed that the political constellations, in terms of parties, interest groups and administrative agencies, are of paramount importance in getting reorganization on to the political agenda and getting it implemented. The tensions between policy requirements and ideological elements are played out in the political arena, the actors being the interpreters of the various structural trends. A structural analysis, as has been presented in this chapter, has therefore to be supplemented with a behavioural one. But it is hard to see how we might understand the reshuffling of Scandinavian local government, and how a more general theory of reorganization can take shape, without a differentiation between types of reform, phases in the development of the public sphere and ideological principles surrounding the institution.

Note

This chapter is a revised and expanded version of an article previously published in the *Journal of Public Policy*, 5 (1985).

References

Ashford, D.E. (1980) 'Central–local Financial Exchange in the Welfare State', in D.E. Ashford (ed.), *Financing Urban Government in the Welfare State*. London: Croom Helm.

Ashford, D.E. (1982) *British Dogmatism and French Pragmatism. Central–local Policy-making in the Welfare State*. London: George Allen & Unwin.

Bentzon, K.H. (1975) *Den Danske Kommunale Indelingsreform* Copenhagen: Institute of Political Science, University of Copenhagen.

Betænkning (Danish Commission of Inquiry) (1966) *Kommuner og Kommunestyre*, no. 420/1966. Copenhagen. Betænkning.

Betænkning (1968) *Statens Refusjoner af Kommunernes Udgifter*, no. 471/1968. Copenhagen. Betænkning.

Brand, J. (1976) 'Reforming Local Government: Sweden and England Compared', in R. Rose (ed.), *The Dynamics of Public Policy*. London: Sage.

Brandgärde, L. (1974) *Kommunerna och kommunblocksbildningen*. Lund: Liber.

Bruun, F. (1981) *Danske Kommunale Reformer siden 1945*. Aarhus: Institute of Political Science, University of Aarhus.

Chodak, S. (1983) 'Etatisation: its Concept and Varieties', *Research in Social Movement, Conflicts and Change* 5: 259–94.

Esping-Andersen, G. (1985) *Politics against Markets: the Social Democratic Road to Power*. Princeton, NJ: Princeton University Press.

Folketinget (1966–7) and (1968–9): Danish Parliamentary Proceedings.

Flora, P. and Heidenheimer, A.J. (eds) (1981) *The Development of Welfare States in Europe and America*, New Brunswick, N.J. and London: Transaction Books.

Gough, I. (1979) *The Political Economy of the Welfare State*. London: Macmillan.

Gustavson, G. (1980) *Local Government Reform in Sweden*. Umeå: Liber.

Hansen, T. (1980) 'The Politics of Local Planning in Norway', *International Political Science Review* 1(2): 168–86.

Indenrigsministeriet (Danish Ministry of Interior) (1985) Bekendtgørelse af Lov om Kommunal Udligning og Generelle Tilskud til Kommuner og Amtskommuner.

Kjellberg, F. (1983) 'Die Reformen der Kommunalen Gebietskörperschaften und Regionen in Dänemark, Norwegen und Schweden', in F. Zehetner (ed.), *Reformen der Kommunen und Regionen in Europa*. Vienna/Munich: Jugend und Volk Verlag.

Kjellberg, F. and Offerdal, A. (1984) 'L'attuazione delle politiche pubbliche in Norvegia', in B. Dente (ed.), *Le relazioni centro–periferia*. Milan: ISAP-Archivio.

Kommunalinndelingskom (1952) *Om Revisjon av den Kommunale Inndeling*. Oslo: Kommunaldepartementet.

Mackenzie, W.J.M. (1961) *Theories of Local Government*. Greater London Papers, no. 2. London: London School of Economics and Political Science.

Madsen, O.N. (1980) *Kommunale Reformer i Danmark*. Aarhus: Institute of Political Science, University of Aarhus.

Mydske, P.K. (1978) *Regional planlegging 1945–80*. Oslo: NIBR.

NOU* (1974: 53) *Mål og retningslinjer for reformer i lokalforvaltningen*. Oslo: Kommunaldepartementet.

NOU* (1979: 44) *Nytt inntektssystem for fylkeskommunen*. Oslo: Kommunaldepartementet.

NOU* (1982: 15) *Nytt inntektssystem for kommunene*. Oslo: Kommunaldepartementet.

O'Connor, J.R. (1973) *The Fiscal Crisis of the State*. New York: St Martin's Press.

Offerdal, A. (1979) 'Kommunane som iverksettarar av statleg politikk', in H. Baldersheim (ed.), *Lokalmakt og Sentralstyring*. Oslo: Universitetsforlaget.

Olson, M. (1969) 'The Principle of Fiscal Equivalence: The Division of Responsibilities among Different Levels of Government', *American Economic Review* 59(2): 479–87.

Rose, R. (ed.) (1980) *Challenges to Governance: Studies in Overloaded Politics*. London: Sage.

Rose, R. (1984) *From Government at the Center to Nationwide Government*. Glasgow: CSPP, University of Strathclyde.

Rose, R. and Peters, B.G. (1978) *Can Government go Bankrupt?* New York: Basic Books.

Scharpf, F.W. (1978) 'Interorganizational Policy Studies: Issues, Concepts and Perspectives', in K. Hanf and F.W. Scharpf (eds), *Interorganizational Policy-Making*. London: Sage.

Sharpe, L.J. (1970) 'Theories and Values of Local Government', *Political Studies* 2: 153–74.

Shonfield, A. (1965) *Modern Capitalism*. Oxford: Oxford University Press.

Siedentopf, H. (1983) 'Die Reformen der kommunalen Gebietskörperschaften und Regionen in der Bundesrepublik Deutschland: in Österreich und in der Schweiz', in F. Zehetner (ed.), *Reformen der Kommunen und Regionen in Europa*. Vienna/Munich: Jugend and Volk Verlag.

Sørvang, K.P. et al. (1981) 'Det kommunale selvstyre: hva sier partiprogrammene.' Oslo: Institute of Political Science.

SOU† (1945: 38) *Riktlinjer för en revisjon av rikets indelning i borgerliga primärkommuner*. Stockholm: Kommundepartementet.

SOU† (1961: 9) *Principer för en ny kommunindelning*. Stockholm: Kommundepartementet.

SOU† (1974: 84) *Stat och kommun i samverkan*. Stockholm: Kommundepartementet.

SOU† (1975: 41) *Kommunaldemokrati*. Stockholm: Kommundepartementet.

SOU† (1978: 35) *Regionalutvecklingsplanering. Vigdad lensdemokrati.* Stockholm: Kommundepartementet.

Steen, A. (1986) 'Velferdsstat og utjevningspolitikk', *Tidsskrift for samfunnsforskning* 27(3): 528–51.

St. meld. nr. 31 (1974–5) *Om mål og rettningslinjer for reformer i lokalforvaltning.* Oslo: Kommunaldepartementet.

St. meld. nr. 26 (1983–4) *Om et nytt inntektssystem for kommunene og fylkeskommunene.* Oslo: Kommunaldepartementet.

Strand, T. (1985) *Utkant og sentrum i det norske styringssystem.* Oslo: Universitetsforlaget.

Strømberg, L. och Westerståhl, J. (1983) *De nye kommunerna.* Stockholm: Liber.

Tarrow, S. (1977) *Between Center and Periphery: Grassroots Politicians in Italy and France.* London: Yale University Press.

Thoenig, J.-C. (1978) 'State Bureaucracies and Local Government in France', in K. Hanf and F. Scharpf (eds), *Interorganizational Policy-making.* London: Sage.

Thrasher, M. (1982) 'The Concept of Central–local Government Partnership: Issues Obscured by Ideas', *Policy and Politics*, 9(4): 455–70.

Wallin, G. (1978) 'Den kommunala sektorns omfattning och finansiering i Sverige', Paper delivered to the Nordic Conference in Political Science, Bergen.

Widberg, J. (1979) *Från Sockn till Kommunblock.* Stockholm: Kommundepartementet.

Ylvisaker, P. (1959) 'Some Criteria for a "Proper" Areal Division of Governmental Powers', in A. Maas (ed.), *Area and Power.* Glencoe, IL: Free Press.

---

* NOU: Norges Offentlige Utredninger (Norwegian Commissions of Inquiry).
† SOU: Statens öffentliga utredningar (Swedish Commissions of Inquiry).

4

Local Government Reforms and Structural Changes in Public Administration: the Finnish Case

Markku Kiviniemi

Reforms and changes

The purpose of this chapter is to show the linkages between the long-term changes in Finnish local government structures and functions, and the various efforts at reform attempted in different periods. The point of departure of the analysis, therefore, is somewhat terminological. What do we mean with the word reform? Is there a clear-cut distinction between reform and change? The international literature on this point is clear enough: the term 'reform' implies conscious, purposeful, directed action.[1] Reform is a conscious change, or at least a conscious attempt to change.

All social and human activities have both intended and unintended consequences. The initiators of change, that is, the reformers, do have their intentions, but the real changes contain more than these intentions. This happens at the least because there always are social actors whose intentions are not compatible with the proposed changes, that is, the opponents. Furthermore there are still other actors who do not have any defined intention concerning the changes, even if they will later on be confronted with the consequences (these are the outsiders). The consciousness implied in the reform processes calls therefore for an analysis of the actors, who can be grouped in three classes on the basis of their intentions: reformers, opponents and outsiders.

It is easy, however, to find instances of changes in governmental structures and processes which do not have any well-defined subject. This happens because unintended and unanticipated consequences can be the product of the progress of time and/or of the cognitive limits of the intentional actors. More to the point, macro-level transformations arise typically from the interaction of several micro-level changes. For the time being the first conclusion is that reforms are only one type of change. There will always be more changes than reforms, even if the change brought about by one attempt at reform can be less far reaching than hoped by its proponents, or feared by its opponents. The question of what can explain the changes and what can explain the reforms — in the local government field as well as in any other domain — requires two different answers.

This discussion leads on to a more fundamental problem concerning the choice of approach for the study of local government transformations: will we be able to understand more with a process-oriented 'micro' approach, or with a structure-oriented 'macro' one? It seems self-evident that the former is more apt for the study of reforms and the latter is best for investigating changes.

However, if our research problem concerns the relationship between reforms and changes, some sort of integrated approach will be needed. This implies that (1) reforms should be interpreted in the context of long-term structural changes and (2) long-term changes should be regarded as cumulative consequences of several reform activities. In other words, as I pointed out in an earlier paper, the macro-level changes consist of several micro-changes that, together, 'paint the macro picture'.[2] An essential feature of macro-level changes is incremental accumulation.

The existing structure of public administration consists of rules and resources which are in turn outcomes of earlier changes.[3] They both enable and constrain the possibilities for further change. Change can therefore be conceptualized as an implementation process having a selective character, and we can study it by revealing the implementation and barrier structures — the strategically most important bodies of intentional actors — through which it takes place. These implementation structures are sometimes relatively stable (established) and sometimes only temporary.[4]

It seems rational to presume that the most change-inducing areas of public administration are the boundary relationships between the most powerful actors.[5] This implies that the most important implementation and barrier structures will usually be coalitions between those actors. The actors themselves can be classified in three main groups or levels, according to their institutional position: the societal level, i.e. the environment of public administration; the governmental level, i.e. the body of national central administration; and the agency level, i.e. the body of various public sector units including local government.

There are, accordingly, three types of boundary relationships:

1. The relations between the societal level and the governmental level. Here the essential implementation and barrier structures are the political forces mediating between society and government. The activities within these structures are also the classical channel of governmental reforms.

2. The relations between the societal level and the agency level. Here the different 'functional' relations between the administrative machinery and its clients and/or its specific interest groups create the most important boundary structure controlling the processes of change. As a centralized and differentiated governmental structure is often more sensitive to the information coming from its own branches than from other sources, the external relations of a public agency with its main interest groups are more likely to produce changes than the formal political processes at the local level.

3. The relations within public administration between governmental and agency level. Here the practices of the prevailing rules and resources (that is, the administrative traditions) are the central factor enabling and constraining the processes of change. Often reform attempts within governmental organizations have to overcome earlier practices and traditions, as well as the opposition of the actors connected to them.

The possible changes are connected not only to the different boundary relationships but also to factors within each one of them. However, for reasons far beyond the scope of this chapter, we can assume, on the one hand, that these factors are of limited importance as far as the governmental and agency level are concerned, while, on the other hand, at the societal level the most powerful mediating structures selecting and processing change impulses towards public administration are the various economic interests.

Figure 1 summarizes the model of change we have presented, bearing in mind that, for present purposes, the agency level will refer to the basic units of local government, that is, the municipalities.

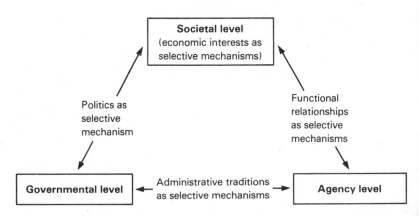

Figure 1   *A model of changes in public administration*

The configuration of local government changes and reforms

Macro-level changes in Finland
The macro configuration of the structural changes can be interpreted by means of a model of growth and differentiation.[6] The model groups structural macro changes in the system of public administration as follows:

1. the growth of public resources;
2. the growth of public rules (norms);
3. the differentiation of public rules;
4. the differentiation of public resources;
5. the multiplication of external relationships of the public bureaucracies;
6. the differentiation of external relationships of the public bureaucracies.

Do these general features also fit the picture of the changes at the local government level? In many respects, they do.

The resources of local government have expanded in Finland, as in other Western industrial countries, in both absolute and relative terms during recent decades. The share of municipal expenditures of GNP (without transfers) was 8 percent in 1950 and 14 percent in 1985. The growth of public rules at the local government level can be seen in the rapid growth of new welfare tasks and duties, stipulating the performance of new public services at the local level. The services are to a considerable extent ruled and planned by the central government.

The growth and differentiation of public rules refers to the strengthening of sectoral powers within the whole public administration. This sectorization implies an increased influence of the different sectoral apexes (ministries, central agencies) in the decision-making structure. It produces a differentiation of public rules because each sectoral apex tends to create its own regulations. Connected with this is the differentiation of public resources, which is manifest in a growing administrative differentiation of the structures as well as in a greater specialization and professionalization of public activities. Local government organization today is bigger, more sectoral and more centrally ruled, and in addition is structurally more differentiated.

The increasing administrative complexity of local government units might be considered as characteristic of their internal dynamics. But growth and differentiation also influence the external relations of local government. This is reflected in a more manifold and more differentiated network of at least three types of relations: the relations between central government and local government, the relations between different local government units, and the relations between local government units and their surrounding communities (local voluntary associations, enterprises and citizens).

The picture of macro changes at the local level is one of accumulated and gradual processes. There is no declaration or expression of goals, which would include a conscious striving for a bigger and a more differentiated local government as an administrative machinery. The planned and conscious efforts to reforms typically have a limited sectoral and functional scope. The macro-organizational dimension has remained latent in the discussions about reforms.

The background of the changes
A mere list of macro-level changes does not give very much insight into their background and dynamics. Some perspective into the relationships between the different features of change is also needed.[7]

The most remarkable and often emphasized developmental feature of the Finnish local government after the Second World War is the increasing influence of central government on municipal affairs. This development reflects the tendency towards a more integrated public economy. It also implies that both the initiation and the production of reforms are more centralized than before. Thus, the growth and differentiation of municipal services and their growing importance for citizens have to be interpreted primarily as an outcome of national policies. The sequence of macro-level changes most often considered in Finnish studies is depicted in Figure 2. The gradual strengthening of central influence on local affairs can be interpreted as a shift from a classical liberalist state to a modern welfare state. The position of local government has undergone a remarkable change in this development.

Local self-government managed by locally elected bodies was the original conception of local government in the nineteenth century.

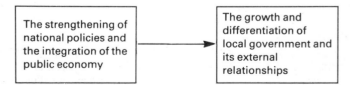

Figure 2   *Macro-level changes in Finnish local government*

This was the prevailing view in Finland at the time when the first laws concerning municipalities were passed (1865–73). However, the functional role of the municipalities was not specified. The relations between the state and the municipalities, as well as between the municipalities and the citizens, were regarded as situationally adjusted, informal and flexible. This was a time of limited public rules and resources

During the last decades of the nineteenth century and the first two decades of the twentieth, the model of a classical liberalist state dominated the development of local government in Finland. In principle, there were great possibilities for local self-government, but the lack of resources at the local level hampered reform activities. This lack of local resources was initially the main argument for state intervention into local government affairs, which originated in the 1920s.

The image of local government changed during the 1920s. The tasks of municipalities were considered to consist of two main types: first, there were the locally defined activities under the principle of self-government; second, there was a group of obligatory duties defined by the central government in the form of special laws. The first functional areas of obligatory municipal duties were public schools and health and social care. The obligatory tasks were financed partly by state aids.

The functional duality of local government is expressed in formal enactments. Since the origin of municipal government, there has been general legislation defining the local societal position and the political formation of municipalities; on the other hand, there are special laws defining different municipal tasks and duties on the base of national policies. This development implied the emergence of a more standardized and uniform system of local government, of its representative political system and of its local services. It also implied the political and bureaucratic segmentation of the classical liberalist state.

The full transition from a classical liberalist state to a modern welfare state took place after the war. The 1920s and 1930s were a mediating period, which, together with the crisis period in the 1940s, created the bases for the development of the welfare state.

The societal background for the development of the welfare state might be summarized in the following way:

- the rise of a centrally managed national economy during the war and the following period of socioeconomic reconstruction;
- the subsequent tendency of centralization within public administration;

- the rise of a widely shared egalitarian welfare ideology[8] in party politics;
- the period of relatively stable economic growth (1950–75), which provided resources for new welfare tasks;
- the relatively stable political leadership (the centre–left coalition) since 1966 and the rise of central planning and the corporatist style of decision-making, especially since 1968.

Both economic and political conditions for reforms, based on an egalitarian welfare ideology, attained their culmination during the years 1966–75. This period witnessed the most rapid reformistic boom in Finnish public administration.

The welfare state period brought with it changes in the societal role of local government. Local government units are, more than ever before, producers and carriers of nationally defined public services. This development has taken place through a number of sectoral and functional reforms, which seem to have as their common goal a greater equality between different districts and a reallocation of resources for achieving it (see Figure 3).

The egalitarian welfare ideology has taken the form of the standardization and equalization of public services at the local level. It also implies a tendency towards strong central control of municipal activities. The forms of control include special laws, sectorally regulated and detailed systems of financial reallocation and several new systems of sectoral central planning.

Since 1975, some new features have been developing which indicate a segmentation of the welfare state. The original welfare ideology has been transferred from political to administrative level. This implies a fragmentation of the political ideology into different sectoral management and planning systems. The background for these changes are:

- the economic shocks (oil crisis) and the subsequent technocratic orientation shared by major bureaucratic centres;
- the increased influence of managerial and professional groups in shaping central and local decision-making and planning;
- an increased reliance on specialized information systems as a means for development.

This latest development has produced a relative stagnation of political decision-making, 'low profiles' in politics, fragmentary corporatist influences and a strengthened technocratic control of different functional sectors. 'Bureaucratization', 'managerialism' and 'professionalization' are slogans to describe these changes. During the segmentation of the welfare state, the strategic boundary relations of

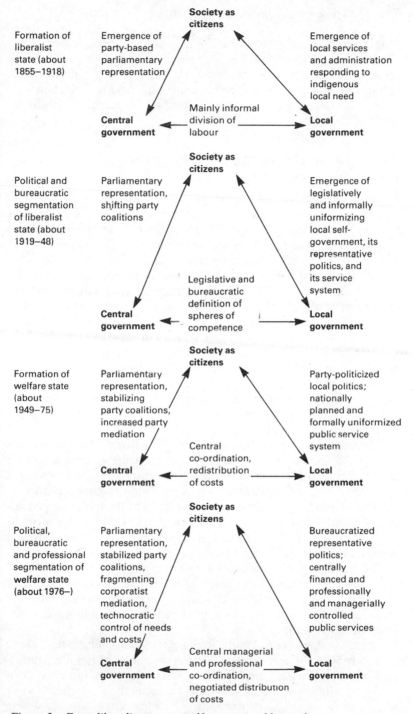

Formation of liberalist state (about 1855–1918)

Emergence of party-based parliamentary representation

Society as citizens

Emergence of local services and administration responding to indigenous local need

Central government ← Mainly informal division of labour → **Local government**

Political and bureaucratic segmentation of liberalist state (about 1919–48)

Parliamentary representation, shifting party coalitions

Society as citizens

Emergence of legislatively and informally uniformizing local self-government, its representative politics, and its service system

Central government ← Legislative and bureaucratic definition of spheres of competence → **Local government**

Formation of welfare state (about 1949–75)

Parliamentary representation, stabilizing party coalitions, increased party mediation

Society as citizens

Party-politicized local politics; nationally planned and formally uniformized public service system

Central government ← Central co-ordination, redistribution of costs → **Local government**

Political, bureaucratic and professional segmentation of welfare state (about 1976–)

Parliamentary representation, stabilized party coalitions, fragmenting corporatist mediation, technocratic control of needs and costs

Society as citizens

Bureaucratized representative politics; centrally financed and professionally and managerially controlled public services

Central government ← Central managerial and professional co-ordination, negotiated distribution of costs → **Local government**

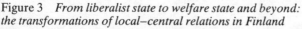

Figure 3 *From liberalist state to welfare state and beyond: the transformations of local–central relations in Finland*

public administration are still more professionalized and technocratized. The original welfare ideology has diffused into public bureaucracies, has lost much of its driving force, and has experienced a routinization in bureaucratic programmes and information channels. A new 'information society' is often said to be emerging as a super-myth of the 1980s.

The central–local relationship as a key factor to modern changes and reforms

Despite changes in its meaning, the basic idea of local self-government has not totally vanished during the time of egalitarian welfare policies and thereafter. As an ideal and as a popular principle it is widely accepted, and complaints about the actual weakening of local self-government have recurred in the 1970s and 1980s. This situation raises the question, What kind of factors have made the development possible? Even if the changes have been gradual, incremental and sectoral, and even if they do not touch the basic structural arrangements between the levels of public administration, it is important to ask, How are the central–local relations organized through different reform processes? Which are the important boundary relations between the central and local levels?

The answer to this question has to be based on some observed 'micro-structural' changes indicating intentional action. There are practically no analyses that might give a detailed empirical picture of reform processes themselves.[9]

One structural change is striking: the growth and differentiation of intermediating boundary structures between the central and local levels. This includes both the rise of new intermediating structures and the growth and differentiation of existing structures. Formally, the intermediating structures are extensions of the basic municipalities. Actually, their position is between the state and the municipalities. A large part of their interactions and communications is directed towards the national central government.

The mediating structures are of two main types. First, at the central level the importance of the national municipal associations and of regulating central boards has increased. Second, at the regional and local level, there has been a strong extension of functional associations of municipalities.

There are three central municipal organizations in Finland: (1) the Association of Finnish Cities, (2) the Association of Finnish Municipalities (mainly rural) and (3) the Association of Finland's Swedish-speaking Municipalities. All Finnish municipalities are members of one of these central organizations. The most important regulating central boards are the Board for Municipal Economy and the Municipal Collective Bargaining Board, both established in the early 1970s.

The central associations of municipalities are considered representatives of local government in most of the reform situations. They are very often represented in governmental commissions and also are often heard by parliamentary committees. Additionally, they can make proposals to the Cabinet. The central organizations of municipalities have had a key position in local reform processes during the last three decades.

The existence of three separate national organizations of municipalities expresses political divergencies in the field of local government. The Association of Finnish Cities has long been dominated by Social Democrats, and, after 1985 by Social Democrats and Conservatives, which is the new Finnish 'red–blue' coalition of the late 1980s. The two other associations are dominated by the political centre. Political divergencies between the central bodies have sometimes deadlocked reforms at the local level.

Given their position as a mediator between the state and the municipalities, the influence of the central organizations of municipalities on local–central relations is considerable. They have a strong pressure–political status in legislative and administrative reform processes. They also have close collaborative relationships with the central government. Moreover, the central associations have an important semi-official role as administrative consultants and reformers in relation to their member municipalities. This includes a quite extensive training of administrative officers, the publication of consultative materials and magazines, the preparation of standards and recommendations for municipal activities, and the adoption of statute models for the municipal organizations. The increased importance of these intermediating and often reforming (or in other cases reform-blocking) activities is clearly evident in the growth of resources in the associations.

In the case of financial relationships between the central level and the local level, a new structure has emerged: this is a co-operative body set up by the state for the financial co-ordination between the state and the municipalities, the Board for Municipal Economy (established in 1973). The central government and the central associations of municipalities are represented in this board, whose main role is to examine, and to plan reforms concerning, the financial relationships between the state and the municipalities. Its perspective is mostly bound to macro-level information about the national economy and the economy of the entire public sector.

The Municipal Collective Bargaining Board was created by law at the beginning of the 1970s. It represents the national employer for the municipalities. The wage decisions reached by this board in bargaining with the central unions of employees are binding for all municipalities.

At the regional and local level, the mediating structures between the central state government and the municipalities have been extended quite largely during the formation of the welfare state. At these levels the functional associations of municipalities have strengthened their status as intermunicipal producers of welfare services.[10] The number of these associations has risen from 180 in 1958 to 416 in 1985. Most of these associations are founded for different health services.

The origin of the associations of municipalities was the need to pool together resources for establishing some public services. This had led (in some cases) to a collaboration between local government units as early as the first decades of this century. The need for collaboration widened gradually, and an institutionalizing law was passed at the beginning of the 1930s. The idea then was a voluntary collaboration between municipalities.

After the Second World War, and in the boom of welfare ideology, the original idea of voluntary collaboration receded into the background and a new idea of centrally planned and compulsory associations of municipalities emerged. Today most of the municipal associations are compulsory, which implies that, according to special laws, each municipality must be a member of some municipal association in the functional areas of several specialized health services (specialized hospitals) and physical planning. Some municipal associations, however, are still voluntary, including functional associations for vocational education and educational advice.

The development of compulsory municipal associations is often interpreted as a strengthening of central government domination over local government. The specialized functional character of both municipal associations and central government regulations express an increased distance from the local government units.

The influence of basic local bodies on the decision-making of municipal associations is often regarded as quite weak. The municipal associations are regarded as products of national planning and as directed mainly by functional specialists.

The present mediating structures between the national central government and the local government include both managing and producing organizations. The positions of the central municipal organizations and of functional municipal associations are important as change-producing and change-inhibiting structures.

This short description points to some established structures in the central–local relations. The nature of these structures can serve as an explanation of the changes of local government. The established boundary-type bodies do have a strong position as implementation and barrier structures. It is a task for further analyses to clarify the actual rationales and action patterns of these structures.

The balance of changes and reforms

The main features of the changes and reforms in Finnish local government are summarized in Table 1. The nature of changes is cumulative in two ways. First, the emerging new features do not abolish the earlier features, but are perceived as 'modern' and salient tendencies. The new tendencies of change must often live together with the

Table 1 *Some cumulative developmental features of modern local government: the case of Finland*

	Liberalist state period	Segmentation of liberalist state	Welfare state period	Segmentation of welfare state
Dominant values concerning local government	Self-government, autonomy of local decision-making	Equality of local resources and possibilities for reforms	Sectoral welfare goals and economic efficiency in the production of local services as carriers of national policies	Emphasis on managerial and professional 'knowledge' and values
The most important local relationships	Local community –local government	Between local governments	Central government–local government	Central government– intermediating systems–local government
Key actors of reforms	Local elites	Coalitions of local elites, Parliament and Cabinet	Central bureaucracy and municipal organizations and associations	Bureaucratic managers and professionals in central government and in associations
Emphasized strategies of reforms	Local initiation	National legislatures and financial aids	National sectoral planning and resourcing	Negotiation between interests, information systems
Emerging main problems of local government	Lack of local resources for reforms	Lack of equality between municipalities	Lack of local autonomy and influence	Lack of capacity to effect real reforms

earlier structures and ideas. This implies that the prevailing structures are usually combinations of old and new practices. Thus, the complexity of local government is growing as new tendencies emerge. Second, the new features can be seen as the common influence of several reforms and reform tendencies.

In the research of reforms as implementation processes, some cases tend to be analysed intensively as to their origins, choices, actors, environments and outputs.[11] At the same time, there is the common pattern of several reform tendencies having some relations between one another. The development of the reform research might profit in considering a frame of reference that includes both the common macro-level tendencies and different cases from the actual field of reforms.

As a short summary of the development of Finnish local government, the following interpretations seem to fit the outputs of research.

1. The dominant values concerning local government have nowadays developed into a triangular situation which implies tensions between different values. The original idea of local self-government was constricted from the beginning by the apparent lack of resources in most of the municipalities. This basic situation led to efforts to equalize the possibilities of reforms at the local level. The equality of local opportunities then emerged as the second value, giving central government the role of equalizer. A growing conception about the responsibility of the national government for the national and civic welfare brought the equalizer under a serious burden of economic stress. This situation led to an emphasis on economic efficiency, which implied strict management of the available resources.

The inherited values of local self-government, the equality of local opportunities and the economic efficiency in the production of welfare goals are quite problematic to combine. During the 1980s the problem has often been transmitted to bureaucratic managers and professionals. This implies more 'professionalism' and 'managerialism' in the production of local services.

2. The most important relationships in local government reforms have been the boundary areas with other institutions. The initial situation implied that most impulses for reform would come from the local communities. The local arena of decisions was regarded as relatively autonomous, and the active groups within the locality were thought to be the reformers. The lack of local resources led to a situation where the collaboration of local units became a typical channel of reforms and a means of solving problems. At the same time, the equalizing role of central government emerged, even if it was restricted at the beginning.

Not until the rise of the new egalitarian welfare ideology was the role of central government strengthened. This development put central–local relations in a powerful position for effecting local government reforms, and led to the rise of strong mediating structures within this area of boundary relations. The newest development can be interpreted as a bureaucratization and professionalization of these intermediating structures.

3. Initially — at the time before strong political parties — local elites were the key actors in local reform processes; they could influence local decisions from their local power position. Later, external relations acquired a key position for reform operations. First, the relationships to other municipalities and to national political elites came into the focus of reforms. But the differentiation of public administration led gradually to a situation in which the sectoral apexes of the central government have quite a strong status, e.g., within the national sectoral planning systems. Thus, the specialist groups of sectoral bureaucrats are a new type of key actors. The representation of local government interests has at least partially been transferred into the hands of specialists in municipal associations. The domination of a sectoral type of decision-making creates distances between the basic local governments and the central government. This distance is filled with sectoral organizations.

The changes of key actors can be regarded as the bureaucratization of local politics. If we think about the three simple categories — local elites, political leaders and top bureaucrats — the most recent period has witnessed the rising status of top bureaucrats and the falling status of local elites and political leaders in local government reforms.

4. The strategies of local reforms were initially considered to be voluntary decisions at the local level. The original idea of local franchise was attached to a conception of representative influence at the local level. Because of local inertia and a lack of resources, the national government took on the role of reformer of local government. Originally, this meant a limited effort to pass reforms through legislation and financial supports. However, the widened ideological press for reforms, especially within the area of welfare services, later led to the strengthening of the central planning systems because of the remarkable economic costs of reforms. The situation changed soon, so that the centrally managed plans began to cover most branches of local government activities, and the efforts to promote reforms became in most cases bound to national plans. The relative inflexibility of centralized plans has led to a tendency to conduct discrete local 'experiments', which in the case of public welfare services are approved and managed by the central government (e.g.

public aid for placing the unemployed in jobs, employment benefits for young persons, public aid for the home care of young children).

5. The principal constraints of local government reforms have continually been the lack of local resources and the weakness of local influence. Generally, this situation can be interpreted as the power of prevailing structures (existing rules and resources) over new tendencies. The creation of local self-government was basically an attempt to increase the possibilities of local influence. Local self-government was, however, no solution to the problem of resources. Later efforts to eliminate the problem of scant resources have in their turn brought on the problem of overregulated local government. The local possibilities to initiate and implement reforms have been quite restricted.

In considering the various consequences of the welfare state development in Finland, Ilkka Heiskanen[12] concludes that there has occurred a development of increased equality and of guaranteed basic services to citizens; but this development has meant a greater concentration of control, more standardization and more uniform reforms, and neglects of specific needs. The capacity to reform is also restricted, and emerging new demands (e.g. environmental problems) suffer a lack of resources also at the central level.

The position of local government in the modern state

The research into local government reforms may have problems inherent to its basic nature. But, in addition, the increased intertwining of local government and national policies makes it appropriate to analyse it as a part of the system of public administration. In the Finnish case, this is because of the strengthened central management of local government activities.

Following the considerations of Juha Vartola,[13] who utilizes the analyses of Jurgen Habermas and Claus Offe,[14] we might take a departure from the problem of modern state government. The opening of state policies and structures to influence from private interests (pluralism) gives the state apparatus the task of balancing economic interests (capital accumulation) and social problems (welfare of citizens).

The formulation of economic policies and social policies constitutes the two main functions of the modern welfare state. Since these functional areas are open to different and conflicting interests, both within themselves and between each other, the 'balance' or 'consensus' is a fluctuating situation, in which the powerful groups (elites) can effect as well as restrain change. In the complex networks of organizational society, coalitions between elites are often necessary conditions for change. Especially with regard to more extensive change, the coalitions have to include elites from different institutional levels (societal interest groups, government heads, local representation). The boundary relations between levels tend to have a key position in more extensive reforms.

Economic policies of the welfare state are managed by coalitions, both public and private, between the national elites. The role of local government is directed more and more towards national social policies that can be interpreted as a legitimizing counterpart of the public care of the prevailing economic interests. The societal functions of public local services are thus connected to the legitimization of political and economic power and to the welfare state vision about the components of human well-being. These societal functions constitute a common tendency of reforms during the last four decades. The functions can be considered as either intended or unintended with reference to various groups of actors in the reform process. A more essential feature is perhaps the selection of reforms for adjustment to the main societal functions (see Figure 4).

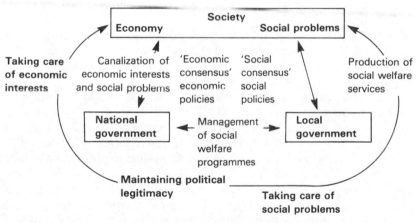

Figure 4   *The position of local government in the modern state*

The selection of reforms by elites has tended to keep the economic functions of the local government (municipal enterprises, municipal aids to private enterprises) at a low level, and to define them primarily as national interests of the state. In the area of social policies, the implemented reforms have also been selected mostly by central elites on the arguments of societal equality and economic efficiency. This structure of reforms implies that the range of local-level decisions is limited, and the responses to local social problems often marginal, if they do not fit the standardized pattern of welfare services.

The capacities of local-level responsiveness are considered too weak, because of the strong influence of the national policies. Thus, the reform tendencies of the 1980s in the area of welfare services have had as their point of departure the strengthening of local possibilities for responsiveness. This is most directed towards the reduction of the central-level influence in the sectoral planning processes. We can, however, ask if central government is the only important factor concerning the problem of local government responsiveness. It is also possible that the local welfare bureaucracies have developed into rigid institutions. Such a sectorized structure of local government often gets support from the hierarchy of public administration. In this situation, the powers of the elected municipal bodies are not necessarily strong, even if the role of central government is limited.[15]

Conclusions

The focus of this exploration has been the study of local government reforms. The central ideas presented above can be briefly recapitulated.

1. The concept of reform is not identical with the concept of change. Reforms are intentional changes, and intentions always refer to some subjects. Only a part of local government changes can be clearly identified as intentional reforms.

2. The position of local government in the political and administrative structure has undergone changes from its liberalist origins to the welfare state and its heritages. This long-term structural change is not an intentional reform, but a development which is connected to societal factors and to the changes in the system of public administration.

3. The general conception of local government has turned from a self-governed local community to a bureaucratic and professional institution, producing public services defined mainly by national social policies. Accordingly, the local–central relationship, and especially the intermediating elements of this relationship, has become a key factor in local government changes and reforms.

The configuration of local reform tendencies, briefly sketched in this chapter, is an interpretation of both societal and governmental macro-level changes. I would suggest that the central–local relationship and its transformation is a useful focus for the study of local government reforms. It would be fruitful to compare processes of reforms and their organizations at different periods of time. How do the values, actors, relationships, strategies and constraints differ from one another in different decades? Alternatively, different reform processes could be studied during one period, with the idea of revealing common values, actors, establishments, relationships, strategies and constraints, and of trying to distinguish them from more situational factors.

Notes

An earlier version of this chapter was presented at the ECPR workshop directed by Bruno Dente and Francesco Kjellberg on the theme, 'Towards a Theory of Local Government Reform', in Salzburg in April 1984. I am very grateful to the participants of the workshop for their valuable comments. Some thoughts have been adopted from another paper by Ilkka Heiskanen and myself entitled 'The Local–central Relationship: the Case of Central Municipal Associations in Finland', presented in the IPSA XIII World Congress, Paris, July 1985. In addition, the author owes special gratitude to Francesco Kjellberg, Bruno Dente and Ilkka Heiskanen for their critical comments and suggestions.

The English translations of the Finnish titles of the publications are in parentheses.

1. See, e.g., Gerald E. Caiden, *Administrative Reform* (Chicago, 1969), p. 65; A.F. Leemans, 'Overview', in A.F. Leemans (ed.), *The Management of Change in Government* (The Hague, 1976), pp. 7–8; and Ferrel Heady, *Public Administration: a Comparative Perspective*, 2nd edn (New York, 1979), p. 114.
2. Markku Kiviniemi, *Research on Structural Changes in Public Sector Organization: Findings and Perspectives*, EGPA Occasional Papers no. 3 (1983).
3. Anthony Giddens, *Central Problems in Social Theory: Action, Structure and Contradiction in Social Analysis* (London, 1979), pp. 65–6.
4. Kiviniemi, *Research on Structural Changes*, pp. 10–11. For a more comprehensive study of implementation structures, see e.g. Benny Hjern and David O. Porter, 'Implementation Structures: a New Unit of Administrative Analysis', *Organization Studies* 3 (1981), pp. 211–27, and Benny Hjern and Chris Hull, 'Implementation Research as Empirical Constitutionalism', *European Journal of Political Research* 10:2 (1982), pp. 105–16.
5. Kiviniemi, *Research on Structural Changes*, p. 9.
6. Ibid., pp. 4–8.
7. The most important sources of the following analysis concerning the Finnish developments are:

Tuomo Martikainen and Risto Yrjönen, *Näkökohtia julkisten palvelusten tuotannosta ja organisaatiosta Suomessa (Considerations on the Production and Organization of Public Services in Finland)*. Publication no. 46. University of Helsinki, Department of Political Science (1977).
Göran Djupsund and Krister Stahlberg, *Finländsk kommunförvaltning i förändring*. Meddelanden fran ekonomiskstatsvetenskapliga fakulteten vid Åbo Akademi, Institutionen för offentlig förvaltning, Ser. A: 162, 1981.
Krister Stahlberg, *Central–local Relations in Finland*. RESPO nr 56 (1980), Åbo Akademi, Statsvetenskapliga institutionen, 1980.
Tuomo Martikainen and Risto Yrjönen, *Central Government Policies and Control Strategies in the Production and Distribution of Public Services: an Evaluative Study*

of the Success in the Change of Policy Strategy in Finland. DETA no. 20. University of Helsinki, Department of Political Science, 1976.
Christer Sanden, 'Kommunal självstyrelse, statsandelssystemet och statlig styrning'. Åbo Akademi, Statsvetenskapliga institutionen, 1978 (mimeo).
Ilkka Heiskanen, On Democracy, Equality, Efficiency and Justice as Criteria for Developing Local Government and Designing Linkages between the Central and Local Levels of Government. DETA no. 17. University of Helsinki, Department of Political Science, 1975.
Tuula Salmela, 'Kunnallinen demokratia ja ympäristönhoidon suunnittelu' ('Municipal Democracy and the Planning of Environmental Policies'). University of Helsinki, Department of Political Science, 1981 (mimeo).
Hannu Lappi, Korporatiivinen etujen välittyminen ja konsensuksen muodostaminen: sosiaali- ja terveydenhuollon valtionosuuksien tasaaminen eli ns. VALTAVA-uudistus (Corporatist Transmission of Interests and Consensus-building: the Reform of State Transfers in Social and Health Administration). Ministry of Social Affairs and Health, Research Department, Helsinki, 1985.
Hannu Soikkanen, Kunnallinen itsehallinto kansanvallan berusta: maalaiskuntien itsehallinnon historia (Municipal Self-government the Basis of Democracy: the History of Rural Municipal Self-government). Helsinki, 1966.
   8. The roots of this ideology are clearly international; see e.g. Peter Flora and Arnold J. Heidenheimer (eds), The Development of Welfare States in Europe and America (New Brunswick, NJ, 1981). As to the concept of ideology, I consider the view of Anthony Giddens worthy of citation. As I conceptualize it, ideology refers to the ideological, this being understood in terms of the capability of dominant groups or classes to make their own sectional interests appear to others as universal ones. Such capability is therefore one type of resource involved in domination' (Giddens, Central Problems in Social Theory, p. 6). The hidden interests of the modern welfare ideology are of course quite difficult to explicate. Compare with the short conceptions contained in the penultimate section of this chapter.
   9. One earlier study has attempted to evaluate the position of central municipal associations in pressure politics, and it includes some empirical materials which indicate their strong status. The study in question is Voitto Helander, Julkisyhteisöt vaikuttajina (The Public Associations as Influentials) (Turku, 1971).
   10. The development of the associations of basic municipalities in Finland is documented in Kaarlo Korvola, 'Kuntainliittojen asema julkisessa hallinnossa' ('The Position of the Municipal Associations in the Organization of Public Administration') (University of Tampere, 1978, mimeo). The strong position of the associations of the basic municipalities can perhaps be considered as a Finnish alternative to the fusion of basic municipalities that has been a salient feature in e.g. the Swedish development.
   11. E.g. Lappi, 'Korporatiivinen etujen välittyminen ja konsensuksen muodostaminen'.
   12. Heiskanen, On Democracy, Equality, Efficiency and Justice.
   13. Juha Vartola, Valtionhallinnon rakenteellisen muutoksen ongelmasta (On the Problem of Structural Change in Central Bureaucracy), Acta Universitatis Tamperensis, Ser. A, Vol. 103, esp. p. 178. University of Tampere, 1979.
   14. Jurgen Habermas, Legitimation Crisis (London, 1976); and Claus Offe, '"Krisen der Krisenmanagements": Elemente einer politischen Krisentheorie', in Martin Janicke (ed.), Herrschaft und Krise (Opladen, 1973).
   15. See e.g. the Swedish study: Nils Brunsson and Sten Jönsson, Beslut och handling (Falköping, 1979). In this study the local politicians regard themselves as defensive investigators of the proposals made by local bureaucracies.

5

Local Government Reorganization: General Theory and UK Practice

L.J. Sharpe

The general case for local government reorganization

National states know no logic: they exist and persist in all their multifarious variety because their citizens and leaders, past and present, wish them to persist and other states respect that wish. Even if we take what will be the principal subject of this chapter, the so-called advanced industrial democracies, a highly distinctive group by any measure, and one that would be reasonably expected to display some sort of underlying common rationale, we find that in terms of physical scale they range from Luxembourg (1000 square miles) to Canada (3,845,144 square miles), and the disparity is just as wide for population as it is for economic base. For all nation-states, the variety is of course even greater. In short, nation-states may not be simply accidents of history, but their location and configuration cannot be assimilated to any causal theory, whether it be derived from geography, functionality or scale.

The configuration of states is also very stable. The post-Second World War period of decolonization marked a period of relative boundary fluidity, but what is so remarkable about this quantum shift in the character of the world order of states is the extent to which boundaries did not change; most of the newly emergent sovereign states clung tenaciously to the old boundaries. Such behaviour is perhaps not so surprising since boundary change is, for all practical purposes, a zero-sum game; normally a state cannot change its boundaries except at the expense (or gain) of its neighbour.

Mutability of the sub-national boundaries

In the world of *sub*-national rather than national government, all is different, for such boundary stability and its underlying cause no longer applies in all its full rigour. Boundaries can be changed because sub-national units are, by definition, not sovereign, except in the case of pure federal systems, where national sovereignty is shared by the constituent polities that comprise the federation. On one view, the entrenchment of constituent state boundaries is one of the key distinguishing characteristics of a federal state.[1] Even in the federal case, however, change is not always ruled out; in the United States, for example, which claims to be a federation in which sovereignty is shared, internal boundaries were changed when Virginia was punished for siding with the South during the Civil War by losing the territory that is now the state of West Virginia. Similarly, a new canton was created in the 1970s in the Swiss federation in order to accommodate the aspirations of the francophones of the Bernese Jura. The German federal system, which may be regarded as no less fundamentally federal than the United States or Switzerland, would have countenanced a change of *Land* boundaries had the Badeners voted for the re-creation of a separate Baden *Land* at the 1962 referendum.

At the local government level in federal and unitary states, boundaries are substantially more mutable, since there is no ambiguity about the fact that local government is subordinate government — although there are exceptions that suggests something very close to immutability. In many US states, for example, the stringent conditions that have to be met before local government boundaries can be altered are tantamount to an embargo;[2] and, as we shall see, in certain types of unitary state redesigning the local government system is very difficult to accomplish. For the vast bulk of states, however, local government boundary change is possible, and this means that, unlike nation-states, questions of local governments' purpose, or functionality, can be raised. In other words, the local government system in question can be assessed as to whether it is appropriate in terms of its *configuration*, or its *population*, or its *area*, or its *resources* in relation to the governmental tasks with which it has been entrusted. The essential point is that all four can be altered to meet changes in the role and functions of local government. 'Can be' rather than 'will be', because, although local government does have a distinctive functionality characteristic that distinguishes it from nation- or constituent states, its task capacity is not in any sense the only criterion of its design. On the contrary, it is possible to hypothesize, without doing flagrant injustice to reality, that local governments' primordial role is no different from that of other polities in that it reflects a sense of common identity among its citizens which at its most basic may be defined as the consciousness that they have more in common with each other than they have with people living beyond their community boundary. Such consciousness may be said to be the *sine qua non* of a democracy.

Indeed, it is possible to argue that this non-functional criterion may be stronger for local government since, unlike the national state, it embraces socioeconomic forms that are non-arbitrary. All urban forms, for example — hamlet, village, market town, regional city, metropolitan centre — exist in their own right and by definition generate some socioeconomic interdependencies which may provide a sense of common identity, ready-made, so to speak, irrespective of any other sources of identity. This is what Tocqueville meant by his memorable but characteristically slightly overblown aphorism to the effect that 'man creates Kingdoms and republics but townships seem to spring from the hand of God'.[3]

Be that as it may, it is clear that the rationale for local government has non-functional as well as functional origins, and it is possible to both sharpen the definition of local community consciousness and establish the necessary link between subjective attitude and task capacity, by adding that such consciousness can be given tangible expression (and be tested) by the establishment of a tax on all citizens for the provision of public goods and other forms of collective consumption that the same citizens do not wish to have provided voluntarily or by the market.

It is this duality of role that local government plays within the larger national system which renders the question of the appropriateness of local government design to meet both requirements highly problematic. Which role is to be given priority — the reflector of subjective community, or the provider of services? It is possible to reconcile the two desiderata simply by pitching the local government system at its smallest feasible scale. There would be no dilemmas if it were possible, in the modern democratic state, to design a local government system that need cope only with those collective functions that have no externalities beyond the village community or its equivalent, wherein a sense of community is likely to exist, so that those who benefit from such functions also pay for them. These functions would include, say, the maintenance of local roads and their lighting, a primary school, a meeting hall, recreation space, refuse collection and a non-trunk sewerage system. There would thus be no spill-overs or spill-ins in such local government units, and this internal balance would be buttressed by a shared sense of identity among its citizens.

The functional revolution
There are two major defects with such a model. In the first place, the functional range is far too narrow for what most Western states regard as being appropriate for local government. The dominant trend over the past thirty years or so has been to extend the functions of the local level to embrace a functional load that could not be

feasibly undertaken on the scale of a village community or its equivalent. Today, local government in most countries embraces a wider range of services than ever before. But wide as it is, the range by no means includes all services internal to the state, so the temptation to interpret the postwar functional revolution in local government as reflecting the dominant role it has played in the evolution of the welfare state, much as it may enhance the status of local government, must be resisted. Still less must structural modernization be necessarily linked to the demands of the welfare state.[4]

A universally acceptable definition of the welfare state still awaits its inventor, but if we take the least controversial and simplified view of what it entails we may say that the welfare state is rooted in the alleviation of three types of largely personal inequality. The first is that enduced by the downswing of the trade cycle (unemployment benefits, supplementary income maintenance, regional aid, job retraining programmes); the second, that derived from changes in personal status over the life-cycle (children's allowances, old-age pensions, ameliorative services for the aged); and the third, that arising from general poverty derived from other causes (broadly speaking, all other redistributive state interventions).

Only the last aspect of the role of the welfare state can be said to involve local government in a major way; the modern welfare state outside health is, in a nutshell, largely about central transfers. This has to be the case, if only because the centre always hogs the biggest money-spinner, the progressive income tax. Even among those services that are often provided by local government, determining what is to be deemed re-distributive is by no means an easy task, especially when the service in question is education. Health, too, presents problems, not only because some of its aspects are at best only ambiguously redistributive, but also because it is not an exclusively government function in all Western states.

In short, although local government was important during the early phase of the welfare state it is unlikely to have played a dominant role in its evolution since the 1950s. It is therefore unlikely that local government reorganization as defined in this chapter has been decisively influenced by the functional needs of the welfare state. The roots of local government structural reorganization are likely to lie as much in the urbanization of society as in functional growth.

One of the most remarkable aspects of the growth of the postwar Western state has been that a greater part of that expansion has usually occurred at the sub-national level, as Table 1 demonstrates. Caution is the watchword, since it is highly unlikely that the data for all twenty-two countries listed can be as easily broken down between the centre and sub-national government as the table implies. Nor is it

Table 1   *Central government share in general government expenditure, 1950–73*

	1950	1960	1965	1970	1973
Australia	79.9	70.8	57.99	56.6	55.6
Austria	73.0	48.8	45.5	43.1	37.1
Belgium	66.9	55.1	51.1	49.8	49.0
Canada	54.7	58.0	50.0	42.2	41.9
Finland	61.7[a]	54.5	53.5	48.3	46.9
France	—	53.7	49.2	47.1	45.6
West Germany	35.2	24.4	26.7	22.9	20.9
Greece	77.8	61.3	55.8	59.4	66.1
Iceland	67.1	61.9	55.0	—	—
Ireland	66.8	74.3	65.2	77.6	76.4
Israel	—	82.7	80.2	82.0[b]	—
Italy	58.0	48.2	43.7	40.6	39.9
Japan	56.0[c]	31.7	29.5	30.2	35.4
Luxembourg	86.2[d]	47.0	44.3	39.6	40.0[b]
Netherlands	48.3[c]	35.3	28.8	30.9	28.2
New Zealand	87.0	85.5	82.2	82.8	81.5
Norway	85.8[a]	69.5	69.3	75.6	74.0
Portugal	79.1	75.9	75.0	77.7	70.1[b]
Sweden	54.3	45.1	42.6	33.2	32.0
Switzerland	28.1	42.7	51.6	46.1[e]	—
UK	72.5	64.6	57.4	55.1	56.3
USA	54.4	53.3	50.2	42.8	38.3

[a] 1953 figure.
[b] 1972 figure.
[c] 1955 figure.
[d] This estimate is not strictly comparable with those for 1961 on.
[e] 1969 figure.

Source: C.D. Foster et al., *Local Government Finance in a Unitary State* (London: George Allen & Unwin, 1980), pp. 127–8

likely that the data are commensurate in all cases. But it does suggest a general trend, and there is no reason to suspect that the data are systematically biased. Table 1 covers the period 1950–73 for all twenty-two of the advanced industrial democracies, and it will be seen that in only two countries (Ireland and Switzerland) did the central share of total government expenditure not consistently decline over the period. In the case of Luxembourg the centre's share of total governmental expenditure more than halved over the period, and it came close to doing so in Austria. The median decline of the centre's share for the period for the whole group is 16.1 percentage points.

Some of the twenty-two countries listed in the table are federal states, so not all of the decline in the centre's share is attributable to local government. However, if we compare the federal group with the unitary (for which all central loss must be attributable to local government), the mean decline of the centre's share of total government expenditure for the federal group is only marginally higher: 15.2 as compared with the unitary group mean of 13.4. By 1973, in more than half (thirteen in all, and eight of them unitary) of the advanced industrial states, the sub-national level absorbed a *higher* proportion of total expenditure than the central government. There can be little doubt that the postwar period has marked a decisive decentralist shift on the balance of functional scope, if not necessarily power, in the modern democratic state,[5] and this shift has almost certainly been an important factor in the perceived need to redesign the structure of its local government.

The urban revolution
The second deficiency of the self-contained small-community model of local government for the modern democratic state, a model in which community consciousness, collective benefits and collective costs are nicely in harmony, is simply that, outside almost wholly rural areas, such communities no longer exist. Population growth, the decline in agricultural employment, the onward march of foot-loose industrialization, long periods of annually rising real disposable incomes for the majority, discriminatory tax laws in favour of home ownership, cheaper cars, rapid transport systems, modern roads and the crowding out of residential accommodation in inner cities to make way for the increasing demand for more collective consumption institutions (car parks, shopping centres, sports facilities, telephone exchanges, tertiary industry, etc.) — all this has meant a massive population flight to the suburbs, and throughout the West, society has become increasingly urban or suburban. In extreme cases suburbanization has merged formerly separate towns and created huge urban agglomerations. Suburbanization has, in short, been as much a distinctive characteristic of the postwar advanced industrial democratic state as the growth of the scope of its sub-national government.

The task facing any state that sought to modernize its local government system to meet these two fundamental changes in the context of which the system operates has been ostensibly to strike some sort of balance between their structural implications and the fact of the existing popular local allegiance and sense of identity. It is important to underline the existence of the 'ostensible' caveat lurking in the preceding sentence since, as we shall see when we come to the particular case of the UK, such rational efficiency arguments are not, and in the nature of the case, given the possible political implications of such change, can rarely be, the whole explanation for local government structural modernization in some countries, and certainly not in the case of the UK.

We need also to recognize that the form of structural change is likely to vary, for the category of advanced industrial democracy covers a wide range of countries, not only in terms of scale and economic base, but also in terms of age.[6] For whereas the UK, Belgium, West Germany and parts of the United States have been industrialized for well over a century, all the northern European states — Iceland, Norway, Denmark, Sweden and Finland — are relative newcomers to the fold. All of them, broadly speaking, have industrialized since 1900, and the implications of this difference may be important for the type of restructuring of the local government that has taken place in the postwar period. We may hazard the guess, for example, that among the late developers the principal need was to redesign a structure (outside the big towns) that was essentially related to a purely rural society. In the older industrial societies, by contrast, restructuring is more in the nature of a second phase involving the adaptation of the system to the emergence of urban agglomerations of the kind just noted, that is to say, where formerly separate settlements have coalesced to form continuous or semi-continuous belts of urban and suburban development.

In the case of the UK, where industrialization is nearer two centuries old, the decline in agricultural employment (under 2 percent of the work force) and the flight from even the suburbs into small rural communities have created what may be regarded as a third phase in the evolution of the settlement pattern, a phase in which the distinction between urban and rural society gives way to a form of quasi suburbia which is neither clearly rural or urban in character. This trend is strongly brought out by the fact that since 1950 the UK has dropped from being the most urbanized country in the OECD group, with 82 percent of its population living in towns of over 10,000 population, to eleventh place by 1980, with only 73 percent living in such towns.

The Napoleonic state

The form that local government structural change takes also seems to be affected by the character of the central–local relationship in each country. There seems to be a fairly clear pattern of difference as between what may be called the 'Napoleonic' group of Western states and the rest. By Napoleonic, I mean that group of states that follow, to varying degrees, the pattern that finds (or found) its most pristine form in France and involves the division of the state into fairly uniform jurisdictions that are larger than the basic units of local government and over which nominally presides an appointed central civil servant — the prefect — as a kind of *primus inter pares* in relation to both the elected local government and a series of additional out-stationed central technical personnel who provide local services within the jurisdiction. In this group of states — Belgium, France, Italy, Spain, Portugal and perhaps Greece — redesigning the basic structure of local government, let us call it the 'commune', which is a uniform legal entity and covers all settlements from major cities to hamlets, is not attempted, and in most of these countries the local government structure has remained largely intact. The possible exception may be Belgium, where the number of communes was reduced from 2500 to 596 in the 1970s. It seems likely, however, that the special circumstances of the intense language conflict in Belgium seriously weakened the normal unity of the localities in resisting change and also diverted the other key sources of resistance, the central field services and localist deputies.

Normally in the Napoleonic group, as I shall argue, the combined effect of such an alliance has ruled out major structural change of the local government system. Instead, the imperatives of functional growth and urbanization seem to have been accommodated by inserting an entirely new level of elected local government at the level of a region; that is to say, at a level between the prefectoral jurisdiction and the whole state. In some cases, notably Belgium and Spain, the more immediate motive for the creation of regional government is regional ethnic nationalism. In determining the origins of regional government in Italy, it would be necessary to take into account both the association of decentralization with democracy as a reaction against fascism (hence the regional clause in the postwar constitution), fears of secessionist movements in the immediate aftermath of the war, and the needs of party bargaining in the early 1970s. It may also be that regional government in France owes something to the special circumstances (forty years out of power) that required the Socialists to give decentralization a first priority when they became the governing party in 1982. In Portugal and Greece it is, perhaps, too early to claim that a fully fledged elected level of regional government is certain to emerge. Portugal is in the process of creating 'administrative' regions, and Greece is redesigning its prefectoral system.

Yet it is very unlikely that such particular circumstances in each Napoleonic state are the whole story, for it is difficult to see how the Napoleonic group could all somehow completely escape the twin problems posed for the existing system of local government by service expansion and urbanization. It seems more likely therefore that the new regional structure they have created is a response to not just one problem but a number, among which must be included those of urbanization and service load. In the case of Spain, for example, despite the importance of accommodating Basque, Catalan and Galician aspirations as quickly as possible after the return to democracy, the legacy of neglect in the localities under Franco required some drastic redesigning of the sub-national system. More problematic is why the regional solution rather than local government structural change was chosen by the Napoleonic group.

One possible reason is, paradoxically, the relative weakness of the existing local government system in terms of functional capacity. Because the local units are so small, there is a tendency for only the larger urban centres to employ their own service delivery staff; in the rest of the system this task is usually carried out by the central field services.

The local government system, then, is often not so much a functional system but more a political-cum-representative one. To argue, therefore, that the postwar service and urban revolutions require new, more functionally rational, units of local government is, if not meaningless, at least misplaced. So, freed from the incubus of functionality, the Napoleonic local government system can resist the requisite change — which would involve the disappearance of very many communes — without inhibition and with no holds barred. This is a privilege not open to local government in the non-Napoleonic states of northern Europe. As service providers in their own right, they, by contrast, are directly vulnerable to the charge of functional obsolescence. Moreover, in the Napoleonic state not only is the local government free to defend itself whatever its scale or demonstrable service incapacity, but it has had to develop the art of colonizing the centre — via national parties and the *cumul des mandats* — in order to bypass the control of the prefect as a normal part of its day-to-day activities and therefore can do battle against reform in the most effective way possible at the very heart of the national decision-making process.

Finally, even if the communes did not have these defensive weapons to hand, they have staunch and very powerful allies in the battle against structural change in the form of the central field services, the very *raison d'être* of which is the functional incapacity of most of local government: 'Turkeys don't like Christmas', as the British adage has it, and the central field services have an enormous stake in the status quo, for the very service inadequacy of the local government system enhances their role.

Faced with such an array of forces on behalf of the status quo, the national governments of the Napoleonic states, we may surmise, have been forced to leave the local government system largely untouched, despite the fact that in some cases it may actually be medieval in structure. France before 1982, for example, still had no less than 36,000 local government units, which constituted a reduction of only 3000 over the whole postwar period. In areas where some more rational form of service delivery was the most urgent, and especially where the facts of urbanization had rendered the existing structure most obsolete, a number of organizations were created and instrumentalities evolved to cope, many of them very effective. In France, such was the role of DATAR, the SDAD, the OREAM and the District de la Region de Paris, for example.[7] Financial reforms in the late 1960s were effected which also moderated the consequences of the antiquated structure.

It must be conceded that the relative success of these arrangements, all of which left the basic structure of local government intact, poses an important question about the necessity for local government structural change of the kind under discussion. It is a mode for responding to the two pressures of functional revolution and urbanization, which is not confined to France, but is very common in the USA and has been applied successfully in West Germany, where some of the *Länder* are, strictly speaking, hybrids in terms of being neither purely Napoleonic nor purely functional in their intergovernmental articulation. However, it is the broad contention of this chapter that the pressure to effect more permanent structural change remained. It was given further impetus, especially in France, Italy and Belgium, by the adoption of the regionalized national plan for economic development. This gave the region a new legitimacy and mobilized popular support on a regional basis. It also offered a rationale for linking the two forms of planning that were in operation by the 1960s, namely, the largely spatially determined land use planning of investment, which was centred on the localities, and the planning of investment over time, which was largely confined to the centre.[8]

Some indication of the difference in the extent of local government modernization between the Napoleonic and non-Napoleonic groups of Western states is given in Table 2, which lists the extent of the reduction in the number of municipalities for fourteen states of both types since the 1940s. The table also summarizes the reduction process by means of an 'index of change', and it will be seen that in almost every case the non-Napoleonic state has made a greater reduction in the number of its municipalities over the period than any Napoleonic state. Some caution may be necessary in interpreting this table, since it is not clear what is meant by a municipality in all cases and so there must be some doubt as to how far all the figures are

Table 2   *Structural change of Western European municipalities*

	1940s	1950s	1960s		1970s			Index of change[a]
Austria				3,183 (1966)	3,183 (1970)	2,414 (1972)	2,417 (1974)	24
Belgium	2,670 (1947)			2,663 (1961)		2,359 (1970)		12
Denmark				1,387 (1961)	277 (1970)	275 (1974)		80
France				37,708 (1968)	36,489 (1970)	36,413 (1980)		3
UK		1,347 (1950)	1,349 (1960)	1,288 (1965)	1,357 (1973)	410 (1974)	521 (1975)	61
Greece				5,993 (1962)		6,037 (1979)		1
Italy		7,810 (1950)				8,056 (1972)		-3
Luxembourg		126		126		126		0
Netherlands		1,015 (1950)		994 (1960)	913 (1970)	862 (1973)	811 (1979)	20
Norway					443 (1974)	445 (1975)	454 (1977)	-2
Spain	9,265 (1940)	9,214 (1950)		9,202 (1960)		8,655 (1970)	8,049 (1978)	13
Sweden	2,500 (1950)	1,037 (1952)	1,006 (1963)	848 (1969)	464 (1971)	278 (1974)	279 (1980)	88
Switzerland		3,097		3,095	3,072 (1970)	3,050 (1975)	3,038 (1977)	1
West Germany		24,512 (1959)	24,438 (1965)	24,282 (1968)		14,242 (1974)	8,514 (1978)	65

[a] Difference between first column and last column expressed as percentage of first column.

Source: Adapted from Brian C. Smith, *Decentralization* (London: George Allen & Unwin, 1985), p. 69

comprehensive. However, the broad distinction between the two types of state in terms of local government change is sufficiently marked to dispel any fear that its origins lie in the possibility that definitions are not uniform in all cases: the index of change for the Napoleonic group (Belgium, France, Greece, Italy, Luxembourg and Spain), is 2, whereas that for the rest is 42.

Thus, when we view the Western states as a whole in terms of local government modernization (and leaving aside the USA as being *sui generis*), two distinct groups emerge. The first is what we have called the Napoleonic group, where the response has been to insert a new tier of regional elected government above the existing local government structure, leaving the latter largely intact.

Other West European countries have tackled the pressure to adapt their local government systems somewhat differently because, as I have argued, they have a different internal mode of intergovernmental relations. Instead of functional hierarchies extending down from the centre to each locality, the central and local levels are more like strata, each much more self-contained in its tasks than in the Napoleonic system, and with the local government strata responsible largely for making their own policies and employing their own service delivery specialists quite independently of the centre. The centre, for its part, confines itself to broad policy, technical advice, auditing and financial assistance. The central–local relationship, then, although never discrete and perhaps increasingly less so, is none the less not as interwoven as it has to be in the Napoleonic group.

Also, in the non-Napoleonic group the central–local relationship is fragmented, for it exists for the most part between two sets of specialist bureaucrats in each stratum for each of the service fields covered by the local authority. Both to some extent are insulated from the world of party politics and politicians, and conduct their business according to fairly strict norms of fairness and equity that are usually resistant to political manipulations. Neither level has any particular stake in the status quo, although as specialists in a particular service they *are* interested in functional capacity; that is to say, they see local government largely in terms of its service delivery role.

It is this tradition therefore which, I have argued, facilitates an outright restructuring response to meet specified functional criteria derived, broadly speaking, either from urbanization or from the growth of local services. The primordial political role of local government as a representative body for a local community irrespective of its functional capacity may, as compared with the Napoleonic group, tend to be diluted, especially under growing public pressure for fairness, minimum standards and equality for all in the provision of public services.

The rest of this chapter will be devoted to examining in some detail the local government modernization process in one member of the non-Napoleonic group. The UK is, perhaps, an extreme case in terms of the dominance of the functional capacity requirement, but in its very extremity it may underline the distinctive characteristics of the non-Napoleonic group.

Local government modernization in the UK

The special character of the British system
Before looking at the local government reform process, it is important to emphasize that there may be characteristics of the British
system of government that have a direct bearing on the local government restructuring process that renders the British experience to
some extent atypical. The first is the capacity that the British political system grants governments, if they command a majority in
the House of Commons, to legislate for almost any change in the
governmental system itself, including what in other Western states
would involve constitutional questions, without the need for any
special procedures, least of all bipartisan agreement. This power
is neatly illustrated in the context of this paper by the way the
government in the spring of 1986 abolished a whole tier of local government in England — the metropolitan counties and the Greater
London Council — simply by an Act of Parliament. In short,
quite drastic structural change of local government presents no
particular problems for a British government if it is determined
on such change.

The second key distinctive characteristic of the British system that
may also render substantial local government structural change more
likely than elsewhere is the insulation of the centre from the localities. This, as I have argued, is a characteristic of all non-Napoleonic
functional systems, but it is probably more extreme in the British case
because of the deeply entrenched non-executant tradition of the
British central civil service.[9] This tradition means that the centre
tends to lack a direct knowledge of local conditions, nor does it
command service delivery expertise superior to that of the localities.
When the centre is bent on effecting major and contentious policy
change in local government, it may therefore experience considerable difficulty in achieving its aims, and as a consequence may be
more tempted to contemplate a structural solution than might other
comparable central governments. Such a possibility is probably re-
enforced by the realization that the problem of control deficits that
arises where the centre is accountable for policy change but the
localities are responsible for implementation may be moderated if
the number of local units that have to be co-ordinated for the said
policy change is reduced.[10] Local government modernization, as
we have noted, must almost always involve the creation of larger
local units and therefore a reduction in their number. Thus the
centre — civil servants and ministers — have more than a passing
interest in local government reorganization, which has little to
do with urbanization or economies of scale, but a great deal to

do with easing the co-ordination and management burden of the centre.

In any case, central governments in all democracies have just as urgent a need to aggregate public sector agencies with whom they have to deal as they do private sector ones — indeed, more so, precisely because the centre may be held accountable but may not be responsible for implementation. In the British case, it seems, such needs were more easily met. Reducing the number of local units in England and Wales from about 1400 to something like 420 for high spending and contentious services such as housing, and to less than 100 for education, master planning and transport, was a potentially considerable management gain for the centre. Such gains can be appreciated when viewed, for example, against the virtual dismantling of the local housing function after reorganization during the rest of the 1970s and 1980s. This fundamental change, which was hotly contested, was made all the easier because the centre had less than a third of the housing authorities to deal with as compared with a decade earlier. Similar considerations apply with perhaps greater force to centres' attack on local autonomy in finance during the 1980s. The aggregate motive for local government reorganization is not one that is usually discussed in public, although it was made fairly explicit by the Treasury in its evidence to the Redcliffe–Maud Commission:

> For the future there will need to be much closer working and more frequent exchange of views between the central government and local authorities collectively, in order to secure satisfactory results. This closer working would be greatly facilitated by a reduction in the numbers of the major spending authorities.[11]

Perhaps the best statement of the case for reforming local government so as to reduce the central workload was made by Mr Walker, the Minister who piloted the reorganization bill through Parliament, to the House of Commons Expenditure Committee when it was investigating transport planning in June 1972. He was discussing various aspects of national transportation policy, and a member of the Committee asked how he was going to ensure that local authorities would actually carry them out. The Minister replied:

> After reorganization I shall have six metropolitan areas and 39 counties, and this will be my total relationship in that sphere with the major transport authorities. This does mean that, both at regional office level and in terms of our office in Whitehall, we are able to establish a relationship which I think will be very effective. The ultimate power, of course, which we have is in the expenditure, and I believe that we can develop with local authorities this block grant system so that we can see that the best knowledge is applied to try to bring a total solution to the

areas involved. This will mean that we get basic co-ordination in central and local government thinking and few difficulties.[12]

A third characteristic peculiar to the British system that has a bearing on local government structural change is the remarkable extent to which local government is dominated by the national parties. The vast majority of local authorities operate on the basis of a party system that, if circumstance permit, is just as rigid as the one operating at national level. The majority party controls all the levers of power and, lacking the moderating effect of a unitary executive (mayor or burgermeister) or a tradition of *proporz* in collective decision-making, does so largely without let or hindrance. At the central level there is an equally rigid 'winner takes all' tradition, for the national electoral process and the party system normally produce a clear majority for a single party. Coalitions are largely unknown. Thus, central–local relations are almost always coloured by the fact of party allegiance, and when the centre seeks to enact major controversial policy change, it may be faced with a local government system largely in the hands of the opposition party. In such circumstances the centre may be tempted into a structural change. Such temptation will be enhanced if it can also see in that change not only an advantage in terms of getting its own way, but also a party advantage, i.e. producing a local authority boundary pattern that improves its chances as a political party of gaining and holding power locally. It would be quite impossible to understand the three major structural changes in English local government of 1963, 1973 and 1986 without taking this party-political motivation into account.

These three distinctive characteristics of the British system are important, but it is unlikely that they invalidate the possibility that the British experience can still yield some useful insights into the nature of local government reorganization that have a wider application, especially in relation to some of the distinctive characteristics of the non-Napoleonic model of intergovernmental relations. That is at least one of the working assumptions of this chapter, and it is therefore to the British experience that we must now turn.

The sociogeographic factor

The present local government system in England and Wales was created by the Local Government Act 1972, and for Scotland by the Local Government (Scotland) Act 1972. This chapter is concerned mainly with the England and Wales Act.[13] As we noted earlier, most local government modernization schemes involve two basic objectives. The first is the need to cope with urbanization, what may be called the *sociogeographic* objective. This attempts to bring the boundaries of local authorities more into line with present-day settlement patterns by joining up the continuously built-up area of cities with their burgeoning suburbs and beyond. The second broad objective seeks to enable local units to cope with the increase in their functional scope, what may be called the *service efficiency* objective, which, by increasing their average population size, seeks to enhance the capacity of local units to provide services efficiently to currently acceptable standards.

Put in formal terms, but not necessarily in the way in which the arguments were developed in the actual process of reorganization in Britain, the sociogeographic objective is based on the assumption that the dominant settlement form is now the service centre and its hinterland. The service centre may be defined as the continuously built-up core of a town, and its hinterland as the surrounding rings of satellite communities. These communities may be embedded in a semi-rural environment, but, it is argued, they owe their existence to their proximity to the service centre and its accessibility to them in terms of employment, shopping and a myriad of private and public services. Thus, in socioeconomic terms, the hinterland is said to be just as much a part of the town as the suburbs that form the rim of the town's continuously built-up core.

The pattern of population settlement, this argument continues, is no longer one of urban entities that are sharply differentiated in socioeconomic terms from their rural surroundings, but instead a series of service centres and their hinterlands whose boundaries meet and overlap to cover most of the country. This applies especially to the central population core of England (where over two-thirds of the population live), which runs from Greater Manchester and Merseyside in the north-west to London and the south-east region; in this so-called 'coffin' we may no longer talk of urban and rural, but rather, of different degrees of urbanness.

Translated into local government boundaries, the sociogeographic objective implied the abolition of the old city governments, the county boroughs, which usually did not embrace even the whole of the built-up areas of their respective cities, and their replacement by new authorities that extended well beyond the built-up core to some approximation of its hinterland.

The need to match the local government structure to this alleged reality rested on three grounds. First, the objective linkages of town-plus-hinterland will have already generated a subjective community of interest among the inhabitants of the spread city 'through the links of employment, shopping and social activities'.[14] Second, and more decisively, it was argued that planning and the related functions of traffic management, highways and public transport could be effectively and efficiently undertaken only if their jurisdiction covered the whole of the city and its hinterland, since in planning terms service centre and hinterland are interdependent.[15] The extent of settlement in the hinterland, for example, can directly affect the prosperity of the service centre economy; equally, the level and pattern of public and market services in the centre — employment opportunities, car parks, shopping and service facilities, traffic control, public transport, cultural and educational services — affects those in the hinterland. Third, retaining the old county borough boundaries was inefficient and inequitable. Put in the more formal terminology of public goods theory, there was no 'fiscal equivalence'.[16] That is to say, the public goods that the old county borough provided had effects — conferred benefits or exacted costs — over an area wider than its own area: the decision-making unit, in short, was less inclusive than the collectivity that was affected by the particular decision. These 'externalities' varied from service to service, but they were all well beyond the boundaries of the county borough. Extending the boundary was therefore an improvement on the status quo in the sense that it would come closer to internalizing these service externalities, thus making possible a more equitable sharing of the costs and the benefits of the public goods among those affected and achieving greater allocative efficiency.

There is undoubtedly an attractive quality of economy and precision about the externalities mode of argument for pinpointing some of the alleged deficiencies of the old structure. But there must remain considerable doubt as to whether it is an adequate basis for determining the structure of local government. In the first place, some service externalities — education, for example — may be national in scope; others, such as land use planning or main drainage, may be regional. Neither type offers much practical guidance for determining *local* boundaries. As a level of general government, local authorities will always generate some service externalities. Second, trying to achieve service self-containment, internalizing all the externalities, may be more equitable for the local taxpayers, but it tells us nothing about the population or its socioeconomic structure. Homogeneity of personal benefits and costs is not necessarily homogeneity of civic consciousness or sense of identity, and this is an important consideration in determining local government boundaries, as we have argued earlier. Some would claim that it was vital.

Density and the need for government
An equally crucial aspect of the town-plus-hinterland model concerns the relationship between urbanness and the need for public services. Here again we must stray for a moment from the particular

case of England and Wales and put the argument in abstract terms. If we imagine a rural–urban continuum running from the remote farm to the centre of the central business district (CBD), the need for public services increases as urbanness and population density increases, so that the level of public services is substantially less at the rural end than at the CBD end. The rise in the need for services is not uniform as density increases, since there will be a substantial expansion in such need once the continuously built-up area is reached. There may be other points on the continuum where the need for more government and co-ordination rises sharply. The perimeter of the inner city within the built-up area of the very large urban concentrations is one point, and the perimeter of the CBD itself is probably another.

This link between population density and government is derived mainly from four factors. The first has to do with self-sufficiency. Our isolated farmer does not need, or else can provide for himself, a wide range of services that the central city dweller needs but can obtain only through local government. In short, farmers can fend for themselves for some local government services. Such services can include, for example, refuse collection and disposal, main drainage and sewerage, outdoor recreation facilities, car parks and water supply. The isolated farmer does, of course, sometimes get some of these services from government, but most of them are not usually provided and need not be provided.

The next reason why urban areas tend to need more collective action than rural areas is the requirement to regulate the impact of the negative externalities of individuals, households and firms as population density increases. As Mancur Olson has put it, 'As population, urbanization and congestion increase, external diseconomies almost certainly increase too.'[17] The isolated farmer can breed pigs, burn old tyres in his yard, park his tractor on the highway, dig a hole to dump his refuse in. If the CBD flat-dweller, office manager or shop-owner did any of these things it would have intolerable effects on his neighbours. In some cases — digging a hole for example — the action might bring the whole communication system of the CBD to a halt.

It could also be argued that collective action is required to regulate and facilitate positive externalities, such as the scale externalities that firms exploit by locating in the central city. Government enhances the capacity of such firms to reap such externalities by planning land use and providing, regulating and policing the communication system — roads, traffic and public and quasi-public transport.

The third reason why more government and more integrated government is needed in urban rather than rural areas is derived from scale effects and the fact that the centre of the towns perform a functional role on behalf of the whole built-up area and its hinterland by providing common services. The larger the urban area, the wider the range of services provided by the central city. Many of these services are provided by the private sector and others by central government, but there remains an important range that is usually the responsibility of local government. Such services can include colleges for further education, museums, art galleries, central libraries, theatres, markets, shopping and sports centres, parks and so forth.

The fourth and final reason why population density is positively linked to the need for collective action is related to the last in the sense that it is another scale effect. Some collective services cannot be provided in sparsely populated areas at the level provided in cities because to do so would be prohibitively expensive. Such services include fire, police and public transport.

Curiously enough, then, the detailed exploration of the functional implications of the city and hinterland leads us away from what is usually regarded as the logical institutional response, namely, the creation of a single wider unit that embraces city and hinterland. For such an exploration suggests that an urban area has distinctive needs, not only in terms of requiring more collective action, but also in terms of requiring more integrated government than a rural area. Extending the boundary of an urban unit is, therefore, not merely a question of recognizing the sociogeographic unity of the centre and its hinterland; for that unity also masks a marked disparity in the types of settlement pattern within the area which at the extremes have very distinctive collective needs.

To put the matter another way, the question is not solely one of deciding whether town and country ought to be joined to meet the hypothetical requirements of planning and transport, but whether such a union outweighs the clear benefits of maintaining separate types of authority in terms of other services that are provided by local government which are arguably of equal importance. That is a choice that was seldom posed in the pro-reform literature on British local government reorganization.[18] However, it was recognized to some extent in the new structure that was introduced under the 1972 Act, since, although unified town-plus-hinterland authorities were created, all the more sizeable towns and cities retained a separate local government status, although, in the case of the former county boroughs, with much diminished powers.

Economies of scale
We now come to the second major objective of local government

modernization, that of the service efficiency, which seeks to improve the quality of local government services by enlarging the average population size of local government units. The discussion of this objective in the reform literature is a little vague, and in order to achieve some clarity it is again necessary to introduce a more formal mode of argument than was usual in the case made for change.

There are two assumptions implicit in the service efficiency objective. The first is that the scale of existing units is insufficient to enable them to provide services effectively — that is, to provide the service in its full range to currently accepted standards.[19]

Of course, this is also an efficiency objective, since it would be perfectly feasible to provide services in their full range and to an acceptable standard whatever the size of the local authority, provided there were sufficient resources. But since we may safely assume that citizens in the smallest communities would find the cost of providing a full range of local services prohibitive, it seems sensible to draw a distinction between effectiveness and efficiency.

The second assumption is that the units in the old system were too small to reap all the possible economies of scale, especially economies of scale in management and cost control.[20] The first doubt that arises about the service efficiency objective is its assumption that the geographical distribution of the given population within a local authority does not affect the assumed relationship between population size and service effectiveness, or economies of scale. Yet the possibility that it does is a very strong one. Consider, in the light of our earlier discussion, the different communication costs and the different governmental needs of an authority that comprises a continuously built-up town and one with the same population but embracing, say, a tract of sparsely populated upland.

Another questionable assumption is that population scale is related directly to the scale of resources, that is to say, that an increase in population automatically implies an increase in resources. Obviously, there is likely to be some relationship between population and resources, but since the major components of local resources in Britain — central grants, taxes on industry and households and charges — are themselves only very loosely related to population scale, we may claim with some confidence that the link is not necessarily a direct one.

The economies-of-scale objective raises even more serious doubts. The claim that there were economies of scale to be reaped by reorganization could only be based on the assumption that, beyond some initial threshold, local services incur certain fixed costs irrespective of the population size of the authority; if the local authorities were enlarged so that the average population they served was increased, it followed that unit costs of the service would fall. The difficulty with this assumption is, first, that these fixed costs were never identified in the pro-reform arguments. They were only assumed to exist, rather in the same way that they are assumed to exist in the theory of the firm. But local authorities are not firms, and given that a great deal of what they produce is fundamentally different from what the firm produces — or, rather, from what is produced by the firm assumed under neo-classical economic theory — there must be considerable doubt about the aptness of the economies-of-scale theory for local government reorganization. The key difference between local government goods and those of the firm (in the theory of the firm) is that the former are almost always heterogeneous whereas the latter have to be homogeneous in order that all the conditions for exploiting economies of scale are satisfied. If they are not — that is to say, if the good varies in form or quality — then the theory collapses and new supply and demand curves come into operation.

Further doubts about the applicability of the economies-of-scale thesis to governmental outputs are strengthened if we probe its assumption a little further. For example, it is assumed, apparently, that the long-run cost curve declines for the same level of output for all services — education, social welfare, highways, housing, police and so forth. This is a highly unlikely possibility to say the least. Another extremely dubious assumption is that economies of scale operate over a very wide population range, so that any enlargement of any existing authority would reduce service costs. That fixed costs do not have a limitless fixity — that is, that at some point diseconomies of scale arise — seems to have been a thought that is largely absent from the reform case.

The economies-of-scale assumption would have been considerably more justified had there been any evidence under the old system that it might be correct. But there was little evidence that scale did bring lower costs, and certainly none that would justify the increase in the average size units brought about by the 1972 Act.[21]

In so far as it is possible to assess the effect of change on costs, there are some indications that, instead of falling, as the economies-of-scale claim for reorganization predicts, costs *rose* after reorganization. In the first year after reorganization, for example, as Table 3 reveals, the rate of increase in local government expenditure tripled as compared with the preceding decade. It seems likely, however, that some at least of this increase is attributable to the once-and-for-all costs of the changeover.[22] Whether local government costs rose on a secular basis as a result of the organization, therefore, can be assessed only on the basis of expenditure for subsequent years.

Table 3   *UK growth of local government expenditure*

	Local expenditure as a percentage of public expenditure	Local expenditure as a percentage of GNP
Average annual percentage increase, 1966–75	0.6	0.5
Percentage increase, 1974–5	1.2	1.6

However, a concerted government drive to reduce public expenditure, and local government expenditure in particular, after the financial crisis of 1975 renders it impossible to ascertain whether the reorganization did incur such a quantum leap in costs.

Once and for all, costs apart, there are grounds for suspecting that the simple assumptions of the economies-of-scale protagonists are misplaced. First, it is just as likely that, with a wholesale increase in population, diseconomies of scale will be reached for some services in some localities. Second, we may hypothesize with a reasonable degree of confidence that, for any particular public service at any point in time and at any level of output, the executants of the service (both technocrat and politician, but especially the former) will favour an increase rather than a decrease in the resources allocated to that service. All government agencies, as Wildavsky has emphasized,[23] will always favour having more resources. In the ordinary course of events, such expansionary predispositions are seldom satisfied, owing to the normal processes of financial control. But when the organization comes to an end, which is what happens in a reorganization process such as the 1972 Act, such normal processes of restraint can in the nature of the case no longer operate with their customary rigour, and the new order offers the opportunity for all who want to increase their allocation to do so to an extent that is not possible in a stable institutional setting.

This tendency for wholesale institutional change to engender increased expenditure is powerfully re-enforced by the need to maintain staff morale during the crucial transition period from the old to the new order. During this period there are inevitable uncertainties about who among the staff of the old system is to be found a place in the new, and who is not. Moreover, not only are there uncertainties for the staff, but there are also extra tasks to be undertaken, since the level of services has to be maintained while at the same time the problems of the changeover have to be coped with. Both additional burdens require compensating incentives and rewards for the bureaucracy, and these usually take the form of overmanning in the new system, or increased remuneration, or both.

Where, as is the case in the new British local government system, two conflicting objectives were pursued at the same time — enlarged master planning authorities and larger second-tier units with planning control powers — the exploitation of economies of scale becomes doubly difficult; not only has it proved almost impossible to economize on staffs generally, but land use planning staffs during the initial post-reform period had to be expanded by no less than 70 percent.[24]

It would be erroneous to assume that the case for increased scale was based entirely on the suppositions of the market model. There had been a long line of official reports preceding the reorganization Act, mainly concerning individual local services that, to a greater or lesser extent, recommended the enlargement of existing local authorities, in terms of either population or area. The Redcliffe–Maud Commission on local government reorganization in England, whose report ushered in the 1972 Act, with a perhaps pardonably elastic definition of enlargement, unearthed forty-nine such enquiries that appeared between 1950 and 1968.[25] The vast bulk of these recommendations, however, were mostly subjective claims and were not, in any case, necessarily concerned with cost reduction, but had the somewhat different objective of devising professionally defined optimum conditions for the operation of a particular service.

The obsession with large scale
There can be little doubt that in the reform debate no clear distinction was drawn between the basic needs of a given service in scale terms and professionally defined ideal scale optima which are only too likely to be determined by the need to accommodate some marginal improvement on the service that has been made an essential emblem of professional good practice. This vague but almost headlong embracing of large scale is perhaps best illustrated in the report of a national survey carried out by the Education Inspectorate (HMI) on the quality of local government for education which was submitted to the Redcliffe–Maud Commission by the Department of Education and Science. Its principal conclusion was: 'The probability of good performance from an education authority increases with size, and the probability of below-acceptable performance decreases rapidly with size.'[26]

There had also been a number of more systematic and objective studies, which had attempted to examine the effects of the population size on their service performance as measured mainly by expenditure statistics of local authorities. The Redcliffe–Maud Commission itself conducted or commissioned some of this research. However, after carefully reviewing all of these studies, Newton had concluded that the search for a relationship between population size and service performance

> ... has been conspicuously unsuccessful, whether the performance mea-
> sures have been spending patterns or the quality of type of services
> provided, ... of 73 different attempts to ascertain the effects of size ... in
> 38 of these the impact is statistically insignificant but substantively small,
> and in the remaining 17 cases the effects are significant and of medium
> strength. In no case is size a powerful or dominant variable which can
> explain as much as a quarter of the variance.[27]

Why, it might be asked, did the reforms take the drastic form that they did, given the meagreness of the evidence in support of one of the central contentions of the case for change? Part of the answer almost certainly lies in the fact that the opposition to reorganization was not aware of the frail basis of the economies-of-scale argument. Rather the contrary: the argument was accepted, but was countered by the claim that service efficiency should not be the only criterion for change. This meek acquiescence is yet another reminder of the extent to which half-digested theories borrowed from the neo-classical market model have the capacity to achieve ascendancy in modern democratic politics, a fascinating subject which we cannot pursue further here.

It is of some significance that the Local Government Commission for England, which was the Redcliffe–Maud Commission's immediate predecessor, did experience some difficulties at its inquiry stage in accepting the economies-of-scale claim, as did the Home Office in relation to its proposals (under the 1964 Police Act) to amalgamate police forces. Even more significantly in the latter case, this led to the procedure for hearing evidence being changed so as to avoid any systematic public examination of the economies-of-scale argument, despite the fact that it was put forward as one of the main arguments for creating the present enormous police authorities.[28]

The pure milk of both the sociogeographic and service efficiency arguments were in the final outcome diluted by the creation of a two-tier structure instead of the much larger units of the virtually single-tier system recommended by the Redcliffe–Maud Commission. However, their influence was still sufficiently salient to render British local authorities among the largest in the Western world.[29] Despite the claims of the 1972 White Paper that the new units would be created 'above all else' on the basis that a 'genuine local democracy implies that decisions should be taken as locally as possible',[30] the smallest units of the two-tier system, the districts, are (if we include their London equivalent, the London boroughs) on average in excess of 130,000 population. In some of the remoter rural areas this means that 'genuine local democracy' operates in areas of thirty miles across, and districts where the seat of government is ten miles from quite large population centres within the district are common.

At the county level, to which have been allocated most of the major functions, we are even further from what may be regarded as *local* government. The average population of the English and Welsh counties is in excess of 700,000, and in some instances the seat of government is half a day's travel by public transport from the largest centres of population within the county. In Devon, which is one of the extreme cases, the largest city, Plymouth, is some forty miles from the county seat at Exeter. Some attempts have been made to mitigate the sheer physical scale of the larger counties by creating another tier of local administration based on the division of the county into areas each with its office of outstationed county administration. In some cases, notably in Devon itself, these arrangements are supplemented with area committees containing district representatives.[31]

But the creation of an intermediate tier of this kind, while it improves public accessibility for those services that are deconcentrated, merely underlines the inappropriateness of the new structure. Moreover, it also contradicts one of the most consistent and prominent claims made on behalf of reform, namely, that it would render unnecessary such intermediate schemes, thereby simplifying the system and making it more comprehensible and accountable to the general public.[32]

Comparisons with France are perhaps inappropriate, simply because its local government structure has not been modernized. Nevertheless, it is indicative of just how (comparatively) huge British units of local government are if it is noted that the average population of French communes is about 1300. Sweden as a non-Napoleonic state provides perhaps a better comparison, for it has completed a lengthy and far-reaching restructuring of its local government spread over twenty years which has reduced the number of *kommuner* from 2500 to 277.[33] Yet the average Swedish commune population, which is higher than for any other continental West European country,[34] is still below 30,000. In other words, Sweden's primary unit of local government, which, unlike the English district, is responsible for all the major local functions, has a population some four times smaller than the English average for the lower-tier unit.

One explanation for the enormous size of the new authorities could be that Britain (equally large local units were created in Scotland) has a distinctly different settlement pattern. As we noted earlier, this is to some extent the case, given the third-phase movement of population from urban centres to small rural communities over the past two decades and the consequent decline of population in urban areas.

There are also many more large and medium-size cities in Britain, say, than in Scandinavia. Whether the British settlement pattern is so different from that of West Germany, however, is much more problematic; yet the basic unit of West German local government has an average population of only 2700. Moreover, by one indicator of the settlement pattern — population density — Britain comes fourth behind the Netherlands, Belgium and West Germany.

The explanation for the huge local authorities in Britain, then, is unlikely to lie in any distinctive sociogeographic characteristic. Another factor that could account for larger local government units than elsewhere is the total absence of an intermediate tier of administration between the localities and the central government in England. Being neither federal, like West Germany, nor Napoleonic (with an intermediate level of the central administration), there is no general government alternative other than local government itself for providing non-central local services. It follows that there is much greater pressure on the local government system to be functionally appropriate.

This peculiarity of England could account for some of the difference between British local authorities and those of other comparable countries, but it has to be remembered that the Swedish communes are in any case education and social service authorities in their own right, so they ought to be compared not with the English districts but with the present counties. Since these counties average over 700,000 population, that is to say some twenty-six times as large as the Swedish commune, we may conclude that the relatively large scale of British local units is well beyond what may be attributable to the absence of an intermediate tier.

Apart from the special conditions of the British political system that facilitate major change, noted earlier, we are driven back to some other explanation for the extraordinary scale of British local government. The most obvious is merely that the sociogeographic and service efficiency arguments in the British reform process were exaggerated. As Peter Self has concluded, 'It is only by looking abroad that one realizes how big and remote British local government has become, and how facile and unproven are the arguments for this large scale.'[35]

Nowhere were the two arguments more forcefully deployed than in the Redcliffe–Maud Report.[36] This dominant emphasis on scale effects has meant that the other major requirement of local government, that it should be representative of local community consciousness, is overwhelmed. As a result, many of the local authorities in the new system are too large to correspond to anything that anyone can recognize as a community if by that is meant units that can command a sense of local loyalty from their citizens, or correspond to any existing sense of identity among them, or even their daily patterns of movement.

Functional capacity equals democracy?
To some extent, the over-emphasis on functional criteria at the expense of the democratic can be explained by the assumption that making local government units functionally effective also makes them democratic. The Redcliffe–Maud Report states quite explicitly:

> If, as we have said, a minimum population of around 250,000 is necessary for the efficient administration of services, it seems to us an inescapable corollary that local democracy will be ineffective unless organized in units of at least that size.[37]

The reasoning behind this connection runs something like this. Democracy implies the capacity of the government to act. It therefore follows that enhancing the capacity of a local authority to act — making it more functionally effective — also enhances its democratic character. Bruce Wood has described this conflation of the democratic and functional objectives in the 1972 act as follows:

> 'Responsive' government is government responding to public demands, and 'accountable' government is government seeking judgement on its performance. Both imply that a council has goods to deliver, that it is responsible for the provision of reasonable important public services. Here there is a clear link between the ideas of 'democracy' and those of 'efficiency' or 'effectiveness'. A responsible local authority is one with clear choices to make about the nature of its outputs: it is not one which is too small to be entrusted with a reasonable range of functions by Parliament.[38]

This view is shared by Dahl and Tufte in their book *Size and Democracy*,[39] which is perhaps the best full-dress appraisal of the relationship between the size of the political unit — the polity — and democracy. It therefore warrants special attention, although it must be emphasized that Dahl and Tufte are somewhat more circumspect than the local government reformers in Britain in their espousal of the claim that governmental capacity is a legitimate democratic criterion.[40]

It cannot be denied that representative democracy does imply that government has some capacity to act: such capacity is the essential prerequisite if the notion of accountability is to have any meaning.[41] However, the functional effectiveness of a democratic polity cannot be equated with making a local government system functionally effective. In other words, governmental capacity is not the same thing as system capacity. An English parish council is no whit less democratic than the Copenhagen City Council because its capacity to act happens to be considerably less, any more than the USA can be said to be more democratic than Luxembourg because it has a permanent seat on the UN Security Council, or because it appoints the Supreme Commander of NATO. As Barry has put it when reviewing Dahl and Tufte, 'system capacity is, surely, in itself neither democratic nor undemocratic, since it refers to the range of options open to those who set the policy of the country'.[42]

In short, system capacity is a 'given', which may have been determined by historical accident, war, physical characteristics, language and so forth. One of the features of local government, as we have noted, is that it is likely to be designed with some notion of functionality in mind, but that does not mean that functional capacity has any bearing on the way in which power is distributed within the local authority, that is, on whether it is democratic or not. If a local authority does not provide the services its citizens would like it to provide, this may merely reflect an error in the assignment of functions within the local government system. Moreover, we cannot assume that enhancing system capacity is preferred by the majority of citizens to the accessibility of government, the accountability of that government, or a sense of community within the given polity, all of which may be weakened by the enlargement that is designed to enhance system capacity.

Other advantages of scale cited by Dahl and Tufte when exploring its relationship to democracy include the so-called 'plumber's rule', which argues that occupational interest groups need a minimum base to generate sufficient numbers to make an organized and permanent group feasible. In this way an individual plumber has his participatory potential enhanced. It also seems likely that at the local level larger units, especially larger urban units (as Dahl and Tufte maintain), are able to moderate the participatory deficiencies of scale because they are able to support political parties, newspapers and other media forms.[43] But these scale advantages are a function not of local government units as such but, rather, of the scale of the actual urban entity, and they would not be affected if that entity were divided between more than one local government unit. In any case, they can only moderate the tendency for democracy to be a diminishing function of scale; they hardly add up to an argument in favour of large scale on democratic grounds.

We must of necessity talk in highly generalized terms about what constitutes big and what constitutes small; nevertheless, other things being equal, we may say that at the local government level a small unit is likely to be more democratic than a larger unit for at least three reasons, which in combination override the possible democratic advantage of scale such as the plumber's rule just discussed. First, in small units leaders are more likely to be responsive to citizens' views because they are simply potentially more accessible. Second, a smaller unit is more democratic because a higher proportion of citizens can participate directly in decision-making, although it must be conceded that above a fairly low threshold the differences become very marginal: 30 councillors may be only 0.01 percent of 300,000 citizens but they are still only 1 per cent of 3000. Third, in smaller units there is a greater likelihood of social homogeneity among the citizenry, thus making possible more clear-cut majorities on issues and more popular control of leaders:[44] 'Majority rule will generate the least political externalities in highly homogeneous communities and . . . such homogeneity is most nearly approximated at the extreme local level.'[45]

To emphasize this rarely rehearsed link between small scale and democracy is not to smuggle back into the argument the case for a village community local government, which, as we have noted earlier, can hardly be the model for local government in the modern Western state. Rather, the aim is to counter the assumption that scale is of little importance for democracy — more important still, to resist the attempt to incorporate other values, like the claim for system capacity, under the democratic rubric so that increased scale is interpreted as meaning increased democracy.

Population mobility

If the aim of service efficiency in local government modernization has been exaggerated in the UK, it could be argued that there is a population mobility aspect of urbanization that strengthens the case for large units of local government. It might also be claimed that it also places a question mark against according the community–democratic criterion equal status as a determinant of structure. Such population mobility includes long-term and diurnal (journey to work) mobility, and both, it may be argued, have reduced the importance of locality and undermined the sense of local allegiance in many areas of the country.

This delocalization process has been aided and abetted by the nationalization of politics, the emergence of a national communications system, especially television, and the growth of disposable income, all of which have tended to metropolitanize popular attitudes. Each of these trends, in its various ways, has reduced the importance of locality, and each has been reinforced by the steady centralization of the economic system. Modern society has moved, so it is claimed, from a 'place community' to an 'interest community'.[46]

It would be pointless to deny that such centralizing forces have been occurring and that they have probably undermined the importance of locality in both a subjective and an objective sense. Nevertheless, it would be equally misguided to overstate the extent of the decline of locality consciousness and its impact. Evidence on most of the centralizing processes is hard to come by, but we do have data on population mobility in Britain, and a national survey carried out in 1963 found that almost half (47.3 percent) of respondents had lived at their present address for more than ten years, and that most movement had occurred within the same local authority area and within a distance of ten miles. Only 13 percent of those who moved had done so outside their region.[47]

On this evidence, it could hardly be said that mobility had been at a level that would tear local roots asunder. Moreover, it is not at all clear that the fact of movement alone necessarily affects the mover's relations with his local community, and there is a possibility that there may be a positive rather than a negative relationship between mobility and civic consciousness. Most community studies, for example, reveal the migrant as being more active on local bodies than the non-migrant.

Musgrove, in summarizing the findings of such studies, has concluded that, 'in the leadership of voluntary organizations in local communities, migrant white-collar and professional people have taken over from the locals; ... they are over-represented in the sphere of leadership as they are in the bureaucracy.'[48]

It should not be too readily assumed, then, that mobility necessarily undermines a sense of local identification, and it may be that it enhances those forms that are relevant to local government because movement from one locality to another tends to sharpen the citizen's awareness of the role of the local authority and its possibilities by providing the migrant with what the non-migrant lacks, namely, a 'contrast model' of another local authority and how *it* has tackled a particular service problem. If the migrant is very mobile, he may have a composite contrast model of all that he felt was best in the local authorities where he has lived previously. Alternatively, or in addition, the migrant may join a service pressure group and acquire a composite contrast model, ready-made as it were. Armed in this way, he may become a more than usually active local participant when a particular local service falls short of his model.[49] An example of this phenomenon is the increasingly numerous group of peripatetic professionals who are both geographically mobile and socially upwardly mobile — the so-called 'spiralists' — who may not only take a direct interest in local affairs because of their greater mobility, but also may participate locally all the more easily because their status in each community as a professional is universally accepted.[50]

Where the migrant moves from an urban to a rural area, his impact on local politics may be even more dramatic, as the following quote from a report on an attempt by former urban parents to stop the closure of a Cumbrian village school illustrates. These parents, says the report, 'have fetched with them the equipment of protest and action — the classical tactics of confrontation and lobbying taken for granted in Camden Town or Coventry but relatively unknown in the larger rural counties'.[51]

Similar scepticism must be accorded the imputation that the increase in diurnal mobility weakens a sense of locality. It may be true that if home and work are in the same community there are likely to be the conditions for a strong community identity, but it does not follow that if they are separated there is a corresponding weakening of a local sense of identity. The suburban revolution marks among other things a rejection of the urban, in the British case perhaps underpinned by a profound sense of rural nostalgia. Thus, the sense of home area identity for the commuter may be all the stronger precisely because he lives a considerable distance from his urban workplace.

These are necessarily speculations, but we may say with some confidence that when it is claimed that mobility undermines the case for small-scale local government, what is forgotten is the fact that we all have to live somewhere. The fact of specific domicile means, in short, that we are all consumers of local services, irrespective of length of residence. Above some fairly low time threshold, length of residence is not going to affect very much our interest in these services and how they are administered. The need for local government to be accessible and responsive, it follows, is likely to be much the same whether the citizen lives in the house in which he was born or into which he moved five years ago.

Just as it does not imply that there should have been no boundary change in the British local government system, the preceding criticism does not imply any belief in the benefits of small scale, irrespective of either sociogeographic factors or the requirements of functional effectiveness and efficiency. As I have emphasized, one of the characteristics of the settlement pattern of modern society is the spread of urban centres and a merging of the urban and the rural. If local government is to do its job — that is, if it is at least to recognize the unitariness of a continuously built-up area both in functional and in political terms — it follows that there will be, inevitably, some large and possibly a few very large local authorities. Having said that, however, our discussion so far makes it clear that the scale of British local government is huge beyond any rational explanation that relates structure to socioeconomic reality.

Public choice theory
Another possible explanation for scale of UK local government is that both the sociogeographic and the service efficiency arguments are focused on local government solely as a system of production rather than consumption. This characteristic is clearly brought out if we look at a theory of structural change, or rather non-change, that is diametrically the opposite of the British reorganization process. This is a theory of local government structure put forward by some public choice theorists,[52] which claims positive benefits for small-scale local government that barely entered the long debate on local government modernization in Britain, not even from the staunchest defenders of the status quo.

The essence of their argument is that, whatever the pattern of unreformed local government that exists, it is preferable to any modernized (i.e., enlarged) alternative. Should there be any economies of scale to be exploited, public choice theorists are happy to exploit them by the creation of ad hoc bodies for special purposes following the fiscal equivalence theory, leaving the existing local government structure intact. Such ad hoc bodies would also have what is usually anathema to orthodox local government reformers — overlapping jurisdictions — and if necessary they would be private and profit-making.

Scale economies could also be reaped by the larger of the existing local authorities, which could provide such services to their smaller neighbours on a contract basis. The model for such an arrangement suggested is that of the Contract Services Plan operating in Los Angeles County, whereby thirty-two of the eighty-one authorities within the county have certain services provided for them on a contractual basis by the county.[53] The idea is to create a 'public economy' which will not only provide a wider choice of public servants and public service 'packages' to meet consumer preferences, but would also provide them more efficiently, because the separate units of output would be in competition with each other. Such a fragmented and complex system, which deliberately maintains all the characteristics that local government reorganization of the kind under discussion seeks to eliminate, would also, it is claimed, be better placed to combat bureaucracy by denying the possibility of the abuse of power.[54]

With such an impressive list of benefits, which fall only just short of solving most of the principal ills of representative democracy, it would be profligate not to give the public choice approach very serious attention. However, like the economies-of-scale thesis, much (although not all)[55] of the argument has to be supposition; there is little to test it, as there has not been much of the kind of local government reform under discussion in the USA, despite the fact that it seems to have prompted the public choice attack.

Like the functionalist case, too, the public choice case is buttressed by some large assumptions. These include, implicitly or explicitly, that local government services will determine the individual's domicile; that the co-ordination of cognate services or of adjacent areas is unnecessary, or can be achieved by inter-authority bargaining; that land-use planning is of no importance; that the abuse of power in local government is largely a function of scale; that there is no need for more integrated government as population density increases; and that, in the absence of a market test, public bureaucrats are virtually autonomous.

Far-fetched as these assumptions may seem, there can be little doubt that the reform process in Britain would have been enriched had the public choice theorists participated. This is because one of the most valuable contributions their theory has to make to the reform issue is its claim that production efficiency, that is, the efficiency with which services may be said to be produced, is not the only form of efficiency to be considered: also to be taken into account is distribution or consumption efficiency, that is, the efficiency with which services are delivered to the public. The two forms may be in conflict, so that the possible gains that may be made in production by enlargement can be lost if consumption efficiency consequently falls short of pre-reform standards. Moreover, consumption efficiency implies some notion of public demand — of its preferences and needs — whereas the British reform process tends to make the assumption that an increase in production efficiency is the sole consideration. It is this almost obsessive preoccupation with production efficiency that probably lies at the heart of any explanation for the scale of the present British local government system.

The notion of consumption efficiency has the great advantage that it provides the vital link between what the proponents of reorganization *à l'anglais* see only as opposed objectives — between, that is, the objective of efficiency and rationality (service and sociogeographic) and that of democracy (areas based on a sense of identity among their citizens). The consumption efficiency criterion enables citizens to choose to sacrifice the theoretical gains from, say, minimizing externalities so as to create a more rational boundary for planning, transport, education and highways. Instead, they may favour retaining the existing boundary because it delimits a sense of common identity that the enlarged area does not. In making that choice they would, of course (assuming the theory was correct), pay the consequent price in terms of inefficient planning, transport, education and highway services.

Access and SDI density

Such choices, it must be conceded, present ticklish problems, not least of which is the possible cost of retaining the status quo — effectively, of retaining small scale — since such costs are unlikely to be equally shared by all citizens, i.e. those within this existing boundary and affected parties beyond.

But if it would be absurd to minimize such problems, it would be equally wrong not to recognize some highly important gains that are to be made by releasing the reform debate from the rigid grip of production efficiency. Once the objective of consumption efficiency is recognized, a major value of local government that we have largely ignored so far can be accommodated: namely, that of *access*. By access is meant the ability of citizens to receive or 'consume' local services. This may seem a rather obvious point; unless the intended recipients of a service can actually receive that service, it might as well not exist. However, it has to be recognized that the ability to consume some public service may be dependent on the spatial distribution of the service delivery point. If it is too far away for the intended recipient to reach, because he has no means of personal transport or because it is not on a public transport route, then, to all intents and purposes, the service may not be provided. For such services the spatial distribution of service delivery institutions (SDIs) — schools, branch libraries, clinics, sports centres, old people's homes — may be just as critical a feature of the provision of the service as the content of the service itself.

In the context of local government reorganization, this notion of access is highly relevant, since there may be a direct relationship between the scale of a local authority and the number and distribution of SDIs. This relationship follows from the axiom that the smaller the jurisdiction for a given (mandatory) service involving the need for SDIs, the more accessible the service will be. No matter how small the jurisdiction, it will have to have at least one SDI. Whether the reverse axiom applies is unlikely (i.e., the larger the SDI, the greater the decline in access), since large organizations can usually deconcentrate their operations at will. We noted an example of this in the county of Devon earlier. But it is highly likely that SDI density *tends to decline* with increasing jurisdictional scale, so that, in the local government situation that has obtained in the UK, there is a strong likelihood that overall access has declined. Whether it has and by how much remains a matter of empirical verification that lies well outside the ambit of this chapter.

It is worthwhile, however, unravelling the possible causes of the relationship between access and jurisdictional scale, bearing in mind that the discussion must in the nature of the case be highly tentative. One reason why SDI density is likely to be reduced as a result of the increased scale of local government is that there is no incentive for decision-makers to do otherwise. They will provide as few SDIs in normal circumstances as the 'market' will bear, for to do otherwise is to add to costs and render more complicated the structure of management and control. There may be additional factors that reinforce this minimalist stance, among which must be noted the psychological: the larger the jurisdiction, the less the decision-maker can take problems of distance and access into consideration. The jurisdiction is for him a given; its very existence is its own justification, however big it is. Thus, a federal civil servant in Washington must assume that the problem of providing services over an area that spans a continent from the Gulf Coast of Texas to Alaska is as feasible as it is to provide that service for the District of Columbia. But in making that necessary assumption, he must correspondingly suppress his awareness that distance raises any difficulties that cannot be rectified by administrative deconcentration.

In the case of local government enlargement, there may be added incentives for decision-makers to reduce SDI density, simply because to do so is identified as one of the objectives of the reform. Thus, reduction becomes transformed into an act of 'rationalization' and is seen as one of the tangible *benefits* of reform. Indeed, it may be seen as being precisely one of those 'economies of scale' that the reformers claimed for the change. As a dilution of the quality of output, it cannot be anything of the kind, of course, but such a consideration will be obliterated by the need to implement an SDI reduction policy that the new enlarged jurisdiction might almost be said to be duty-bound to carry out.

The reduction in access is not the only qualitative dilution that is likely to occur, thereby further invalidating the economies-of-scale claim, but it may be interpreted none the less as reflecting such economies. Unless there is a corresponding increase in facilities to match the increase in consumer load, any reduction in SDI density also entails a dilution of service quality — that is to say, larger classes in schools, larger queues at library check-outs and clinics, more crowded sports facilities and larger (and hence more impersonally managed) residential establishments.

The possible reduction in the quality of services consequent upon jurisdictional enlargement, either because of a decline in access or because of dilution, is not uniform in its impact, since the consumption of local services has a tendency to be asymmetric in social class terms. That is to say, the lower paid and the poor may tend, in the UK at least, to have a disproportionate consumption of local services per capita such as housing, various social welfare and old people's services. For those services that are usually delivered by SDIs, such class consumption asymmetry may be even greater. Any reduction in their number, it follows, may tend disproportionately to penalize the lower paid and the poor. This possible negative effect is enhanced by the fact that the lower the income, the greater the importance of distance since car ownership tends to be a function of income. Any increase in distance to be travelled to SDIs — the normal effect of reducing their number — therefore may further discriminate against those citizens who are least able to cope with that change.

The decline in access and service dilution, which may extend to include a reduction in senior specialist staff as well,[56] and its special discriminatory effects against the poor, add up to an important and usually ignored deficiency of local government reorganization. It is likely to be worse where reorganization reaches the scale of the present British local government system, but it is likely to be a deficiency of more modest reorganizational schemes as well. At the very least, there is always the danger that it will tend to occur when jurisdictions are enlarged.

Conclusions

It is difficult to summarize adequately the preceding necessarily wide-ranging discussion, so it might be preferable to set out briefly the possible conclusions that ought to be drawn from it. The first is the importance of the distinction that needs to be drawn between the Napoleonic and non-Napoleonic groups of states if we are to account for at least some of the major variations in local government modernization. The second is the importance of spatial factors in such modernization. There is a tendency in modern social science, and especially perhaps in political science, to understate spatial or territorial factors, or to transform them into a non-spatial form, and hence perhaps a tendency to root the rationale for local government modernization in the service requirements of the welfare state rather than in the urban revolution.

Within the group of non-Napoleonic states, the special character of the British political system must be emphasized, and not the least important element in this special character is the remarkable power of the centre to undertake fundamental institutional change. Of almost equal importance is the temptation in the British context for the centre to resort to structural change for reasons that have little to do with the local government system as such. Such motives can arise either because of the centre's non-executant insulation, which can make co-ordination of the localities extremely difficult,[57] or in order to promote party-political interests. Perhaps, too, some account needs to be taken of the comparative maturity of the UK in terms of industrialization. Again, the territorial dimension must not be forgotten, and the emergence of a quasi-urban society and the continued decimation of the inner city in large tracts of central England and other parts seems likely to have a bearing on the extraordinarily large scale of British local government. In this sense the British experience could be of some value for the future pattern of local government in the older industrial societies.

How far the British local government reorganization offers lessons for the more newly industrialized countries is more problematic; but it is not too far-fetched to claim that, like all extreme cases, it does force us to examine more carefully the premises and principles of structural change of any kind — in this case, the relationship between functional capacity and democracy and the possible crucial impact of sociogeographical factors on what, after all, modern democratic government is largely concerned with, namely, the successful delivery of services to those for whom such services were intended. To this extent, the British experience is both a warning and a lesson.

Notes

1. Preston King, *Federalism and Federation* (London: Croom Helm, 1980).
2. For a discussion of the need for local government reorganization in the USA and some of the problems that such reorganization can encounter, see *Modernizing Local Government* (New York: Committee for Economic Development, 1966).
3. Alexis de Tocqueville, *Democracy in America* (London: Fontana, 1962), vol. 1, p. 73.
4. For an explicit linking of the functional needs of the welfare state and local government reorganization, see Francesco Kjellberg, 'Local Government Reorganization and the Development of the Welfare State', *Journal of Public Policy*, 5:2 (1985). Also see Douglas Ashford, *British Dogmatism and French Pragmatism* (London: George Allen & Unwin, 1982), especially chs. 1 and 3.
5. See L.J. Sharpe, 'The Growth and the Decentralization of the Modern Democratic State', *European Journal of Political Research* (forthcoming), for a discussion of sub-national governmental growth in Western democracies. Also see L.J. Sharpe, 'The Failure of Local Government Modernization in Britain: a Critique of Functionalism', *Canadian Public Administration*, 24:1 (1981), which overlaps the present chapter.
6. For summaries of local government modernization in various countries, see *Administration Aspects of Urbanization* (New York: United Nations, 1969); A. Hauck Walsh, *The Urban Challenge to Government* (New York: Praeger, 1969); A.F. Leemans, *Changing Patterns of Local Government* (The Hague: International Union of

Local Authorities, 1970); E. Kalk (ed.), *Regional Planning and Regional Government in Europe* (The Hague: IULA, 1971); Donald C. Rowat (ed.), *International Handbook on Local Government Reorganization* (Westport, CT: Greenwood, 1980); Arthur B. Gunlicks (ed.), *Local Government Reform and Reorganization: an International Perspective* (Port Washington: Kennikat, 1981). For the best short appraisal, see Kjellberg, 'Local Government Reorganization'.

7. F. D'Arcy and B. Jobert, 'Urban Planning in France', in Jack Hayward and Michael Watson (eds), *Planning, Politics and Public Policy* (Cambridge: Cambridge University Press, 1975).

8. P. Viot, 'Through Regional Planning towards Regional Administration', in Kalk (ed.), *Regional Planning and Regional Government*.

9. Ashford, *British Dogmatism and French Pragmatism*.

10. For further discussion of central co-ordinative strategies designed to minimize control deficits in the British context, see L.J. Sharpe, 'Central Coordination and the Policy Network', *Political Studies* 33:3 (1985).

11. *Royal Commission on Local Government in England* (henceforth RCLE), *Written Evidence of H.M. Treasury* (London: HMSO, 1967), p. 5.

12. *House of Commons, Second Report of the Expenditure Committee, Urban Transport Planning. Vol. II Minutes of Evidence* (London: HMSO, 1973), p. 507, para. 2444.

13. The 1972 Act reduced the total number of units in England and Wales from 1391 to 422. The various types of authority before and after reorganization (London excluded) may be summarized as follows:

Old system		New system	
Counties	58	Metropolitan counties	6[a]
County boroughs	83	Metropolitan districts	36
Boroughs and districts	1250	Shire counties	47
		Districts	333
Total	1391		422

[a] Abolished in 1986.

14. White Paper, *Local Government in England*, Cmnd. 4584 (London: HMSO, 1971), p. 6, para 8.

15. For a succinct account of this argument, see RCLE, *Written Evidence of the Ministry of Housing and Local Government* (London: HMSO, 1967), pp. 60–6.

16. Mancur Olson, 'Strategic Theory and its Applications: the Principle of Fiscal Equivalence: the Division of Responsibilities among Different Levels of Government', *American Economic Review, Papers and Proceedings* 59 (1969), p. 482. Also see J. Stefan Dupre, 'International Relations and the Metropolitan Area', in Simon Miles (ed.), *Metropolitan Problems* (Toronto: Methuen, 1970), and F.W. Scharpf et al. (eds.), *Control Deficits in Multi-level Problem Solving* (Berlin: International Institute of Management, 1975).

17. Mancur Olson, *The Logic of Collective Action* (New York: Schocken, 1971), p. 121. Also see Walsh, *The Urban Challenge to Government*, p. 7, who also underlines the need for more government and planning as population density increases.

18. The main document of this debate in the RCLE *Report*, Cmnd. 4040 (London: HMSO, 1969).

19. For a discussion of the service effectiveness case, see RCLE, *Written Evidence*

of Ministry of Housing and Local Government, paras 256–62; and *Written Evidence of Department of Education and Science*, paras 83–102.

20. For a discussion of such economies, see RCLE, *Written Evidence of H.M. Treasury*, paras 8–10.

21. See the RCLE's own research findings on scale in RCLE, *Research Studies* nos 3 and 4.

22. *The Cost of Reform* (Chester: Cheshire County Council, 1970).

23. A. Wildavsky, *Budgeting* (Boston: Little, Brown, 1975).

24. J.R. James, 'Lessons from the Past', *Town and Country Planning* 43 (1975), p. 165.

25. RCLE, *Report*, vol. III, appendix 9.

26. Ibid., appendix 11.

27. K. Newton, 'Community Performance in Britain', *Current Sociology* 22 (1976), p. 54. Also see R.A. Dahl, 'The City in the Future of Democracy', in L. Feldman (ed.), *Politics and Government in Urban Canada* (Toronto: Methuen, 1981). In this article Dahl concludes: 'there is no worthwhile evidence that there are any significant economies of scale in city governments for cities over 50,000' (p. 54).

28. R.E. Wraith and G.B. Lamb, *Public Inquiries as an Instrument of Government* (London: George Allen & Unwin, 1971), p. 273.

29. The Scottish reorganization was derived from the *Report of the Royal Commission on Local Government in Scotland*, Cmnd. 4150 (Edinburgh: HMSO, 1969).

30. *Local Government in England*, p. 6.

31. See Peter G. Richards, *The Local Government Act 1972 — Problems of Implementation* (London: George Allen & Unwin, 1976), p. 84.

32. See RCLE, *Report*, *passim*.

33. Lars Stromberg, 'Sweden', in Rowat (ed.), *International Handbook on Local Government Reorganization*, p. 308.

34. See Brian C. Smith, *Decentralization*, table 4:2, p. 72, for the average population of local government units for nine Western European states.

35. Peter Self, 'Local Government: a Lesson from Sweden', *The Times*, 17 December 1976.

36. The Report lists ten principles on which its proposals are based, seven of which are derived from the urbanization, and service efficiency arguments. See RCLE, *Report*, vol. I.

37. RCLE, *Report*, vol. I, para. 272, p. 2. Also see Derek Senior's *Dissenting Memoranda*, vol. II, paras 178–80, p. 44. The Redcliffe–Maud Report's notion of 'democratic strength' is also essentially a conflation of the functional and the democratic criteria. See RCLE, *Report*, vol. I, pp. 145–6.

38. Bruce Wood, *The Process of Local Government Reform: 1966–74* (London: George Allen & Unwin, 1976), p. 24.

39. Robert A. Dahl and Edward R. Tufte, *Size and Democracy* (Stanford: Stanford University Press, 1974).

40. 'A rational and reasonable democrat who wished to maximise the chances of attaining certain of his goals might well trade off personal effectiveness for some gain in the capacity of the system to attain them' (Dahl and Tufte, *Size and Democracy*, p. 23). Not only are Dahl and Tufte cautious about the relationship between system capacity and democracy; later in the book they appear to concede that it may even be a red herring: 'Differences in the autonomy of a democratic country do not necessarily produce differences in the power of the individual citizen' (*Size and Democracy*, p. 133).

41. For a more detailed discussion of the link between governmental functional

128   *The Dynamics of Institutional Change*

effectiveness and democracy, see L.J. Sharpe, 'American Democracy Re-considered, Part 2', *British Journal of Political Science* 3:2 (1973).

42. Brian Barry, 'Size and Democracy', *Government and Opposition* 4:9 (1974), p. 495.

43. For similar arguments, see K. Newton, 'Is Small Really so Beautiful? Is Big Really so Ugly?', *Studies in Public Policy* no. 18 (Glasgow: University of Strathclyde, 1979).

44. Barry, 'Size and Democracy', p. 497.

45. Jerome Rothenburg, 'Local Decentralization and the Theory of Optimal Government', in Julius Margolis (ed.), *The Analysis of Public Output* (New York: Columbia University Press, 1970), p. 32.

46. These terms were coined by Melvin Webber, who has an important influence on the decline-of-locality thesis. See his 'The Urban Place and the Non-place Urban Realm', in Melvin M. Webber et al., *Exploration into Urban Structure* (Philadelphia: University of Pennsylvania Press, 1963), and Melvin M. Webber, 'Order in Diversity: Community without Propinquity' in Lowden Wingo (ed.), *Cities in Space* (Baltimore: Johns Hopkins University Press, 1964).

47. A.I. Harris, *Labour Mobility in Great Britain*, Government Social Survey (London: HMSO, 1966), tables 6, 12 and 14.

48. Frank Musgrove, *The Migratory Elite* (London: Heinemann, 1963), p. 12.

49. Margaret Stacey et al., *Power, Persistence and Change* (London: Routledge & Kegan Paul, 1975), p. 65.

50. W. Watson, 'Social Mobility and Social Class in Industrial Communities', in Max Gluckman (ed.), *Closed Systems and Open Minds* (Edinburgh: Oliver and Boyd, 1964), p. 147. For a discussion of the role of outsiders in stimulating local participation in the USA, see G. Suttles, *The Social Construction of Communities* (Chicago: Chicago University Press, 1972) and Matthew A. Crenson *Neighbourhood Politics* (Cambridge: Harvard University Press, 1983).

51. Ian Breach, 'For Whom the School Bell Tolls', *Guardian*, 3 May 1978.

52. For the earliest and perhaps the most explicit application of the public approach, see Vincent Ostrom et al., 'The Organization of Government in Metropolitan Areas', *American Political Science Review*, 55 (1961). Also see Robert L. Bish, *The Political Economy of Metropolitan Areas* (Chicago: Markham, 1971); Vincent Ostrom and Elinor Ostrom, 'Public Choice: a Different Approach to the Study of Public Administration', *Public Administration Review* 31 (1971); and Robert L. Bish and Vincent Ostrom, *Understanding Urban Government: Metropolitan Reform Reconsidered* (Washington: American Enterprise Institute for Public Policy Research, 1973).

53. For a description of the Contract Services Plan, see James F. Horam and G. Thomas Taylor, *Experiments in Metropolitan Government* (New York, Praeger, 1977), ch. 6.

54. Bish and Ostrom, *Understanding Urban Government*, especially chs. 4, 5 and 6.

55. For examples of empirical analysis which substantiate some of the public choice school theories, see Elinor Ostrom and R. Parks, 'Suburban Police Departments: Too Many and Too Small?', in Louis H. Masotti and Jeffrey K. Hadden, *Urban Affairs Annual Review: the Urbanization of the Suburbs*, vol. 7 (Beverly Hills: Sage, 1973); Elinor Ostrom et al., *Community Organization and the Provision of Police Services* (Beverly Hills: Sage, 1973), and Roger S. Ahlbrandt, *Municipal Fire Protection Services: Comparisons of Alternative Organizational Forms* (Beverly Hills: Sage, 1973).

56. E. James, 'Frontiers in the Welfare State', *Public Administration* 44:4 (1966).

This is one of the very rare pieces of systematic research that examines the negative effects of increasing jurisdictional area in the provision of local government services.

57. For a discussion of this aspect of the British system see Sharpe, 'Central Coordination and the Policy Network'.

6

Radical Reforms and Marginal Change: the French Socialist Experience

Yves Mény

Since 1958, France has not gone through a single year without the government attempting to reform the local system, and without the opposition heavily criticizing excessive centralization or 'dictatorship' from Paris. Few countries have seen so much debate, so much reform — and apparently so little change, even after the far-reaching reforms attempted by the Socialist government from 1981 to 1986. Fundamental characteristics seem to remain.

First — and this is the feature most often stressed — the French system is traditionally a centralized, structured, hierarchical system. Initiative is regarded as coming from above, with the base of the system having in principle only a minor role, being controlled by the central government. Guidance is the function of the ministers, and in each of the ninety-six départements the prefects, as agents of central power, keep an eye on the proper functioning of the whole administration. This 'spider's web' network was aimed at giving the centre control over the periphery, at diffusing its values and establishing its leadership. This situation has given rise to very diverse evaluations, whether critical, such as that of Lamennais, which condemns the 'apoplexy at the centre and paralysis at the extremities', or much more favourable, like Michelet's analysis: 'French France had attracted, absorbed, amalgamated the English, German and Spanish with which it was surrounded. She had southernised the North and northernised the South.'[1]

Second, centre and periphery are not perfectly distinct, autonomous poles. The most striking feature, at least up to the recent reforms, has been the osmosis between the institutions and officials of the central power and those of local government. The prefect was simultaneously the government's representative and the département's executive, and the mayor, who is elected by the commune, has the task of 'implementing the laws' at the local level. As Hayward has written, 'the two leaders who dominate French local government . . . exemplify in their different ways the enduring triumph of bureaucracy and democracy.'[2] The fact that central and local functions were handled mainly by the two appointed or elected authorities illustrates likewise the tendency to personalize power at the local level. Even when the institutions of 'imperial' type were swept away at the central level from 1870 onwards to make room for less personalized forms of government, the local institutions did not cease to be dominated by a single-headed executive which was, in any case, a leadership more in line with the traditions of rural society.

Third, by contrast with many European states, France has proved incapable, at least at first sight, of reforming in depth a local system created for a rural, peasant society, and ill-adapted to the requirements of industrial and urban development. The French local authority map looks like an old-fashioned jigsaw cut on no rational basis, and puts the famous French Cartesianism to a severe test: 36,000 communes, of which 28,000 have less than 2000 inhabitants; 96 départements in a country less populated than, for example, Italy, Germany or Britain. The local political–administrative system seems 'fossilized' in the form it had last century, despite the urgency of reform and the endeavours of the governments of the Fifth Republic. Not even the creation of twenty-two regions in 1972 contradicts this immobilism, since the regions had only residual powers and were made subservient to the coupled or divergent objectives both of central government and of the départements and communes. The only Western country that has to face similar complexity is the USA, which with its federal system has less means of manipulating the local authorities than the French government.

Finally, relations between local authorities, which vertically are characterized by richness and density, horizontally are often conflictual or, at any rate, very difficult. Co-operation between communes or between départements works well only sectorally and fails when further attempts at integration are made. Thus, the regions have often found it very difficult to establish budgets that are anything more than simple reallocations of resources among départements on an egalitarian basis. The reforms of local taxation have largely foundered on this reef, and central government has assumed an impossible task of equalization, for instance, at the level of conurbations. This situation, no doubt explained by the strength of community sentiment, by 'parish-pump spirit', likewise originates in the mutual hostility that has long prevailed between town and country. The antagonism, which has long constituted the fundamental division in all French politics,[3] remains present in the institutions, even if it has become largely blurred in people's minds as a result of massive urbanization and the economic, cultural and perhaps political integration of the countryside. For example, until 1943 a local tax, the *octroi*, was levied on all goods coming from the country to the towns.

The linkages between centre and periphery

Links between centre and periphery take on different forms: they may be established principally through the interplay of political parties (as in Italy or Belgium), through functional administrations (as in Britain) or through an overlapping of tasks and institutions (West Germany). The exchanges between centre and periphery in France pass through political and administrative channels, but their uniqueness comes particularly from the 'to-ing and fro-ing' that is constantly going on in the system. This situation, and its development over recent decades, means that a 'traditional model' of regulation can be counterposed to an 'innovatory model'. What is the scope of this distinction, and, in particular, does it fully respond to the interpretation of present relations between government and local authorities?

The main political channel in France does not run through the parties. Except for the Communist Party, which until recently was the only party with a solid local organization throughout the country, the political parties have never sought, or managed, to give themselves real roots at the local level. For instance, at the municipal elections of 1971, the Socialist Party, which admittedly was going through a bad patch, had a number of problems in many towns in finding enough members to fill the slate! Likewise, the Gaullists, triumphant in national elections until 1974, were not able to acquire solid local positions before the end of the 1970s.

This weakness in party structure, to be sure, has ideological or sociological reasons (rural mistrust of Parisian parties), but it has much more to do with the institutional cumbersomeness of the system. The parties have practically never been in a position to be instruments of the distribution of resources. From well before the French Revolution, the administration has always enjoyed that monopoly, but this role was strengthened and rationalized by the Napoleonic reforms. By contrast with Italian mayors, who turn to the political parties to secure the advantages they seek for their communes, French mayors know that the channel they have to take is that of the state administration, which is locally represented by its 'field services'.

Recourse to the political parties is not essential, because the system supplies the necessary way around administrative blockages, in the form of local bigwigs with a network of influence, who are local representatives and at the same time (in the case of the most important of them) national representatives. MPs who are also local representatives are, to use Tarrow's expression,[4] 'policy-brokers', who mediate between centre and periphery and attenuate by their intervention the dysfunctions of the system. More than 85 percent of senators and deputies in the present Parliament have a local seat, and many of the others have tried to get one or have given one up at the end of their careers. This osmosis makes changes in the institutional and relational setup more difficult: neither the Senate Reform in 1969 nor the reform of the local authorities was possible, since notables proved hostile to any radical changes in the local system, and local representatives mobilized to prevent the disappearance of the Grand Conseil des Communes de France. In turn, central government is interested in the overlapping of the two areas: it can be certain that policies will be debated, defended or criticized within the departmental or municipal assemblies by those of their members who have national seats. The 'nationalization' of local political life remains incomplete, but the regional or municipal peculiarities are tending to disappear, as the regional elections of 1986 showed. The national character of the representatives has even acted as a counterweight to the development of the regional idea. In 1972, to avoid the regions being tempted to become too autonomous, especially under the influence of new elites, the government decided that deputies and senators would automatically be regional representatives. In 1986 the differences between national and regional outcomes in the elections of March were marginal. Only 6 regional councillors (out of 1800) belong to regional parties.

The administrative channel is the other important link between centre and periphery. Its importance and solidity depend not only on the presence of the prefect or the field service in the départements and communes, but also on the duplication of functions by state representatives: before the reform of 1982, the prefect, as already stressed, was the executive in the département and technical employees of the state are available, at extra pay, to départements and communes for the preparation and implementation of investments by these units. These employees find themselves simultaneously in a situation of actors (they act on behalf of the communes) and supervisors (they have to give a favourable opinion on behalf of the government on the projects they have prepared). It is almost impossible to break out of this circle. There is a reciprocal complex overlapping, which was analysed by Worms in terms of complicity,[5] although Thoenig probably got closer to the truth by talking of a 'honeycomb structure'.[6] None of the actors — administrative or political — holds all the cards in the game alone. It is only through conciliation, compromise and mutual exchange of advantages or concessions that each can reach his goals. The solidity and good operation of the system are due precisely to this interdependence. It is exceptional for the decision to be taken exclusively along one or the other of the channels: on the contrary, they call for cross-intervention and arbitration by higher-level protagonists in the other channel.

This interdependence results not only from the duality of roles played by the protagonists, but also from the resources they have for putting pressure on their partners: the mayors know that they need the support of the government's field services for their policies. But the latter, 60 percent (and even sometimes 90 percent) of whose time is spent on work for local authorities,[7] must be on good terms with the representatives in order to continue to receive the fees that supplement their state salaries. Likewise, general councillors and mayors depend on the prefect for inclusion of their projects in the plan, and the prefect needs the councillors and mayors for local policies to be in line with national objectives, and for support or neutrality (for instance, a favourable opinion on a major infrastructure project such as a nuclear power station).

Although there is no doubt that these two channels exist and overlap, it remains true that the combinations may be manifold. We may seek to analyse them by asking about the significance of the interpretive models given of them.

Models of linkage
Research about centre–periphery relations in the last few years has in general distinguished two principal modes of linkage: the traditional model, and a new model in the process of formation, which some discern mainly in the towns and call the 'urban model'.

The traditional model is based on a formal linkage which most observers, from Tocqueville to Crozier, consider as the 'factor of general immobilism' and as an informal linkage that 'compensates unevenly for bureaucratic dysfunctions'.[8] Grémion, who did a systematic analysis of these relations within the local political–administrative system, ranges them round what he considers to be the central pivot, namely, the power of the leading citizens.[9] This power is essentially linked to property and repute, two key values of rural communities and of traditional liberal societies. Was it not Benjamin Constant who was content to demand the right to vote for those who had 'riches and light'?

In 1977 almost half the mayors (45 percent) were still farmers, 15 percent were heads of firms and 13 percent were in the liberal professions or were teachers or civil servants. Workers and employees made up only 5.5 percent of the total number of local representatives. Even if the proportion of farmers has declined since 1977 (to 34 percent), and that of managers, white-collar workers and teachers has gone up, statistics show that very many local representatives (and this is even more true of general councillors) belong to social groups whose power perpetuates itself despite their numerical decline. (The percentage of active farmers fell from 26.8 percent in 1954 to 9 percent in 1980.) These data tend to confirm the hypothesis that it is not election that makes one a leading citizen, but rather that election confirms a social status already acquired.

In this traditional model, the leading citizen takes the function of conciliator and mediator: conciliator within the community to preserve local consensus, mediator with the outside world and in particular with the centre (represented by its local agents). To retain this role, the leading citizen keeps political parties and ideology out of the local scene and takes refuge in an apolitical stance. This stance has a dual function. There is the endogenous function, which enables the leading citizen to present himself as the 'man of the people', the only one able to overcome divisions in the interests of all. In a certain sense he symbolizes (as does the prefect at his level) the public good, which in the French conception cannot simply be the sum of individual interests. Then there is the exogenous aspect of the apolitical stance, which almost symmetrically duplicates the restraint the state imposes on its officials. No one is fooled by this frequent and very convenient hypocrisy. It enables open conflict with official representatives of a politically marked central administration (radical or socialist, later Gaullist) to be avoided, and, in the event of real political connivance, masks possible party favouritism. This traditional political model is still very much alive, as is shown by the resistance of categories in numerical decline or by the community's rejection of candidates dropped in by the political parties or by the government.[10] It still dominates in the rural communes and in small and medium-sized towns: mayors, general councillors, officials of the field services, prefect and deputies play a game that is two centuries old and was brought to perfection by the radicals under the Third Republic.

The 'innovatory' model is presented and analysed in a more differentiated manner.[11] Some writers stress the goals that are aimed at through the setting up of the new model: a strategy of change and development that is apparent mainly in the towns (to the detriment of the general councils, the prefect and even the deputies) and at regional level. The appearance of this new model is alleged to coincide with the emergence of new elites (regional and sometimes urban) or with the adaptation of the most dynamic local notables to new social needs.

In constructing these models, the emphasis is put more on changes at the periphery than on those that affect the centre. For example, by contrasting the role in the big towns of the former leading citizens with that of the new ruling elite, stress is placed on the new strategies that these new mayors are developing: they approach the centre directly, short-circuiting the general council and sometimes even the prefect and the member of Parliament, to seek the maximum advantage and the maximum resources for their town. The political weight they represent, and the requirements of urban development (to which general councillors with a rural background are indifferent or hostile), are thus held to have enabled the emergence of a new model of linkage. It seems from these analyses that it is essentially at the local level that we find the responsibility for the passage from the traditional model to the innovatory one.

Given this dual system of relationship between centre and periphery, one may wonder what differentiated effects the reforms have on local government and what kind of social and political change they have brought. From this point of view, the socialist reforms, the most ambitious since the end of the nineteenth century, are a good case for testing the impact of central intervention upon the functioning of the politico-administrative system.

The Mitterrand reform: 'la grande affaire du septennat'

The decentralization and regionalization policy launched by the Mauroy government on the basis of Mitterrand's commitments and programme were presented as one of major socialist reform.[12] But does the reality match the promises?

Until recently it was possible to claim, without being contradicted by the facts, that decentralization was a promise made when in opposition and soon forgotten on coming to power, and that the left was fundamentally characterized by Jacobin options. This time, however, the new majority seemed to be wanting to disprove the old chestnut of electoral betrayals and disappointed hopes. As Mitterrand stated, the left intended to carry out the whole of its programme and nothing but its programme. This fidelity is all the more remarkable because neither electoral debates on the matter (or rather the absence of debates) nor the hierarchy of needs seemed to justify the absolute priority given to decentralization and regionalization. Certainly, it was easier to draw up a draft framework law on this aspect, where everything had been said and prepared for twenty years, than on the complex thorny problem of nationalization. But additionally, experience and political perspicacity enabled Defferre, the Minister for the Interior, to realize that on such a disputed issue he would require the trump-cards to be produced during the initial 'honey-moon' phase.

The opponents of decentralization and regionalization ranged from the top civil servants, local notables satisfied with a system that gave them influence and discharged them from the burden of exercising power, to the parliamentary opposition and some local and departmental elected representatives. With knowledge of both the internal divisions in the Socialist Party and the opposition between traditionalists and regionalists, one might have expected the postponement of promises to more favourable times. But the renewal of the Socialist Party had weeded out the most Jacobin or old-guard elements; furthermore, the gains of the left in the communes and départements had given the party a solid local base, and conflicts between local representatives and the central administration had made government control and interference increasingly unacceptable. The traditional centre–periphery conflicts were thus strengthened by (and in the end became identified with) the antagonisms between majority and opposition, right and left, at least in the towns and in many départements or regions. For the first time in a century, the coincidence of the 'central' majority with the 'local' majority in 1981 had attenuated (without completely eliminating) the bias against decentralization and regionalization.

This allowed the socialists to adopt and implement several hundred bills, decrees and *circulaires* in the span of four years. By 1985, most of the reforms were being implemented more or less easily. From a purely quantitative point of view, the balance sheet is impressive.

— The executives of the départements and regions are to be elected by elected bodies, the regional council of each of the twenty-two regions being itself elected by direct suffrage (for the first time in March 1986).

— Prefects are to be known as *commissaires de la République* and are the representatives of the state in the départements and regions. But they cease to be the executives of these territorial units.

— The a priori supervision of the prefect and the representative of the Ministry of Finance in the decisions of communes, départements and regions is to be replaced by a posteriori legal control exercised by administrative tribunals or the new regional courts of accounts.

— New powers are transferred to the three levels of local government (commune, département, region) in the areas of town planning, housing, professional training and social matters. Although each level has the main responsibility for certain areas, the transfer of the requisite powers has by no means led to a clear division of respective roles.

— Corsica and the French overseas regions (Guyana, Martinique, Guadeloupe, Réunion) are granted specific statutes, which will result in a number of new institutions rather than the acquisition of important new powers.

— The cities of Paris, Lyon and Marseilles have been divided into separate units with mayors whose task is to run local services, and new electoral systems have introduced partly (communes) or fully (regions) proportional representation.

— In the place of a fiscal reform, which has been shelved, the government has transformed a number of specific subsidies into a block grant and has guaranteed the transfer of the necessary resources to enable decentralization to be effective.

— New patterns of recruitment, promotion and career have been set up for the local civil service. (But the new Chirac government has more or less 'frozen' this part of the reform.)

This collection of legal texts (and a first glance at their implementation) allows only a tentative assessment of the general outlines of the reforms, but it enables a number of hypotheses to be formulated on the potential implications for the politico-administrative system as a whole and centre–periphery relations in France in particular.

1. Radicalism or pragmatism?

The reform bears witness to the belief of the new government in structural reform as an instrument of social change. Decentralization and nationalization are considered essential parts of the policy of economic, political and administrative change that the Socialist government is seeking to pursue. From this point of view, the new rulers have not adopted an attitude or strategy that is any different from that of the Debré government in 1958. The major structural reforms were adopted during the first six months after Debré's taking office, and, since he lacked a coherent disciplined majority such as that elected in 1981, he acted using the full powers allowed by the Constitution for a six-month period. The experience of the initial phase of the Fifth Republic was to provide some guidance for those who, twenty-five years later, ventured along the same path: in many sectors, particularly in respect of decentralization, the structural reforms had remained a dead letter. It took fifteen years to make a start on implementing the local taxation ordinances, and twenty years to bring the number of municipalities down from 38,000 to 36,494.

One might therefore rightly wonder whether the Defferre reform will go any further than the symbols it abolishes and those it sets up, and, if so, what the consequences of the new provisions for centre–periphery relations will be. The law on 'the rights and liberties of municipalities, départements and regions' introduces several changes that at least appear to constitute serious breaks with the past: government control over the acts of local authorities is abolished, with a posteriori checks through the courts replacing a priori administrative and political censorship; the prefects cease to be the executives of the départements and the region and become mere 'commissioners of the Republic', responsible for the co-ordination of the field services of the state; and local authorities can now take measures to ensure 'the protection of the economic and social interests of the regional population'.

These three major changes seem to be radical, and the opposition has not failed to bring out the usual skeletons from the Jacobin cupboard: 'threats to the unity of the Republic', say some; 'waste, disorder, and muddle', cry others. In truth, the reform deserves 'neither that honour nor this indignity', if looked at from a realistic viewpoint.

On the suppression of the preliminary supervision, the Defferre law completes a development that began in 1959 and continued during the 1970s; that is, the reform consigns to oblivion an archaic supervisory system that has become pointless. It is, for instance, hardly any use to check administrative financial measures for their legality when it is well known that in most municipalities they have been prepared by the field services of the government itself. The crucial question in recent years has not been supervision by the prefectures, but supervision by the Ministry of Public Works or the Treasury. On the other hand, although checks through the courts theoretically ensure more guarantees, it is not certain that these guarantees will differ substantially from previous administrative control. The administrative tribunals and the future regional courts of auditors, by virtue of their composition, will both be steeped in the values and traditions of the administration. Finally, the personal responsibility of elected representatives, which ought to be the logical accompaniment to the elimination of the supervision, has been rejected by MPs of both right and left.

The transformation of the prefects into commissioners of the Republic has certainly constituted the most spectacular aspect of the reform. One cannot wipe out with impunity two centuries of such solid and continuous tradition. However, the 'revolutionary' nature of the change is moderated by several considerations. In the first place, Socialists and Communists had already provided, in the 1946 Constitution, for the elimination of the prefect as executive of the département; yet that reform was never put into practice. To be sure, the present majority, in contrast with former governments of the Fourth Republic, had time on its side. However, one may wonder whether such a change will not be vulnerable in the event of a political or social crisis. In the second place, many presidents of departmental councils will be tempted, as in the past, to leave things to the prefect, who, behind the scenes, will retain the central role he has exercised hitherto.

However, this possibility is not likely to be the case in the most urbanized and industrialized regions or départements, where leaders of national stature will take full advantage of the new rules of the game. One possible consequence might be the development of patronage relations and the strengthening of the parties at local level. This 'Italianization' of French political life would, however, meet with resistance from the state administration, which is still very powerful at local level. Only a few big cities, départements and regions have sufficiently well staffed services to counterbalance the state administration. Elsewhere, the latter will retain its primacy except that the triangular relations between prefect, departmental ministries and elected representatives will probably give way to a bipolar confrontation — between representatives of the ministries and the commissioner on the one hand, and between the administration and the elected representatives on the other.

The third major aspect of the innovation is the authorization given to regions, départements and municipalities to take measures in the economic sphere. The reform in fact ratifies practices that the previous Giscard government had sought to prevent, but had not been able completely to forbid. Both Mauroy at Lille and Defferre at Marseilles, to cite only two examples, had thought up and created numerous instruments and procedures aimed at circumventing the prohibition so as to come to the aid of firms in difficulties. Now, the same policy can be extended and applied without encountering a veto from central government.

Apart from the inevitable partisan and political aspects, the reforms themselves showed great prudence, despite symbolic and spectacular gestures such as the 'suppression' of the prefect. Even though the Socialists are often accused of being inexperienced and dogmatic, it seems that, at least in the area of decentralization, they have demonstrated pragmatism and have clearly shown that they can learn from experience. The experience in question comes first of all from the Fifth Republic, which for more than twenty years has considered radical reforms in regrouping communes. Failure had been so obvious (after twenty years there were still more than 36,000 of the original 38,000 communes in France) that all the politicians had rallied to the politics of the status quo. The cry is 'hands off the communes'. This total consensus of opinion confirmed that, at least in the matter of fusion and regrouping communes, local reform could not be introduced over the heads of the local elected representatives — a large pressure group (approximately 500,000) of whom virtually all are from the rural areas. Their influence in the appointment of senators, and the local links of national politicians (85 percent of whom hold local elected office), all contribute to a fossilization of the present situation. Just as the communal map cannot be redrawn, so the government has been unwilling — or unable — to decide which is the more important, the département or region, or a radical reformation and extension of the basis of inter-commune co-operation — especially in urban areas (districts and urban communities). The changes therefore were only marginal, and were achieved more by encouragement than by constraint, and more by addition than by suppression.

The experience of previous governments is not the only factor to have inspired Socialist reformers. A large number of the changes introduced were based on the experience gained in local affairs by the Socialists in the large towns and the départements. The reforms introduced reflect as much the past exasperation of locally elected representatives with the men and methods of the central power as any traditional conception of the exercise of local power in France. The absence of reform on citizen participation is ample demonstration that there exists a considerable area of agreement among politicians as to the 'untouchable' elements of the political system, despite all the election speeches and ministerial promises to the contrary.

In other respects, the reform is indeed merely a legal recognition of former practices of the elected representatives — particularly the Socialists — in the most dynamic urban areas or départements and regions.

Put another way, the Minister of the Interior, Gaston Defferre, and the Prime Minister, Pierre Mauroy, have legalized the practices used in large cities, which worked well but were hindered by the rules and regulations that the past central government.and its local representatives used from time to time to make things difficult. This view is supported by a number of empirical observations. The mayors of the big towns, the chairmen of influential *conseils généraux* and some chairmen of regional councils had already made for themselves powerful local bases from which to apply strong pressure to their advantage on the prefectoral administration, the local administrators and the financial and accounting services.[13] A study from Lille and Valenciennes has confirmed just how powerful the innovating notables were, how ingeneous and inventive their extra-legal practices were and how powerless the administration was to control this policy of continuous harassment from local elected representatives.[14] In short, the state administration, despite its theoretical and traditional *imperium*, is exploited by the most powerful local notables. As may be seen, such a perception is at odds with the contention that most of the power and the source of the so-called *mal français* is to be found in the central administration. In the struggle between the 'boss' (the mayor) and the 'manager' (the prefect), it is the former who, during the last two decades, has got the better of the latter, now downgraded from the prestigious title of prefect to the more prosaic 'Commissaire de la République'.[15]

In the same way, the suppression of prefectoral supervision over the regional, departmental and local authorities is less revolutionary than supporters and opponents would like to admit. Prefectoral supervision was no longer the meddlesome nuisance often described, but it had increasingly become a source of legal guidance particularly useful to the small communes. For instance, in the département of the Somme, the number of decisions that have been annulled in any one year by local councils has varied from three to twenty-two for 783 communes (out of a total of over 36,000), and in 1975, for example, only two were annulled. At the national level the figures given in the debate in Parliament were of the same order.

In spite of the legal reforms, the situation has not radically changed. Indeed, the prefect is not denuded of any means of intervention, even in relation to cities, départements or regions. In the first place, although he no longer enjoys the right of *tutelle*, he retains a key position in the new monitoring system on local authorities. It is the prefect, after all, who may demand that the (regional) administrative tribunal consider appeals against acts by local authorities — and the prefectoral services have been substantially reinforced to cope with the mass of local acts that must be sent to the state's local representative. According to statistics from the Ministry of the Interior, nearly 3 million such acts (2,915,015 to be precise) were sent in 1983 — as well as 327,547 budgets. Out of this mountain of documents, only 1,293 cases went to administrative tribunals. But two figures allow us to measure the prefect's crucial role: 72,740 'observations' were communicated to local authorities, and half the appeals were settled out of court.[16]

In other words, as in the past but under new forms, the prefect still wields real powers of influence and negotiation. The use he makes of it depends on the different actors concerned and on the social and political context — and it is here that uncertainties appear. Some prefects prefer to keep a low profile in the current climate (the number of appeals was one or none in fifteen départements in 1983), while others, especially in the most urbanized départements, practised more aggressive policies (74 appeals in Yvelines, 60 in Var, 45 in Bouches-du-Rhône and 39 in Essonne). Going to court thus becomes the prefect's ultimate deterrent, and elected officials hardly like being dragged into a legal process that lasts two years on average (further appeals aside) and risks serious financial repercussions.

Finally, in the framework of the contractual procedures so beloved of central governments over the past ten years (and reinforced in 1981), the prefect retains his crucial role at the interface between central government departments and local authorities. Conscious of the amputation of its traditional prerogatives, and of the inexorable nature of this development, the prefectoral corps has defended the functions that remain to it all the more stoutly, against field services and elected officials alike. If their former roles as executives of regions and départements definitely belong to the past, the resulting diminution of authority does not necessarily correspond to that suffered by the Italian prefect. The 'Commissars of the Republic' still have, it would appear, a number of opportunities open to them.

2. *Conflict or consensus?*

If the reform was de facto, if not de jure, gradualist and differentiated, it was also of a highly consensual nature. It constitutes, indeed, a sort of 'Common Minimal Programme of the Left and the Right'. If the wording seems excessive to some readers, it may be supported by several arguments. First, it is perfectly clear that the Socialists' ambitious — and even, in some eyes, utopian — reform programmes of before 1981 have been very unevenly applied. Not the remotest trace of *autogestion* will be found in the 300 or so legislative and regulatory texts that have been passed.[17] It was not, apparently, thought worthwhile even to write in the magic word as a sort of posthumous tribute. The same could be said of the ambitious plans that were put forward before 1981 to reform the local tax system. The resources of local authorities have undergone some modifications, but in the direction started by Valéry Giscard d'Estaing as Finance Minister twenty years ago. And the *taxe professionnelle* (the local business tax), although described as an absurd levy by Mitterrand, is still very much alive and kicking. The Defferre Acts are socialist only because they were elaborated by a Socialist government; as to the rest, they are pure French politico-administrative classicism.

The reform was consensual in a second sense, in that it was grounded to a considerable degree on the experience of previous governments and the conclusions that they had drawn from it. There was near-unanimous agreement that small communes (in default of a better solution) should be kept, as should the *cumul des mandats*, and that prefectoral *tutelle* should go. For evidence of this convergence one need look no further than the process by which the bills were drawn up. Those responsible freely admitted that the points of departure had been the project produced by Giscard's Interior Minister Bonnet as amended and modified by the Senate in 1980–1. Moreover, it was the same men at the Direction Générale des Collectivités Locales (DGCL) who prepared the (abortive) reform of Giscard's term and the successful one of the Socialist government.[18] Gaston Defferre, initially mistrustful of the civil service, started by setting up a 'cell' of Socialist university professors charged with preparing the reform for him. As early as September, however, the professors had demonstrated that they were not a satisfactory substitute for the specialists of the DGCL, and were sent back to their books.

The third indication of the consensual approach was the effort made to avoid, as far as possible, obstacles and oppositions. The reform was 'smooth', and its few controversial points (such as the possibility of holding mayors personally responsible for their administrative decisions) were eliminated during the parliamentary debate. In this respect, Defferre's strategy was no different from that of Giscard, even if the style was. Some years ago we called this strategy that of the 'line of least resistance'.[19] In other words, both Giscardian and Socialist governments drew the same lesson from the defeat of the Gaullists: no reform is possible which is not accepted by the notables and by their most eminent representative body, the Senate. As P. Sadran underlines, 'what the reform did not say is as important as what it did'.[20] Thus, the law avoids any incentive to merge communes, suggests without conviction new forms of intermunicipal co-operation (which appear to have become a dead letter before any attempts to put them into practice), and refuses changes in both regional boundaries and the hierarchy between the different local authority levels. No settlement of the long-standing quarrel between regions and départements was reached, and the attempt to tackle the *cumul des mandats*, that most solid convention of French political life, was in effect modest. As much for what it is not as for what it is, then, the reform constitutes a triumph for the notables. The title of the book on the subject edited by Jacques Rondin, *Le Sacre des notables*, is much more than a pretty turn of phrase: it is a correct assessment of political power relations.

3. Administrative efficiency or democratic legitimacy?
Compared with what happened in other European countries in the last two decades, the 1981–3 French reform was not principally justified by questions of public management, even if the problems of the division of labour, of laws and of personnel management did play an important role. In the eyes of the left, the local system, quite independently of its hiccoughs, suffered from two main problems: a

lack of democracy in its institutions, and the arbitrary character of state intervention. 'Changer la vie, changer l'Etat' meant that at the local level priority should be given to changes that were considered indispensable to justifying the activity of local elites. Put another way, even before modifying or extending the powers to be devolved to the various decentralized levels, the left considered it essential to invest it with a new legitimacy. In this respect, the beliefs of the left are well known and have been reasserted in two centuries of political combat: the election is the source of all powers, and the rule of law is protection against the arbitrary. The left, taken together (Socialist Party, Communist Party, Radical Party), since the last world war has not ceased to demand 'democratization' of the local level and to denigrate central control. The Constitution of the Fourth Republic, which was considerably influenced by the left, was the first in French history to express this political aspiration, but it was never put into practice. It was therefore no surprise that the reforms of 2 March 1981 gave formal recognition to the democratic beliefs repeatedly voiced by the left.

The legitimacy of power is therefore assured henceforth at all local levels by recourse to an election; local, departmental and regional assemblies are now all elected by direct universal suffrage, and they appoint their own executives. The innovation that is involved in the general recourse to election should not conceal the fact that the other mechanisms open to society for the control of decisive members were not considered: referenda, public hearings, neighbourhood councils and, more generally, all the other means of practising a participatory and responsive democracy are totally absent. One might, in certain respects, be glad about this, since some of these latter methods are less than perfect: they are too often manipulated by unrepresentative pressure groups, and they are administratively disruptive. But it must be said that the channels for expressing opinions and applying pressure in society are singularly limited.

Furthermore, the control of local authorities will henceforth be governed by a judicial system, as is the case in most other Western systems; that is to say, the local authorities are answerable to a judge. The organization of centre–periphery relations tends therefore to model itself, at least at the formal level, on the example of the majority of Western countries. The experience of these other countries leads us to expect at least two sorts of difficulties in putting such a new system into operation. On the one hand, there is a great lack of flexibility in the exercise of jurisdictional control (as seen in England) compared with the margin for manoeuvre and negotiation that always characterized prefectoral supervision; on the other hand, there is a considerable risk of a politically motivated supervision from one tier of local government to another, right across planning procedures and the subsidizing of investment projects. These possible developments represent very real fears for numerous mayors, especially of small communes. Something similar has already occurred in Italy, where municipal and provincial elected representatives complain, *mezza voce*, that elected regional representatives have replaced the prefect in exercising supervision. But, as has been shown before, it seems that the prefectoral control remains in a disguised fashion and that the judicial control is not as effective as expected.

This process of legitimization is not however going so far as to modify the 'personalization' in the exercise of power and to alter the 'government by delegation'. Since many politicians hold multiple offices and cannot exercise all of them effectively, they often have recourse to *éminences grises*. The latter are the real managers of day-to-day affairs (and often more), since the mayor and the chairmen of the Conseil général and the regional council are simply unable, through lack of time, to accomplish all of their tasks.

Well staffed private offices (*cabinets*), which have already been in existence in the big towns for some years, are now being set up at departmental and regional level. Already, about sixty prefects and sub-prefects run things in départements or regions on behalf of the new elected representatives after having been seconded from the prefectoral corps. Thus one now sees a strange game of 'musical chairs', with one part of the old prefectoral corps removed, but reappearing in other slots. And the local system is run by public servants even more than before. Numerous observers have already pointed out the part played by public servants in the elective functions at local and national level in the last few years. But the phenomenon is even more striking if one looks at what has happened in the most important functions. Overall, barely 10 percent of the mayors are also public servants — although the proportion is greater in larger and more urbanized towns.

We are witnessing, therefore, a situation where local government posts are increasingly being taken over by public servants by two means: *sociologically*, by the candidates elected, and *functionally*, by the growing practice of public servants carrying out the administrative and policy tasks of elected representatives. It is interesting, incidentally, to note that the reform of the local public service provides, among other things, some form of solution to the problem of legitimation, by applying to local public servants the rules governing recruitment and careers similar to those of state civil servants. The period when the elected representatives could recruit just whom they wanted, 'selon leur bon plaisir', seems to have disappeared — at least in principle.

Apart from its democratic virtue, decentralization has, according to its supporters, another important advantage, namely, that it simplifies administrative procedures by placing decision-making at the appropriate level. Such a hypothesis would need to be looked at carefully, if only because of the transformation of the tasks of local government, the fiscal system, the interdependence of territorial units of government and the fact of externalities. It is worth pointing out that the experience of federal states reveals that the relations between the centre and the constituent states, far from being simple, are becoming increasingly complex. It would be more correct to argue about the administrative unwieldiness (*lourdeur*) that is inherent in the excessive centralization of decision-making. Central ministries, which are theoretically omnipotent by virtue of their regulatory and supervisory powers, are often incapable of proper implementation of their policies. Decentralization therefore would be a means of making the bureaucracy more efficient and of simplifying the decision-making process. However, for such a thing to occur, the implementation of a policy of decentralization should be sensitive to the ends to be achieved; and the present reforms do not appear to be concerned with simplification and efficiency.

The new powers transferred to the regions, départements and communes concerned urban development, ports, waterways, teaching, school transport, social welfare and health, the environment and cultural affairs. The government and the legislators seem to have pursued, more or less with success, two particular goals: the transfer of homogeneous 'blocs' of power, and the precise definition of the respective responsibilities of each territorial level. In practice, this redistribution of powers has been carried out more or less successfully according to a number of rather approximate criteria, such as the physical mass or cost of investments. In certain respects, the boundaries drawn between regional and departmental responsibilities appear highly artificial: can river ports be considered as somehow more 'regional' than the seaports, whose construction, management and development fall under departmental jurisdiction (with the exception of 'independent ports' (*ports autonomes*) and ports of particular national importance)? Equally, it is far from clear why 'assistance to sea farming firms' is financed and allocated by the region, while 'assistance for sea farming infrastructure provision' is financed and allocated by the département.

The complexity of the decision-making process concerning school buildings is another product of the new system created by the transfers. For example, while the regional council can decide on the location of schools, it has to draw up the programme of investments to be made in collaboration with all the territorial authorities affected

148 The Dynamics of Institutional Change

by such planning. Finally, although the state is no longer involved in building matters as such, it may still exercise a right of veto. 'The representative of the state decides on the annual list of buildings or building extensions *related to appointments which it considers necessary to make.*' In other words, at the risk of building schools for which there will be no teachers, the regions or départements cannot formulate plans that do not have the approval of the state services!

In this 'share-out of the spoils', the département has taken the lion's share, particularly if the financial transfers connected with the transfers of powers are taken into account. However, the roles of the regions and communes are far from negligible, and this reflects the absence of a clear choice in the reform among the various decision-making levels. France seems condemned to having one of the most reticulated administrative networks in the West.

Conclusion

In an earlier article on the Defferre laws,[21] I asked if they represented a reform of society or a reform for the elites. The first three years of their application have dispelled none of the doubts I expressed at the time. On the contrary, they appear to confirm that only the political and administrative elites were affected by the changes. True, the election of all decision-makers by universal suffrage has reinforced their legitimacy — but it has not changed the ways in which society controls and participates in local and regional administration.[22] Far from tending towards the dismantling of the state, the reform is rather an element of consensual integration, which associates local elites with the administration while marginalizing the most radical nationalist or regionalist dissenters. But instead of bringing government closer to the governed, as the reform's supporters on all sides hoped it would, decentralization as it has been put into effect has complicated procedures, and has made the workings of the administrative machine heavier by complementing state services (which have generally been maintained) with new local ones.

Notes

1. Quoted by J. Hayward in *The One and Indivisible French Republic* (London: Weidenfeld & Nicolson, 1973), p. 17.
2. Ibid., p. 19.
3. S. Tarrow, 'The Urban–Rural Cleavage in Political Involvement: the Case of France', *American Political Science Review* 65 (1977), 341–57.
4. Ibid.
5. J.P. Worms, 'Le Préfet et ses notables', *Sociologie du travail* 3 (1966), 249–75.

6. J.Cl. Thoenig, 'La Relation entre le centre et la périphérie en France', *Bulletin de l'Institut International d'Administration Publique* 3 (1975), 77–123.

7. F. Dupuy and J.Cl. Thoenig, *L'Administration en miettes* (Paris: Fayard, 1985).

8. J. Becquart-Leclercq, 'Réseau relationnel, pouvoir relationnel', *Revue Française de Science Politique* 29 (1979), 102–28.

9. P. Grémion, 'Introduction à une étude du système politico-administratif local', *Sociologie du travail* 1 (1970), 51–73.

10. Y. Mény, 'Partis politiques et décentralisation', *IFSA, Cahier 18* (Paris: CUJAS, 1979).

11. P. Grémion, *Le Pouvoir périphérique* (Paris: Editions du Seuil, 1976).

12. D. Ashford, 'The Socialist Reorganization of French Local Government: Another Jacobin Reform?', *Environment and Planning — Government and Policy* 1 (1983), 24–38.

13. J. Lagroye, *Société et politique: Jacques Chaban-Delmas à Bordeaux* (Paris: Pédone, 1973); Y. Mény, 'Permanence and Change: the Relations between Central Government and Local Authorities in France', *Government and Planning* 1 (1983), 17–28.

14. J. Hayward and Y. Mény, 'Economic Incentives in Lille and Valenciennes', working paper, Princeton University, 1981.

15. H. Machin, *The Prefect in French Public Administration* (London: Croom Helm, 1977).

16. Quoted in *Rapport d'Information du Sénat par M. Poncelet*, session ordinaire 1984–5, 19 December 1985, no. 177.

17. M. Kesselman, 'The Tranquil Revolution at Clochemerle: Socialist Decentralisation in France', in P. Cerny and M. Schain (eds), *Socialism, the State and Public Policy in France* (London: Frances Pinter, 1985), pp. 165–6.

18. J. Rondin, *Le Sacre des notables* (Paris: Fayard, 1985).

19. D. Ashford, *British Dogmatism and French Pragmatism* (London: George Allen & Unwin, 1982).

20. P. Sadran, 'L'évolution des relations centre–périphérie en France', unpublished paper delivered at the conference of the International Political Science Association, Paris, July 1985.

21. Y. Mény, 'Decentralisation in Socialist France: The Politics of Pragmatism', *West European Politics* 7:1 (1984), p. 69.

22. See V. Schmidt, 'Decentralisation in France, Past and Present: Myth or Reality?', paper delivered at the 1985 American Political Science Association meeting, New Orleans, September 1985; and M. Kesselman, 'The End of Jacobinism? The Socialist Regime and Decentralisation', *Contemporary French Civilisation* Fall/Winter (1983–4), 48–70.

7

The Political Economy of Local Government Reform in the United States

Thomas J. Anton

Local government is by far the largest, the most varied and quite probably the most dynamic portion of the US public sector. Nearly 83,000 units of local government exist in the United States at the present time. Most of these (38,000) are municipal governments, offering a broad range of public services to their residents, but special districts providing only a single service abound (26,000), as do local school districts (16,000). Understanding this system of public authorities is an extraordinarily difficult task, not only because of its size and variety, but also because of its dynamism. Changes in local activities occur constantly, and structural changes are made every year. Between 1942 and 1977, for example, more than 3300 changes in local government were made each year, and thousands of additional changes have been made since 1977 (Anton, 1984). US local government is thus constantly changing, in response to forces that reflect both social and governmental imperatives. Identifying those forces and demonstrating their significance is the main purpose of this chapter.

The American context

Local government enjoys a special place in the *belief systems* of US political elites. The revolution that separated the original American colonies from the British empire was a revolt against centralized authority in favour of a governing system more responsive to the special needs of local populations. As the United States grew from a poor agricultural outpost to a modern industrial state, the original hostility to central authority became a distrust of 'big government' in any form. Successive generations of US politicians self-consciously used that distrust to shape US governing institutions. Local government became the preferred vehicle for public action because it was 'closest to the people' and could thus be more easily controlled by the people. The larger and more distant state governments were tolerated because they were essential elements of a federal union, but their ability to act was carefully circumscribed by frequent elections, large legislatures, fragmented executive agencies and, in the newly settled areas, many provisions for citizen initiatives to counter unwanted government actions. With little to do, the national government in Washington did not even levy a tax until the middle of the nineteenth century. Not until the present century was local government domination of the US public sector challenged, and even now, the ideological appeal of local government as a democratically controlled alternative to 'big government' remains powerful.

American elites also value local government because they value citizen participation in public affairs. In most of the United States, local governments are created through the voluntaristic actions of citizens who come together and petition state legislatures for permission to incorporate themselves as legal entities. These petitions have many sources, but their common element is a desire among local populations to obtain services such as zoning or police protection that would otherwise not be available. Having been created voluntaristically, local governments continue to operate through the services volunteered by millions of citizens who participate without pay in the boards, commissions and authorities through which local government decisions are made. Local governments are thus an important vehicle for expanding opportunities for citizen participation in government. To a considerable extent, this explains why there are so many local governments: Americans value participation and thus create a great many public authorities to structure participatory opportunities. While traditionally wary of *big* government, Americans nevertheless are clearly in favour of *many* governments.

Participation and limited government are enduring values in the US polity, but they are not the only values that affect local government. Americans also value efficiency in the delivery of public services and accountability for the officials who operate public programmes. Both of these latter values are often in conflict with the former. Maximum feasible participation is a worthy goal in the United States, but pursuit of that goal through a large number of governments causes service duplication, high costs per unit of service and excessive employment levels, none of which contribute to efficiency. Americans generally have chosen to live with inefficiencies and political confusion as acceptable costs for securing a high level of participation in constrained local governments. From time to time, however, efficiency and accountability values become dominant, fuelling cycles of reform designed to reduce costs or improve performance. As we shall see, the results of such efforts can be very significant indeed.

The major institutional framework that shapes the behaviour of these many local governments is *federalism*. Under the US Constitution, powers are allocated to both the national government and the fifty state governments. Because these allocations are expressed in extraordinarily vague language, the assignment of governmental responsibilities between the national government and the states is a matter of continuous political controversy. The federal Constitution makes no mention of local government, however, leaving the fifty states entirely free to design and implement their own systems of local governance. Within the fifty different systems of local government designed by the American states, local governments have a legal status not unlike that of local agencies in unitary states: they are entirely dependent on state action for their authority; the 'pieces' of authority available to them are carefully defined and strictly interpreted; and their existence can be terminated at any time by action of the various state legislatures. Despite their legal inferiority, local governments in the fifty states operate with considerable autonomy and continue successfully to resist efforts to impose major structural reforms. None of the states, for example, has attempted local government reforms comparable to the massive restructuring of local and regional governments enacted recently by several nations in Western Europe.

The substantial degree of operational autonomy enjoyed by US local governments is based partly on tradition and partly on pure political influence. Throughout New England and the mid-Atlantic states, local government jurisdictions predate the federal Constitution by a hundred years or more. Towns and boroughs of colonial origin, celebrating 300 or 350 years of continuous existence, reflect the continuing vitality of a tradition older than the nation itself. Quite apart from that tradition, local governments and their associated interests are powerful forces in every state legislature, on guard against efforts to weaken local authority. In states with large urban centres, political leaders from those centres are often better known than are most state leaders. Mayor Koch of New York City, for example, was a far more significant figure in Albany and in Washington, DC, than the relatively obscure state senator who defeated the Mayor in a race for governor. Koch remains an important figure, even though former state senator Mario Cuomo has now achieved national prominence as governor of New York State. Mayor Daley of Chicago certainly was far better known — and conceivably far more influential — than any Illinois governor of his time.

Even in states without influential big-city mayors to represent local interests, those interests are not without effective representation. State municipal leagues, township associations, school district associations, municipal employee organizations, real estate boards, construction unions and a host of other organizations whose interests overlap the interests of local governments are a permanent presence in state capitols, offering not just opinion but expertly produced information to buttress opinion. The substantial operational autonomy enjoyed by local governments, in short, is in good measure a product of their political power. State governments do not impose stronger constraints or major organizational reforms because they are largely unable to mobilize sufficient political support for stronger or more comprehensive controls. Legally dependent on state governments for their very existence, US local governments nevertheless operate with a considerable degree of political independence.

Because each of the fifty states organizes its own system of local government, the independence actually exercised by local units varies from state to state. However, one overriding historical–cultural condition imposes discernible national patterns on this variety. *Regionalism* defines patterns of difference along both north–south and east–west dimensions. In general, the states of the northern tier, strongly influenced by settlers from northern and western Europe, created systems in which most governmental taxing and spending powers were allocated to local governments. The states of the south, strongly influenced by settlers from Great Britain and southern Europe, created systems that allocated preponderant authority to the state governments themselves, leaving local governments in a relatively weak position (Elazar, 1972).

From the east–west perspective, states that were derived from the original colonies inherited a tradition of strong and comprehensive local government. Local governments along the eastern seaboard, accordingly, generally performed many different functions and enjoyed broad taxing authority to support those functions. As population spread westwards the new states tended to create more specialized systems. Local schools, operated by governments in the East, became the responsibility of separate school districts in the Midwest and West. Special districts were created all over the Midwest and West to perform many functions, ranging from water supply to fire protection, typically performed by municipal governments in the East (Liebert, 1975). As the American population spread across the continent, therefore, local authority became less comprehensive, more specialized and more fragmented.

The existence of large numbers of US local governments, often quite small in size, has three important political consequences. One is that these governments often 'bump into' one another in the course of pursuing their normal responsibilities. A second consequence, following from the first, is that local government purposes often cannot be achieved without co-operation from other governments; thus, much local government action is intergovernmental in quality. Finally, both 'bumping' and resort to multi-governmental interactions to resolve problems are extraordinarily important sources of political dynamism. Even under benign social and economic conditions, thousands of local governments 'bumping' into one another will produce conflicts, and resolutions to those conflicts will often require changes in structures, procedures or both. Whether or not 'reform' occurs, change is an unending characteristic of the US local government systems.

Eras of change

During the twentieth century, US local governments have experienced three periods in which operational changes were far greater than normal. The first occurred during the Great Depression of the 1930s, when the financial collapse of many local governments led to the emergence of a much stronger and more influential national government. For convenience I will refer to this period as the *era of nationalization*. A second *era of capacity-building* began in 1945 and continued for a quarter-century. During this period, local and state governments were restructured and millions of professionally trained people became new local government employees. The third period, which began roughly in 1970 and continues to this day, may be thought of as the *era of national integration*. During this period, distinctions between local, state and national responsibilities have become blurred and new patterns of joint action have emerged. Each of these major eras deserves some consideration.

To appreciate the magnitude of the transformation that occurred during the 1930s, it is necessary to recall that until that time most government services in the United States were delivered by local authorities. Taxes on real (land, buildings) and personal (automobiles, furniture) property provided most of the revenue used by local governments to support public services, and these property taxes constituted by far the largest portion of total government revenues in the country. In the 1930s, however, these relationships were totally changed. As portrayed in Figure 1, local government revenues fell from 46 percent of all public revenue in 1929 to 36 percent in 1939 and to less than 15 percent in 1949. The change in the significance of federal revenues, derived primarily from the income tax, was even more striking, rising from less than 34 percent of total revenues in 1929 to nearly 70 percent in 1949. Since that time, local government revenues have remained at roughly 15 percent or less of total government revenues, state government revenues have in-

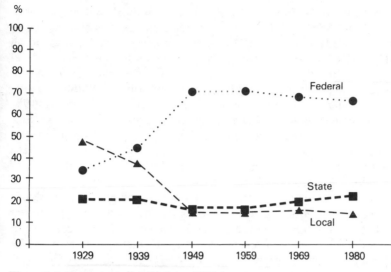

Figure 1 *Percentage distribution of US government revenues, by level of government, 1929–80 (ACIR, 1986: 11)*

creased slightly, and federal revenue has generally remained at nearly two-thirds of all government revenue until a recent slight decline during the Reagan administration.

It would be impossible to overestimate the significance of the transformation that occurred during the 1930s. Faced with cities and states whose resources were far too limited to deal with the consequences of massive unemployment, the national government was driven to act. New programmes providing jobs, income for unemployed persons, assistance for mothers with children, retirement pensions, food assistance, housing and other components of 'welfare' were enacted, vastly expanding the scope of federal government activity and laying a foundation for the US welfare state. Virtually all of these programmes previously had been regarded as either state/local responsibilities or private sector obligations, rather than national government responsibilities. By assuming them, the federal government not only increased its spending but also established the legitimacy of social assistance on a national scale. No longer would federal politicians be reluctant to confront major social issues. And no longer would local politicians be reluctant to call for assistance from Washington to help them solve local and regional problems. A system in which local governments paid for most public services had been transformed into a system in which the national government paid for most public services.

The transformation was given powerful support by US entry into the Second World War, which provided an additional stimulus to increased federal spending. Interestingly enough, federal spending did not decline significantly after the war ended. Instead, federal politicians found new ways to maintain or increase the significance of the national government: a full employment policy in 1946, a massive new housing bill enacted in 1949 and amended in 1954, a 1956 interstate highway bill that became the largest public works programme of the century and many others. In short, having discovered the benefits of distributing benefits, national politicians continued to enact programmes that maintained the dominant fiscal position of the federal government.

The new postwar position of the federal government as the dominant source of public revenues and expenditures did not mean that local governments fell into stagnation or decline. On the contrary, it is important to recognize that local governments, as well as the federal government, grew substantially after 1945 as part of an overall pattern of comprehensive public sector expansion. From the local point of view, this was the period of capacity building, when population growth combined with the expansion of metropolitan areas around large US cities to create problems that required professional solutions. New suburban communities required engineers to lay out streets and sewer systems. Expanding school systems required teachers and administrators. Larger populations required more doctors, lawyers and social service professionals, many of whom were employed by growing local governments. Thus, as I have noted elsewhere (Anton, 1985), local and state government employment expanded rapidly during the 1950s, averaging some 200,000 new employees per year from 1951 to 1959, 80 percent of whom were local government employees. This was in stark contrast to federal government employment trends, as I have also noted:

> Between 1955 and 1979, fewer than 500,000 employees were added by the federal government — indeed, federal employment actually declined by some 130,000 workers from 1970 to 1979. During the same 1955–1979 period, however, more than eight million new employees went to work for state and local governments. Nearly 3.7 million people (up from 1.5 million in 1955) now work for state governments, while more than 9.4 million (up from 3.8 million in 1955) work for the cities, counties, townships, and school districts that comprise American local government. From the 1950s through the 1970s, state and local governments were the major growth industries, with federal employment in a state of comparative decline. (Anton, 1985)

Put differently, whereas federal government employees comprised a third of all public sector employees in 1950, by 1980 they amounted to fewer than 18 percent of public workers; local government employees, on the other hand, increased from 50 to 59 percent of all public sector employees in the same period.

The results of the era of nationalization and the era of capacity building thus seem paradoxical, if not contradictory. Local governments in the United States generate only 15 percent of all public revenues, yet they employ nearly 60 percent of all government employees. The federal government, which generates nearly two-thirds of all public revenue, nevertheless accounts for only 18 percent of all employees. How can these assertions be true? The answer, of course, lies in a device that became increasingly popular during the third era of national integration: the federal grant-in-aid.

Federal grants-in-aid distribute funds to state and local governments who agree to carry out programmes designed by the national government. Grants thus allow the national government to pursue national purposes without the use of national government employees; federal agencies provide the funds, but state and local agencies provide the employees who actually operate the programmes. From the point of view of state and local governments, federal grants allow them to offer services that do not require support from local or state tax revenues. Local officials can thus appear both innovative and responsive without taking the political risk of asking for tax increases to fund so many programmes. From the point of view of the system as a whole, federal grants increase the total services available to citizens and spread the costs of many of those services across a national tax base that is both more productive and more progressive in its incidence than most state and local tax systems. Given these advantages, it is not surprising that many observers regard federal grants-in-aid as a uniquely important tool of American governance.

Although federal grants have a long history of use, both their number and their total dollar value have increased dramatically in recent years (see Figure 2). Indeed, federal grants-in-aid may be regarded as the most important defining characteristic of the era of national integration that began around 1970. In 1950 federal grants amounted to less than $2.3 billion, and they were less than $6.4 billion ten years later. During the 1960s, however, grants to state and local governments more than tripled, reaching nearly $22 billion in 1970. President Lyndon B. Johnson's 'Great Society' vision, which led to hundreds of new grant programmes to achieve a variety of social goals, was clearly the driving force in this increase. Rapid as it was, this increase was overshadowed by the even more dramatic four-fold increase that occurred in the next decade, when federal grants rose from $22 billion in 1970 to $91 billion by 1980 (US

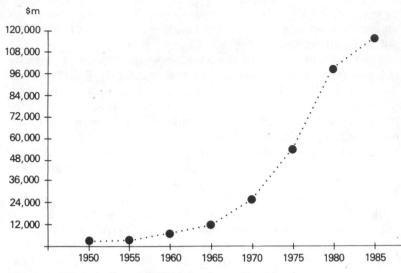

Figure 2   *Historical trend of US federal grant-in-aid outlays, 1950–85 (OMB, 1986: H-19)*

Treasury, 1985; OMB, 1985). President Reagan's efforts to reduce federal spending, including federal grants, temporarily slowed the rate of increase in federal grant expenditures, but grants have once again begun to increase, reaching a level estimated by the Office of Management and Budget (OMB) to be $107 billion in 1986 (OMB, 1986: H-20). Federal grants-in-aid clearly have become an important and permanent source of local government revenue as well as the hallmark of a newly integrated fiscal system.

Perhaps the most significant component of this new system was General Revenue Sharing (GRS), enacted in 1972. GRS was certainly not the largest grant programme of this era. Expenditures amounted to $6 billion annually for the first five years, but this amount was later scaled back to $4 billion per year — in contrast to programmes such as Aid to Families with Dependent Children (AFDC) ($8–10 billion), the Comprehensive Employment Training Assistance (CETA) ($6–8 billion) or Medicaid ($14–17 billion). What made GRS genuinely significant was not so much the dollars distributed but the structure of the programme itself. Unlike other grant programmes, which distributed funds only to cities that applied for assistance, GRS funds were allocated *by formula* to all states and all general-purpose units of local government in the country (school districts and special districts excluded). Since only the larger and more professionalized local governments had participated extensively in the numerous programmes that required cities to apply for

funds, the effect of GRS was to extend direct federal financial assistance to thousands of cities, counties and towns that had never before
received such assistance. For the first time in American history, the
federal government had established a direct and continuing financial
relationship with the 38,000 general-purpose local governments in
the United States.

GRS was immediately popular among local officials because there
were essentially no federal constraints on how the money could be
used. The legislation itself stated a number of different purposes, but
the main purpose was simply to provide a subvention, to be used as
local (and state) officials desired. Reporting requirements were
minimal, amounting to nothing more than the provision of written
assurances that GRS funds were expended for 'legal' purposes. Freed
from federal constraints, local officials across the country applied the
funds in a variety of ways, from the construction of new tennis courts
to the support of essential services such as police or sanitation
(Nathan et al., 1975; Nathan and Adams, 1977; Juster, 1977).

Beneath its widespread popularity was a fundamental political
fact: GRS provided local governments with an interest in further
participation in the federal aid system. Recent studies have shown
that previous participation in federal grant programmes has been an
important determinant of current levels of federal aid (Rich, 1985;
Kramer, 1985; Stein, 1981). Thus, distribution of quarterly GRS
cheques to the 37,000 local governments that had previously had little
or no contact with the federal government provided both a resource
and an incentive for further participation. As Stein (1981) has shown,
GRS did in fact lead to increased local participation in other federal
aid programmes. Local governments thus have become more integrated into a national system of programmes and financial support,
just as the national government, through programmes such as GRS
or the Community Development Block Grant, have become more
concerned with local and regional issues. Local officials now routinely take federal policies into consideration in framing their own
actions, and federal officials routinely act on matters of local significance. Policy boundaries have become blurred in a system that
increasingly treats local, state and national issues within similar programmatic frameworks.

In the US context, a more integrated national–state–local system
of governance does not necessarily imply a loss of local autonomy,
nor does it imply a significant increase in national policy control.
Although many officials have expressed concern over these issues in
recent years, observation of the main instruments of national integration makes clear that local autonomy remains strong and national
control remains undeveloped. Recall that the principal instrument of

integration has been the national grant-in-aid. An important secondary class of instruments of national policy have been the regulations that are typically attached as conditions to the several hundred grant programmes. Important as they have been in establishing programmatic frameworks for national political debate, neither grants nor their attached regulations have substantially altered the US tradition of local self-governance.

For political reasons, it is difficult to establish a national grant programme that imposes strict controls on either state or local governments. Grant programmes must be enacted by Congress, which means that majorities in both the House and the Senate must be organized. Since majorities are difficult to mobilize for narrow purposes, grant programmes typically are couched in legislative language that is either vague, or expansive, or both. Vague language often characterizes statements of programme purposes, which express general goals that can accommodate a large number of specific actions. The purpose of the Law Enforcement and Assistance Administration programme (1968), for example, was 'to improve and strengthen law enforcement' (Anton, 1980). If programme purposes are expressed in more specific language, expansive eligibility rules are often attached, broadening the potential beneficiary base. Thus, more than 80 percent of the 3145 county governments in the United States were declared eligible for disaster assistance from the Farmers Home Administration in 1978 as a result of expanded legislative language adopted in the previous year (Oppenheim, 1983).

Vague statements of purpose and expansive eligibility standards obviously have been effective in attracting votes for grant-in-aid programmes, which increased in number by several hundred between 1965 and 1975 (ACIR, 1978). But ambiguous programme designs have made it virtually impossible for the federal government to control the uses of federal dollars once they have left Washington. Again and again, local governments have been able to impose their own interpretations on the loose language of federal grant programmes, often pursuing local objectives that seem only distantly related, if at all, to the ambiguous objectives of federal programmes (Anton, 1985; Larkey, 1979). Federal programme managers, sensitive to the political imperative of maintaining support for the programme (and their jobs!) and lacking the personnel adequately to monitor local uses of federal dollars, are typically reluctant to use the enforcement powers they have (Stenberg, 1980). Congressmen are less reluctant to act, but often are frustrated in deciding how to act. In a Congressional hearing devoted to the record of the Law Enforcement and Assistance Administration, Congressman Smith clarified both the problem and the frustration.

What I am really getting at is this — and other members tell me that they hear the same thing — it's not a matter of illegal expenditure of funds. In fact, the act itself is very vague. The guidelines are rather loose. If you are too strict in enforcing guidelines, they complain about red tape. If you are not strict enough, anybody who wants some money comes in under the name of law enforcement and makes application. This is what has been happening. . . . What goes on is that they find out the big money now is coming from LEAA. So if they need some money, they figure out an application which can be put under that program. These local people know where the money is coming from and where the big increases are. They try to get in under it. (US Congress, 1972: 1126)

Congressional action to adjust federal programmes occurs with some frequency, but often such action leads to less rather than more federal control. Programmes that are initially narrow in focus are broadened to attract more political support by substituting vague language for specific language. Later, congressional efforts to exert greater control lead to more restrictive language, which has the effect of changing, and possibly threatening, the base of support for the programme. If the base becomes restrictive enough to lose a majority, broader and vaguer language will again be substituted in an effort to retain majority support. Federal grant programmes thus tend to move through natural cycles of change in which programme purposes are adjusted to meet changing political demands (Rich, 1985; Stein, 1984; Oppenheim, 1983; Anton, 1980). The result, as I have argued elsewhere (Anton, 1980), is that programme goals are inherently unstable through time. Even if federal programme managers were more interested in controlling local uses of federal funds, therefore, the standards available to them for exerting control are subject to frequent and not always predictable changes. This is not to say that federal agencies are entirely unable to constrain local decisions (Dommel and associates, 1982). Under conditions of programme instability, however, in a system of complex and dispersed power, achieving federal control is bound to be extraordinarily difficult (Fossett, 1983).

Federal control need not be pursued solely through statements of purpose and eligibility, of course. Regulations attached to grants-in-aid provide what many observers believe to be even more powerful instruments of control. Federal regulations rely on the legal superiority of the national government to prohibit state and local governments from taking specified actions, or to order that certain actions be taken, under penalty of law (ACIR, 1984). Some regulations prohibit employment discrimination based on race, sex or age in programmes funded with federal dollars, or prohibit denial of access to the benefits of such federal programmes based on racial or sexual discrimination. Other regulations require state and local governments to meet federally defined standards for air, water or other environmental pollution — and impose financial as well as legal sanctions on governments that fail to meet those standards. Still others impose sanctions on one programme for failure to meet standards imposed by another programme. For example, in an effort to stop the damage caused by drunk driving, the national government recently enacted legislation that reduces federal highway construction grants to states that have failed to raise the legal drinking age to twenty-one. In all, some fifty-five different regulations are attached to various federal grants, in various ways, creating a system of federal regulations that rivals the grant system in complexity (ACIR, 1984).

Most grant programmes are voluntary; state and local governments may choose to participate or not participate. The regulations attached to grants, however, are both legally binding and coercive; if a local government chooses to accept a grant, it is bound by regulations attached to the grant, whether or not the regulations have anything to do with the purposes of the grant. Accepting a federal grant for housing construction, for example, binds local governments to a number of anti-discrimination, environmental and procedural regulations that technically have nothing at all to do with housing. Because these regulations can be legally enforced in federal and state courts, local officials and others frequently complain that they are not only being coerced by the federal government, but that the instruments of coercion are uninformed judges who are beyond the reach of the political process. Federal regulations thus have been widely criticized as a usurpation of local authority.

Despite these criticisms, many studies of federal regulations have made clear that the regulatory bark is worse than the bite. For one thing, regulatory policies have been plagued by ambiguities of purpose that are very similar to the ambiguities found in the goals of grant programmes. A number of regulations have been adopted in great haste, often in response to desires for symbolic reassurances on the part of mass publics that have developed deep concerns over some set of issues. For example, Earth Day, an environmental 'teach-in' patterned after the anti-war demonstrations of the 1960s, took place on 1 April 1970 and provided a catalyst for rapid congressional action on air and water pollution (ACIR, 1984: 67). In some cases legislative action has been so rapid that rules implementing new regulations could not be written. Section 504 of the Rehabilitation Act 1973, prohibiting discrimination against handicapped individuals, was passed without a word of debate; Congress was thus forced to enact a retroactive statement of legislative intent in the following year before the process of rule development could begin (ACIR, 1984: 75).

Given the haste with which many regulations have been enacted, it is not surprising that implementing rules typically have taken years to write — as much as nine years for Section 504 rules! Even after they are written, regulatory rules are subject to the same political and administrative difficulties that plague efforts to strictly enforce grant programme goals, namely, ambiguity and resource limitations. Local governments thus remain far less coerced by regulations than is often thought, leading one analyst of various health, safety and environmental regulations to conclude that 'there is no solid evidence that the regulatory programs are even modestly effective' (Crandall, 1981). Local governments, in other words, retain considerable freedom to interpret federal regulations, just as they retain considerable latitude in choosing the purposes to which they put national grant dollars.

If federal control over local governments does not appear to have increased in any operational sense, it is nevertheless true that local governments are now operating in a much more integrated national–state–local policy environment. As noted earlier, General Revenue Sharing gave all local governments a financial interest in federal policies and encouraged thousands of local officials who had never before dealt with federal government to seek various forms of federal assistance. Participation in federal programmes has led to the creation of new administrative agencies within local political environments to provide the new services often funded by federal dollars (Yin, 1980). Federal officials responsible for the distribution of national dollars for a variety of local purposes have developed permanent communication networks that allow them to interact with these organizations and thus participate in local decisions on a daily or weekly basis. Local (including state) officials now routinely impact on national policies and, on the other hand, national officials routinely impact on local decisions through these established networks. Although some issues continue to be confined to one level of government or another, important issues are increasingly dealt with simultaneously, by all levels of US government. In this sense the influence, if not the formal power, of local governments has grown.

Sources of change: piecemeal modernization

If one asks whether the changes brought about in US local government during this century were the result of some 'policy' or 'plan', the answer clearly is no. To speak of 'a' plan or policy is of course misleading in the American context, since each state operates its own local government system. Efforts to change local government in some comprehensive fashion thus could not occur at the national level but instead would have to occur in the fifty states. Such efforts have been exceedingly rare among the states, which typically have preferred piecemeal and marginal changes rather than comprehensive reorganization. During each of the three major eras of change, however, state systems of local governance were subjected to common national pressures. Since these pressures fell into recognizable patterns, it is not surprising that responses also were patterned, whether or not they represented 'policy'.

During the era of nationalization two issues were at stake: the appropriate size of the public sector, and the legitimacy of national government action. By adopting a number of employment, pension, housing and social service laws, US governments assumed responsibility for many activities previously regarded as private sector obligations. Although these new public obligations were not rationalized as welfare state policies — indeed, they were justified as policies that could preserve the existing capitalist system — their effect was to provide a foundation for later government expansion into a full range of welfare state programmes supported by a much larger public sector. By locating these new programmatic initiatives within the national government, furthermore, national action in these programmatic areas was legitimized. This legitimization was important because, to the extent that welfare programmes were regarded as public responsibilities at all, they were thought to be local or state — but not federal responsibilities. None of these new programmes was derived from a plan to alter local government. Their cumulative effect, however, was substantially to reduce the significance of local government by activating the localized policies of a large and resourceful national government.

If massive unemployment was the condition that stimulated the era of nationalization, population and economic growth were the underlying stimulants for the era of capacity building. This era, too, dealt with two major issues. One was the perceived need for professionalization in local government administration. Growing cities, booming suburbs, exploding schools and rapid infrastructure development all defined an environment in which professional skills were both required and obtained. Closely related to this was the issue of efficiency: professional skills could hardly be used to good advantage if the structures within which they worked were poorly arranged. After the Second World War, therefore, state systems of local governance were subjected to substantial — almost revolutionary — changes, as Table 1 shows. Structural changes most nearly approached revolutionary proportions in public education. Between 1942 and 1952 more than 41,000 school districts were eliminated, and another 33,000 school districts disappeared over the next decade. By 1982 the

Table 1 *Types of government, USA, 1942–82*

Type of government	Number of governments[a]								Change in number 1942–82
	1982	1977	1972	1967	1962	1957	1952	1942	
National	1	1	1	1	1	1	1	1	0
State	50	50	50	50	50	50	50	48	2
County	3,041	3,042	3,044	3,049	3,043	3,050	3,056	3,050	−9
Municipal	19,076	18,862	18,517	18,048	18,000	17,215	16,807	16,220	2,856
Township	16,734	16,822	16,991	17,105	17,142	17,198	17,202	18,919	−2,185
School district	14,851	15,174	15,781	21,782	34,678	50,454	67,355	108,579	−93,728
Special district	28,588	25,962	23,885	21,264	18,323	14,424	12,340	8,299	20,289
Total	82,341	79,913	78,269	81,299	91,237	102,392	116,807	155,116	−72,775

[a] Alaska and Hawaii are included from 1952 on.

Source: US Bureau of the Census, *Statistical Abstract of the USA: 1986*, 106th edn (Washington, DC, 1985), p. 262

number of local school districts in the United States had fallen to less than 16,000 — a reduction of more than 93,000 units in less than forty years!

Curiously, these massive structural changes across the nation have been largely ignored by US scholars. None the less, it seems clear that the ideology of efficiency was the central motivating force. Most of the school districts eliminated were tiny systems located in rural areas that were losing both population and tax resources to the rapidly growing metropolitan areas. The elimination of these tiny districts in favour of much larger units with more adequate property tax bases thus made good sense economically, as well as educationally. Efficiency also appears to have been the driving force behind the other major change revealed in the table, the large increases in the number of special districts that occurred during this same period. Rather than create new multi-function governments to produce some desired local service, local populations in the Midwest and West increasingly chose the special district mechanism, which provides a legal vehicle through which a single service (i.e. fire protection, water, etc.) can be provided and charged against the consumers of that service.

Although not revealed in these figures, it should be noted that this was also a period in which proposals for more efficient metropolitan governments were widely debated by academics, and actually implemented in cities such as Miami, Florida, and Nashville, Tennessee. Except for these metropolitan experiments, which were quite rare, the era of capacity building generated no state policies specifically aimed at local government reform and certainly no national policy. Instead, underlying population and economic changes motivated officials in the fifty states to realign local government structures in order to produce a more efficient delivery of public services. The result was far fewer local governments, but governments with more employees, better educated employees and more adequate tax resources.

Local government competence provided a fertile soil for the era of national integration. President Lyndon B. Johnson's 'Great Society' programmes of 1964–8 had generated hundreds of new federal grant programmes to remedy a variety of problems in education, housing, welfare and employment. None of these programmes was designed to stimulate local reform, but, by enlisting local governments as administrators of national programmes, they did in fact stimulate new activities, new structures and a new level of local influence in programme design. It was left to President Richard M. Nixon to formalize and institutionalize the new position of local governments in federal policy-making.

Although President Nixon entered office with a 'New Federalism' plan which emphasized a more powerful role for local governments as well as more influence for 'generalists' rather than specialists within those governments, his achievements were a function less of the plan than of ad hoc political arrangements. Indeed, it is important to remember that, while Nixon pressed for a larger local government role, he was also responsible for a considerable expansion of central government power over grant programmes. The Food Stamps programme, which had been a relatively small experiment, was nationalized under Nixon and quickly became one of the largest welfare programmes. Similarly, three programmes previously administered by the states — Old Age Assistance, Aid to the Blind and Aid to the Disabled — were nationalized under Nixon in a new programme called Supplementary Security Assistance (SSI). Nevertheless, during the course of the Nixon administration, local empowerment became an important thrust of national policy in three related ways.

First, Nixon proposed, and Congress passed, a number of grant programmes that allocated federal funds directly to local governments. Traditionally, most federal grants provided funds to state government, which in turn distributed those funds to local governments. Most grant programmes, in fact, continue to operate this way, but President Nixon successfully introduced several programmes — Comprehensive Employment Training Assistance (CETA), Community Development Block Grants (CDBG) and others — that avoided the states and channelled funds directly to local agencies. Second, Nixon ultimately helped to secure the adoption of General Revenue Sharing, which provided a direct financial link between all general-purpose local governments (38,000) and the federal government. While passage of GRS had nothing to do with local government reform (Dommel, 1974; Derthick, 1975), the programme itself not only provided additional resources for local governments, but also stimulated closer relationships between the national government and the nation's cities and towns. Third, Nixon was a strong proponent of 'block' rather than categorical grants in federal aid programmes. That is, he proposed that groups of programmes in different functional areas be 'blocked' together and allocated to local governments, rather than continuing to distribute funds according to separate programme categories. Categorical distribution meant that federal officials made most of the decisions regarding amount and use; blocked programmes allowed local officials to make most of those decisions. The CDBG programme, for example, required all local applications to be approved by the Department of Housing and Urban Development unless they could show that the local proposals were clearly in conflict with national policies (Dommel and associates, 1982).

Despite the lack of an explicit national policy for local government reform during the Nixon administration, therefore, local government influence was in fact expanded during this period. More importantly, perhaps, it was during the Nixon and, later, Ford administrations that federal grant expenditures really began to accelerate, heading towards the four-fold increase in such expenditures that took place between 1970 and 1980. Having developed improved capacity in the postwar period, local governments now gained more authority over federal programmes and many more federal dollars. As before, these changes did not occur because of some over-all policy or national plan for the reform of local government. Instead, they were a by-product of national government efforts to do something about a variety of social and environmental problems, using local governments to administer programmes funded primarily by national tax dollars.

The future of US local government

President Ronald Reagan entered office carrying with him his own version of a 'New Federalism', which was in some ways similar to President Nixon's ideas. Mr Reagan's preferences for a smaller federal government and greater freedom for state and local governments led to proposals for several new block grants, a 'swap' of health and welfare programmes between federal and state governments, and a 'turnback' of responsibility for some forty other programmes back to the states. Nine new block grants were created during the first euphoric year of Mr Reagan's first term, but no action was taken on either his 'swap' or 'turnback' proposals. In part, failure to enact these proposals was due to Reagan's own lack of commitment to them. In part, it was due to the determined opposition of state and local officials, who saw clearly that the main objective of the proposals was to reduce federal spending rather than to enhance their authority (Stockman, 1986). Meanwhile, other developments during the Reagan administration have had the effect, again unintended, of diminishing the influence of local authorities.

To begin with, President Reagan's determined efforts to reduce federal spending for social service programmes substantially reduced the flow of federal dollars into local governments. In some areas state governments replaced some of the lost federal dollars, but most state governments were either unable or unwilling to do so, leaving local governments with significant reductions in overall resources (Nathan and Doolittle, 1983). Second, Mr Reagan's block grants returned to the traditional pattern of allocating block grant funds to state governments rather than local governments. Whereas Nixon had designed grant programmes that enhanced local authority, Reagan's programmes in health, education and community development enhanced the authority of state governments.

Third, and somewhat ironically, the so-called tax limitation movement of 1978–80 also had the effect of enhancing state government authority at the expense of local governments. In both California and Massachusetts, citizens initiated referenda to reduce and limit the taxes that could be levied against property. These referenda were successful, and several other states also approved statutes or referenda that were designed to limit local taxation. By limiting the property tax, which remains the major source of local revenue, citizens also limited the ability of local governments to manage their own affairs. In both California and Massachusetts, state governments were forced to allocate large sums to make up for lost property tax revenue; and, having assumed control over the bulk of local finance, the state governments also assumed control over much of local policy (Sears and Citrin, 1982; Kirlin, 1982). Thus, President Reagan's initiatives in support of enhanced state government authority entered an environment in which a substantial amount of state fiscal centralization was already under way. For local governments in the United States, the Reagan administration has meant reduced revenues, diminished authority and greater state government control.

Like the changes that have occurred in previous periods, these recent developments are no more than by-products of policies designed for other problems; in that sense they should be regarded as temporary rather than fundamental. What is fundamental is the enhanced professional capacity that local governments now enjoy and their full integration into the political life of the nation, as well as the states in which they operate. Although local resources and authority may be temporarily diminished, local officials remain powerful within their states; they are well represented in the national capitol, both through their own activities and through their national organizations such as the US Conference of Mayors or the National League of Cities; and they are collectively an important voice in the shaping of national as well as local policies. If there is no single 'reform' that can be identified as a source of local government modernization, that is because reform is seldom accomplished in US politics. Change, on the other hand, remains the most enduring characteristic of a local government system that is as dynamic as it is varied.

References

Advisory Commission on Intergovernmental Relations (ACIR) (1978) *Summary and Concluding Observations: the Intergovernmental Grant System*. Washington, DC: US Government Printing Office.

ACIR (1984) *Regulatory Federalism: Policy, Process, Impact and Reform*. Washington, DC: US Government Printing Office.

ACIR (1986), *Significant Features of Fiscal Federalism, 1985–1986*. Washington, DC: US Government Printing Office.

Anton, Thomas J. (1980) 'Federal Assistance Programs: the Politics of System Transformation', in D.E. Ashford (ed.), *National Resources and Urban Policy*, New York: Methuen.

Anton, Thomas J. (1984) 'Intergovernmental Change in the United States: an Assessment of the Literature', in T.C. Miller (ed.), *Public Sector Performance: a Conceptual Turning Point*. Baltimore: Johns Hopkins University Press.

Anton, Thomas J. (1985) 'Decay and Reconstruction in the Study of American Intergovernmental Relations', *Publius: the Journal of Federalism* 15: 65–97.

Crandall, Robert W. (1981) 'Has Reagan dropped the Ball?' *Regulation* (September/October): 15–18.

Derthick, Martha (1975) *Uncontrollable Spending for Social Services*. Washington, DC: Brookings Institution.

Dommel, Paul R. (1974) *The Politics of Revenue Sharing*. Bloomington: Indiana University Press.

Dommel, Paul R. and associates (1982) *Decentralizing Urban Policy: Case Studies in Community Development*. Washington, DC: Brookings Institution.

Elazar, Daniel J. (1972) *American Federalism: a View from the States*, 2nd edn. New York: Harper & Row.

Fossett, James W. (1983) *Federal Aid to Big Cities: the Politics of Dependence*. Washington, DC: Brookings Institution.

Juster, F. Thomas (ed.) (1977) *The Economic and Political Impact of General Revenue Sharing*. Ann Arbor: University of Michigan Press.

Kirlin, John J. (1982) *The Political Economy of Fiscal Limits*. Lexington, MA: D.C. Heath.

Kramer, Kevin (1985) 'Fifty Years of Federal Housing Policy: a Case Study of How the Federal Government distributes Resources'. PhD thesis, University of Michigan.

Larkey, Patrick D. (1979) *Evaluating Public Programs: the Impact of General Revenue Sharing on Municipal Government*. Princeton: Princeton University Press.

Liebert, Roland J. (1975) 'The Partial Eclipse of Community Government: The Trend Towards Functional Specialization', *Social Science Quarterly* 56: 210–24.   ˙

Nathan, Richard P. and Adams, Charles F. Jr. (1977) *Revenue Sharing: the Second Round*. Washington, DC: Brookings Institution.

Nathan, Richard P. and Doolittle, Fred C. (1983) *The Consequence of Cuts: the Effects of the Reagan Domestic Program on State and Local Governments*. Princeton: Princeton University Press.

Nathan, Richard P., Manvel, Allen D. and Calkins, Susannah E. (1975) *Monitoring Revenue Sharing*. Washington, DC: Brookings Institution.

Office of Management and Budget (OMB) (1985) *Special Analyses, Budget of the United States Government*. Washington, DC: US Government Printing Office.

OMB (1986) *Special Analyses, Budget of the United States Government*. Washington, DC: US Government Printing Office.

Oppenheim, John Edward (1983) 'Federal Response to Natural Disasters: a Spatial Political Analysis', PhD thesis, University of Michigan.

Rich, Michael (1985) 'Congress, the Bureaucracy and the Cities: Distributive Politics in the Allocation of Federal Grants-in-Aid for Community and Economic Development'. PhD thesis, Northwestern University.

Sears, David O. and Citrin, Jack (1982) *Tax Revolt: Something for Nothing in California*. Cambridge, MA: Harvard University Press.

Stein, Robert M. (1981) 'The Allocation of Federal Aid Monies: the Synthesis of Demand-side and Supply-side Explanations', *American Political Science Review* 75: 334–43.

Stein (1984) 'Growth and Change in the US Federal Aid System', paper presented at the Southern Political Science Meeting, Savannah, Georgia, November.

Stenberg, Carl W. (1980) 'Federalism in Transition: 1959–1979', *Conference on the Future of Federalism: Reports and Papers*. Washington, DC: US Advisory Commission on Intergovernmental Relations.

Stockman, David A. (1986) *The Triumph of Politics: How the Reagan Revolution Failed*. New York: Harper & Row.

US Congress (1972) Hearings of the House Subcommittee of the Committee on Appropriations, Washington, DC.

US Treasury Department, Office of State and Local Finance (1985) *Federal–State–Local Fiscal Relations: Report to the President and Congress*. Washington, DC: US Government Printing Office.

Yin, Robert K. (1980) 'Creeping Federalism: the Federal Impact on the Structure and Function of Local Government', in Norman J. Glickman (ed.), *The Urban Impacts of Federal Policies*. Baltimore: Johns Hopkins University Press.

8

Local Government Reform and Legitimacy

Bruno Dente

This chapter attempts to give an interpretation of local government reform processes as responses to the need for legitimacy of contemporary states. To this purpose I will (1) present a typology of different forms of legitimate power, derived from the Weberian tradition; (2) describe the character of public administration and local government within each type; (3) isolate the main trends in local government reform; and (4) refer these trends to the shifts in the forms of legitimacy.

A preliminary remark is necessary. Although this approach refers to local government reform, it should be equally valid for other instances of institutional change. The fact that local governments are reformed more often than central administrations can be seen as a further indication that the main rationale for restructuring local government has to do with the problem of political power. To alter the existing arrangements of local governance seems easier than to change national political institutions (e.g. the relations between parliament and government, or the electoral law). On the other hand, a local government reform is a politically more sensitive matter than the mere restructuring of bureaucratic structures (Brand, 1976).

The Weberian legacy: the legal–rational model

Obviously, one has to start from the Weberian typology of legitimate power (Weber, 1922). As is well known, in *Economy and Society*, Weber defined political power as legitimate when there was a general belief about the need for obeying its orders. It is important for our purpose that the Weberian notion is not normative: a power is legitimate when empirically there is a widespread belief — i.e. a psychological attitude — among citizens that it is. (This is why Weber's concept of legitimacy is called empirical/psychological.) Furthermore, Weber argued that the existence of a stable political power was virtually impossible without a successful claim to legitimacy. Accordingly, I shall use the terms 'legitimacy', 'legitimate power' or simply 'power' in this chapter in an undifferentiated way. The existence of a reasonably stable political system implies a widespread conviction among its citizens of the need to obey its orders.

Of Weber's three 'pure' models of legitimate power — the traditional, the charismatic and the legal–rational authority — one can quickly dismiss for the purpose of this chapter the relevance of the first two — not because they are irrelevant, or because their importance is fading away, but rather because they do not imply a specific form of routinization of power, i.e. a single specific bureaucratic structure. The basis for the legitimacy in traditional authority is the fact that the power situation has 'always' existed. The administrative rules therefore are partly regarded as untouchable and partly seen as results of the will of the political leader: in neither case is there a possibility of considering administrative reforms. In the case of charismatic authority, legitimacy depends upon the personal qualities of the political leader, who is therefore free to organize the public affairs at will. Here too, it is impossible to deduct the essential characters of a 'charismatic administration'.

Therefore only the 'most perfect' form of domination, in Weber's own terms — the legal–rational legitimacy, requiring a bureaucratic administration — serves the purpose of this chapter.

I will not summarize here the Weberian theory of bureaucracy, but will only recall, albeit very briefly, its main aspects: the basic role played by the law (general and abstract norms); the principle of office competence; the organizational principle of hierarchy (that the competence of the superior includes the competence of lower levels); the very existence of a bureaucracy (i.e. a body of permanent employees, recruited on the basis of their abilities in order to carry out professionally specific tasks, within a given competence and a given hierarchical chain).

In order to get a full picture, one has to bear in mind that legal–rational authority and the organizational arrangements work within a more general system-frame in which the state, first, must restrain itself in order to allow for the maximum individual freedom; second, has to guarantee the (formal) equality of all citizens; and finally, achieves these two goals solely through regulatory policies (in Lowi's terms, the policies where the likelihood of coercion is high and it is applied to the individuals: Lowi, 1972).

The entire legal–rational scheme is, in Weber's own mind, closely linked with the liberal state, with the idea of laissez-faire and the doctrine of *Rechtstaat*, where the regulation through general and abstract norms is aimed at guaranteeing maximum possible freedom and equality to a bourgeois class, worried about undue interference in the free market. This rough picture can be regarded as a description of the essential characteristics of the nineteenth-century European continental states.

There would be many points to add in order to provide a full account of the legal–rational model, but for our purposes it is more important to ask what consequences this kind of legitimacy has for the local government system.

Municipalities and other levels of administration pre-existed the bourgeois revolution and often successfully resisted the Jacobinian attempts to abolish all the *corps intermédiaires* between the individual citizen and the state. One might even argue that the main rationale for maintaining a politically responsible local government system was the lack of the organizational and communication technology necessary to establish a sufficient number of field agencies for the enforcement of national regulatory policies. The survival of the 'old' structures can be seen as a necessity more than a choice.

In fact, since the most conspicuous feature of the legal–rational administration is its centralization, one cannot expect local governments to have a significant degree of autonomy in this context. However, centralization is not without purpose: it is aimed at securing a uniform and impartial interpretation of the law, a necessary condition for an equal treatment of citizens. If a way could be found of reaching the same result, there could well be room for a politically responsible local government system. Such a way was found in the doctrine and practice of the *tutelle*, i.e. the idea that measures taken by the local governments have to be supervised by a field office of the central administration, to be enforced only after their approval.

This kind of relationship between the municipalities and the state, historically embodied in the French and Italian prefectoral control, has some important characteristics (Dente 1985a). First, it takes place measure by measure; it is the single administrative decision that can restrict the citizens' freedom, and therefore it is at this level that a guarantee is needed. Second, it is more often concerned with the decision-making process than with the content of the decision. When the administration's powers are restricted concerning the substance of the action, the possible courses of action being strictly typified, the legality of individual measures is endangered more by the procedural arrangements. Third, although this supervision can be done both on legal and on political grounds (i.e. controlling the legality of the decision or its merit), in fact, legal control is by far the most important and frequent, because it is more closely linked with the overall rationale of the system (providing a uniform and impartial enforcement of the centrally decided regulatory policies).

The result is that, under a pure legal–rational rule, local agencies, albeit elected on political grounds, are, in the case of the regulatory policies, little more than field agencies of the central administration, with the prefectoral supervision taking the place of the hierarchy characteristic of state organization.

However, this picture would be misleading if we forget another important aspect. Since in the liberal state the franchise at all governmental levels was restricted to the upper classes, and in particular to the property-owners, the space for the local government system and local functions could easily be regarded as a mere extension of the principles of laissez-faire, i.e. the idea that the individual citizen–owner is free to do whatever he wishes with his money and/or land. The rationale for a local government system then becomes a sort of joint-ownership: the municipalities are free to perform those policies that do not restrict the freedom of their citizens, provided that the local community can fully pay for them. All sorts of distributive policies, and in particular the development of public services, are therefore possible. Local agencies act in a 'separate' capacity in front of the central administration. Moreover, the general provision that the main source of local revenue is property tax reinforces the claim for local autonomy. Obviously, the legal control, or prefectoral *tutelle*, affects these distributive policies in a very different way, with the degree of freedom enjoyed by the local authority being much greater than in regulatory policies. The American tradition of self-government, emphasized by Tocqueville, is a case in point; but the relatively strong development of 'municipal socialism' at the beginning of the twentieth century in Italy provides a further example of this often underestimated aspect of the liberal tradition.

Post-Weberian legitimacy: clientelistic power

The Weberian typology, however, does not exhaust the possible forms of legitimate power. I will argue that there are two other possibilities, namely, clientelistic power and functional power.

Both are instrumental. This means that the consensus or mass loyalty of citizens is a reflection of the fact that they have an advantage in being loyal. One could argue that the same is true in the legal–rational legitimacy: the bourgeois class has an interest in having a very carefully regulated political power, on the assumption that only the freedom of individuals, notably economic freedom, is able to provide the maximum well-being for the national community. In all cases, legitimation of power has to be investigated within a utilitaristic framework, even if we cannot dismiss lightly the importance of ideology.

A clientelistic system can be defined as a situation in which the legitimacy of a power structure lies upon its ability to exchange specific measures in favour of individuals with the political support of the recipients (Graziano, 1976). Under a clientelistic rule, particular segments of the political system have special relations with particular groups of the population. The latter will assure their consensus to the extent to which the former are able to satisfy their particularistic needs and demands. It is important to bear in mind that this exchange takes place between the political structure (boss/faction/party) and the population (individuals/groups). The process is highly competitive and conflictual at both ends of the relationship.

The consequences for the administrative structure are:

1. a large amount of fragmentation, in order to secure the largest possible number of political factions to be represented at the administrative level;
2. a high degree of politicization (i.e. a pervasive presence of politicians in the administrative machinery and decision-making), in order to secure the factional grip over the administration;
3. a partisan bureaucracy, both because access to it is an important trade-off for the clientelistic exchange and because it enables the political leaders to count on the readiness of the officials to follow the political orders;
4. a large amount of discretion, in order to allow for all possible courses of action according to the changing political needs;
5. a low level of efficiency and effectiveness, because virtually every output must be negotiated on a case-by-case basis.

In such a situation, the importance of a local government system is quite evident. First, local organs are elected and therefore politicized. Second, they are numerous, thus allowing for many possible overlaps, duplications and superimpositions.

The relationship between centre and periphery will be confused and scattered, because the different responsibilities will not be allocated straightforwardly. Furthermore, because the fragmentation is present at the central as well as the local level, the relationship will certainly not be zero-sum. After all, both levels of the political system will have their own legitimation needs and will be interested in trade-offs with the same population group on separate basis.

As far as the policy type is concerned, one can argue that all kinds of distributive policies will be appropriate. This does not mean that in a clientelistic situation only distributive policies will be performed, but rather that every policy (even a regulatory or a redistributive one) will be performed 'as if' there were a distributive policy, i.e. with an eye to its economic substance. The reverse is obviously true in a legal–rational situation, where distributive or redistributive policies are implemented 'as if' they were regulatory policies. (For the distinction see Lowi, 1972.)

A 'pure form' of clientelistic power is unlikely to shape the actual structure of governance in any country. This is true not only because of the ideal character of the type sketched above, but for an additional reason. A peculiarity of clientelistic domination, unlike the legal–rational and the functional ones, is the fact that it is often presented as an exception, if not a pathology, within a system supposed to work on a different and more 'respectable' basis. However, it is well known that within Western democracies clientelistic behaviour is quite frequent. Pertinent examples are the US machine politics and spoils system, the importance of French 'notables' (Grémion, 1976) and the clientelistic electoral market in Italy (Graziano, 1973; Belloni et al., 1979).

Post-Weberian legitimacy: functional power

We shall define a power situation as one dominated by the functional legitimacy when the mass loyalty of the population towards the political/administrative system is a consequence of its ability to satisfy the demands and the needs of the population. In this case the state, as a whole, is held responsible for the well-being of the entire population. Put in different terms, the legitimate power of the political system is the reflection of the success of public programmes in meeting the expectations of their clients (Ronge, 1974).

The difference between functional power and legal–rational legitimacy is apparent. In a liberal society, the state is not responsible for the well-being of the population, but only for the respect of the individual freedom and equality.

The difference between functional power and clientelistic power is also clear, particularly on two counts. First, in the case of the clientelistic power, the main relation takes place between the citizens and the political parties or party factions, while in the case of functional legitimacy what matters is the degree of the citizens' satisfaction with the policies carried out by the administrative structure. Furthermore, in the clientelistic case the demands of the citizens are particularistic, while they tend to be universalistic and collective in the functional case.

Functional legitimacy is often associated with the welfare state. Its consequences on the administrative machinery are easy to identify: strong professionalism, and therefore strong sectorization; emphasis on 'rational' decision-making and planning; and popular participation at the administrative level, as a way of understanding the needs, collecting the demands and providing feedback to policy-makers and implementors. The dominant value is effectiveness, defined as the optimal relationship between needs and policy outcomes. Consequently, the rationale for a 'functional' local government is to be found in its ability to improve the institutional performance of the system, mainly in the provision and delivery of public services, the typical welfare state policies (Castells, 1976).

There are several possible facets to this statement. First, one might argue that the pre-existence of a local government system could provide a useful and inexpensive organizational framework for the implementation of public policies; this might be true, but it is certainly not the most important aspect. Second, since effectiveness is defined as the best way of meeting citizens' demands, implementing policies at the local level makes it easier to adjust them for local differences. Third, territorial representation increases the legitimation value of policy success and splits the responsibility for the failures between local and central actors.

Unlike clientelistic legitimacy, functional legitimacy calls for a well defined and 'rational' system of central–local relations. A system based on the need for meeting the demands for services dramatically increases the scope of local policies. The importance of municipalities increases greatly in the welfare state, since many social services are delivered at this level. There are of course important variations between the Western societies, but there is little doubt that local agencies in the 1970s generally were much more involved in such policies than previously.

However, to the extent that local services have consequences for the legitimacy of the system as a whole, the need for central control also increases. We have seen such a need in the legal–rational case in connection with regulatory policies, but in the welfare state this aspect is much more important. Sooner or later, central departments will activate some form of policy control; i.e., they will involve themselves in all stages of the policy process, on the assumption that an effective policy requires a better co-ordination, a larger constituency, and a faster rate of change in order to meet the needs of a changing population. Certainly, the rationale for a local delivery will remain, but more complex forms of central–local relations (e.g. various forms of policy planning) will be put in operation in order to secure a necessary link for improving effectiveness.

There are other factors explaining central intervention:

— The ideology of equality in substantive terms, all policies requiring positive discrimination and/or the establishment of minimum standards of service, are examples of this central responsibility for securing equal opportunities for all the social groups. This equalization ideal entails a central financial involvement in local policies so as to secure a minimum level of services, even in the poorest communities.

— The growing importance of local policies, as well as the impact of central grants, has another important consequence. Since the control of public expenditure is generally accepted as a central responsibility, the concern of the national government with the 'correct' sharing of resources, mainly in a period of inflation, reinforces a trend towards greater central involvement in local affairs.

Local government reforms and legitimacy

The preceding paragraphs have summarized the first two steps of the analysis in presenting a typology of legitimate power and describing the characters of public administration and local government within each model. The following section will present the main argument of the chapter, identifying the major trends in local government reform and referring them to the changing legitimacy needs of contemporary states. In doing so, I shall draw extensively from the current literature on the different national systems, even beyond the references provided at the end of the chapter.

The reform processes will be divided into four different types:

1. reforms affecting the number of local units;
2. organizational reforms;
3. financial reforms;
4. functional and procedural reforms.

Reforms affecting the number of local units

The first type of local reforms that took place since the 1950s in many European countries affected the number of local governments, i.e. modified the size of municipalities and/or intermediate levels of government. The territorial reform in England, Federal Germany, Sweden and other countries reduced the number of municipalities through amalgamation. The main justification for such a course of action was the functional ideology, the assumption that the efficient and effective provision of local services required larger constituencies and bigger administrative departments in order to avoid spillovers and profit from scale economies.

This reform trend is therefore closely linked to the importance of functional legitimacy, the rationale being an increase in responsiveness, a desire to improve the performance of the system as a whole and, at the same time, an attempt to enlarge central control. (A few big units are more 'visible', and therefore more controllable, than many micro-communities.) Obviously, functional legitimacy was already dominant in these situations, in order to set in motion the reform process and to overcome the resistance of the more traditional forces of parochialism and patronage. It has been argued, to the contrary, that the impossibility of reducing the number of communes in France and Italy can be explained on the basis of the strength of *notables* and party clientelism, which accounted for the strong opposition to the abolishment of such a large number of elective positions (Ashford, 1982; Rotelli, 1981).

However, territorial reform is by no means the only reform affecting the number of units. The creation of intermediate tiers of government, often in the form of regionalization, is another. This has occurred in France, Italy, Belgium and Spain, among others, and has been explained officially by the need to provide new and adequate machinery for planning and for co-ordinating locally implemented policies. Here, too, there is seemingly an idea coherent with the functional legitimacy. The reality may be more ambiguous: municipal consolidation had the effect of reducing the number of elected local officials, while regionalization created new elected councils with ample room for party representation and electoral bargaining.

One could suggest that the creation of regions or different forms of intermediate-level administration had the effect of strengthening the clientelistic ties between the population and the party system. The fact that, for instance, in France the regional councils were and are dominated by the same *notables* that are present at the national as well as the local and departmental level, through the practice of the *cumul des mandats*, is a further clue in this direction (Wright, 1979). Another indication is the political suicide of de Gaulle in attempting to jeopardize the power of the *notables* with a different regional system (Hayward, 1969). And in Italy, the very creation of the regions in 1970 has been successfully explained strictly in party-political terms (Rotelli, 1974), as a way of reinforcing the traditional politicization of Italian local government (Tarrow, 1977).

The same is true in connection with the third possible reform trend affecting the number of local units: the proliferation of different local agencies, often at the lower level (service delivery level), sometimes with a general competence (e.g. neighbourhood councils), but generally with specific tasks (special districts), and very often with a participatory purpose, most of which are indirectly elected, but some of which are appointed or directly elected. It is possible to identify some such administrative or quasi-administrative units, most of which were established during the 1960s and 1970s, in most countries. (For the neighbourhood councils, see Kjellberg, 1979, and Magnusson, 1979.) They have the same ambiguity as the regions, having been established with the intention of improving service responsiveness and effectiveness and at the same time enlarging the space for political intermediation and therefore clientelism. In Italy, behind the mushrooming of special districts during the 1970s, there were the two conflicting ideologies of functional and clientelistic power, both interested in breaking the uniformity of the previous legal–rational orthodoxy (Dente, 1985a). After the creation of these agencies, however, the two conflicting rationales, and the actors sharing them, entered a struggle from which there emerged a winner and a loser. As far as Italy is concerned, I would say that, all in all, the clientelistic legitimacy gained advantage over the functional one, even if in few instances the reverse was true (Dente and Regonini, 1980).

Summing up, the different national cases can be roughly divided into two groups: the first where the number of local units is today smaller than twenty years ago, and a second where the opposite is true. In the former case one can hypothesize a strengthening of functional legitimacy; in the latter, a reinforcement of the clientelistic one.

Organizational reforms

Another important aspect of the reform processes affecting local government is the internal structure of the local unit. This might include the major internal bodies (the role of the mayor, the executive board or the council), the decision-making process (the legal requirements for a valid decision, the role of public participation, the need for a 'rational' planning process), or the organizational structure (legal rules about the personnel, and/or organizational principles to be followed). In most European states there has been some sort of central intervention in such cases, even if it may be difficult to indicate a clear trend.

The shift towards functional legitimacy might explain some important aspects of this type of reform. The introduction of corporate planning in Britain, clearly supported by central departments, is but one example. In other countries, such as Italy, interventions in the personnel field were officially aimed at improving the efficiency of local administrations. And the emphasis on public participation, in order to enhance the responsiveness of local governments, points in the same direction. However, the latter example, as well as all the attempts to strengthen the role of political intervention in the decision-making process, can also be viewed as a way of reinforcing the grip of the political system over society as a whole, thus making clientelism possible.

In Italy there have been several examples of such reforms with apparently a functional and modernizing rationale. Their support by some sectors of the party system can be explained very well by the need to reinstate party control over a changing society, which is trying to find autonomous channels for its demands (Rotelli, 1981). And in any case, a widening space for clientelism can be easily discerned among the outcomes of such reforms — as in the case of neighbourhood councils (Dente and Regonini, 1980). In the same way, the generalization of the mayoral role to the *departements* and the *regions* in France has been regarded as reinforcing the power of the political leaders and the grip of clientelistic links (Thoenig, 1982).

Finally, although many examples of internal structure reforms were in fact aimed at softening the rigid uniformity characteristic of the liberal legacy, one cannot rule out the possibility that some changes, mainly in the decision-making process, are a reaction against an illegal use of administrative powers (corruption practices, for example) in order to re-establish the rule of law. For instance, the most recent anti-Mafia legislation in Italy has established very rigid guidelines for local government contracts, emphasizing the priority of legality even before efficiency and effectiveness. A rationality aimed towards a legal–rational administration can therefore clearly be discerned. However, the most striking case of a reform process of the organizational aspects of local agencies, aimed to break clientelism in favour of a functional legitimacy, is the Efficiency and Economy Reform movement in the USA. The rise of the city manager might easily be interpreted in these terms (Ostrom et al., 1984).

Financial reforms

A most important chapter in the history of recent local government reform in Western countries concerns finance. This aspect has been widely investigated, even on a comparative basis, and it is often regarded as the most important feature of the reform process (Ashford and Thoenig, 1981; Newton, 1980; Sharpe, 1981). These studies, however, have regarded financial reforms as an example of modifications of the central–local relationship, and not as a response to the need for new legitimacy.

In many countries, the main effect of the financial reforms was an increase of the central role in providing resources for local authorities (Dente, 1985b). The justifications for this course of action were several, ranging from the alleged central responsibility for the level of public expenditures to the need to equalize the level of services in localities, all clearly coherent with functional legitimacy. In other cases — like Britain — the most recent reforms have resulted in a weakening of the central role, with local services being increasingly financed through local taxation and a recourse to fees and charges (Karran, 1986).

This might be seen as a consequence of the same type of legitimacy, arising from the central will to reduce public spending as a whole. Furthermore, a national policy opposed to the present level of welfare will only need to withdraw the financial support, on the assumption that local authorities simply will not be able to run some services only with the revenue of local taxes. But the same situation can be explained, under other circumstances, in a different way. It might very well be that the main rationale for the fading away of central financial intervention is an attempt to re-establish some kind of market mechanism in the provision of public services, in order to ascertain the preferences of the clients. In this case, we would probably be in a classical legal–rational situation, with the municipality or local agency acting as a representative of the citizens/taxpayers, and totally separated from the central government. I suspect that in some countries this type of reform, clearly inspired by the so-called 'public choice' school, is actually taking place.

A third alternative to the increase or decrease of central intervention in local finance is the modification of the mechanisms through which central money is channelled to local authorities. A possible example is the process of block-grantization in USA, where it seems that the system is retreating from a clear-cut functional ideology towards a relative indifference on the part of central government about the way in which the money is actually spent.

It seems, therefore, that there is an attempt to reintroduce the separate capacity in service provision by local authorities, somewhat typical of the liberal state. On the other hand, the fact that the new block grants are distributed through the state legislatures, instead of being given directly to local authorities, introduces a further level of political intermediation, which can be seen as a step in the clientelistic direction (Kelley, 1984). Other examples of block grants, consolidating the previous categorical grants, are subject to different interpretations; but in general, one might suspect that such experiments in some cases are inspired rather by an attempt of central government to wash its hands of the possible dissatisfaction of the citizens for the quality or the quantity of services, and not so much by an increasing respect for local autonomy. In other words, they can be seen as an attempt to move away from functional legitimacy.

Functional and procedural reforms
The last group of local reforms is somewhat heterogeneous, as it includes changes both in local government's functions and in the

procedural links between central government and local administration.

Starting with functional reforms, the first aspect to be emphasized is that most of them occur on a policy-by-policy basis. Quite specific local tasks may be nationalized, or particular decision-making processes decentralized to local elected bodies. From time to time, however, a major reorganization occurs, in the sense that the overall distribution of tasks is reshuffled in accordance with some sort of doctrine. A paradigmatic example is the English reorganization of the 1970s, where there was an attempt to reconcile the need to keep service provision as close as possible to the client with the efficiency argument allegedly calling for larger constituencies. Both principles clearly referred to an overall functional legitimacy. In other cases it may be more difficult to discern the connection between functional legitimacy and redistribution of tasks. In general, however, one might safely suspect that this is often the case.

But there are exceptions. For instance, in Italy the implicit rationale for decentralizing national functions — mainly distributive policies — has been the enlargement of political intermediation, a condition clearly connected with the development, or at least the survival, of clientelism. On the other hand, behind many attempts to nationalize regulatory policies, or to put severe constraints on local discretion — such as land use planning in Italy — there was a wish to achieve greater uniformity and impartiality, thereby strengthening the legal–rational legitimacy of the system as a whole.

The allocation of tasks is also influenced by the procedural links between central and local administration. Two major trends can here be discerned. The first is the abolishment of prefectoral control in France and Italy. Generally speaking, this must be regarded as a move away from the liberal administrative tradition, and therefore away from legal–rational legitimacy. However, in order to understand the real sense of the trend, one has also to consider the substitutes to prefectoral control. Thus, in Italy, the creation of a political body in charge of the control activity is usually regarded as one of the most effective instruments for political control, and one of the most clearly clientelism-oriented changes (Vandelli, 1984). Still, the parallel rise of the administrative tribunals both in France and Italy shows that the legal–rational legitimacy is profoundly embedded into the system, and cannot easily be done away with.

More clearly in line with functional legitimacy is the second trend: the introduction of policy planning systems in order to strengthen central control over the efficiency and effectiveness of local services delivery. Normally these procedures work on a sectoral basis, but this too can be an improvement compared with the traditional link on a programme-by-programme basis.

Concluding remarks

The first part of this chapter has attempted to use a Weberian framework — the concept of legitimate power, and the empirical–psychological notion of legitimacy — in order to sketch some ideal types of local government. In the second part I have tried to refer some of the major changes in local government to the different forms of legitimacy. In doing so, the limits of the framework for empirical purposes became apparent, as is always the case with ideal types. Many reforms are ambiguous in both their objectives and their effects, and can easily be distorted in various ways according to the different actors and their relative power position.

However, the exercise has not been totally useless. First, it has shown that behind many reforms there might be much more than technical rationalizations or simple adjustments to changing needs. Some of the proposed or actual changes were quite extensive, in so far as they tried to alter the very foundations of the political system, i.e. its legitimacy. As pointed out by Weber, the quest for legitimacy is a permanent feature of the political system. This might be more prominent in some historical periods because of their open conflicts or anomic tendencies, but in fact, legitimacy represents the real basis for the existence of the state.

This recognition implies the need to evaluate the importance of local reforms also outside the local arena. If every institutional change can be regarded as an alteration of the 'rules of the game', of the 'structure' of political power, it follows that the fact of taking place at the centre or the periphery of the administrative system is quite unimportant. From this point of view, some local reforms have represented — more or less consciously — a sort of bottom-up approach to constitutional change, at least in their overall aims. The Italian regionalization, and the high expectations of its achievements, is clearly an instance of a sub-national reform whose importance should be evaluated in a broader perspective than simply measuring the performance of the new elected bodies (even if this is a necessary step towards a better understanding: see Putnam et al., 1985). And the same goes for the much discussed English reorganization (Goldsmith, 1986), and the Mitterrand decentralization in France (Mény, 1983).

Most of the reforms referred to in the previous section pointed towards a growing importance of the functional legitimacy. This is hardly surprising, given the rise of the welfare state after the Second

World War and the central role in service delivery played by local authorities. One could go further and say that the ideology of local reform during the 1960s and the 1970s was in fact a welfare-oriented set of values, an embodiment of the basic principles of functional legitimacy.

However, the ideologues of the 1970s often underestimated the weight of the tradition, and notably the importance of the local political systems, with their clientelistic practices and their personal links between the politicians and the electorate. The French *notables*, the US 'machine' and the Italian *clientele* not only have often successfully resisted many attempts to institutional reform, but also have been able to turn some proposals in their favour. The increase in political intermediation brought about by some reforms can be better evaluated in this perspective. And one might also predict that the end of welfare expansion — experienced in virtually all Western societies — will give to the clientelistic legitimacy a greater impact — even without a greater appeal — than in the recent past.

Following this line of argument, the most puzzling question is whether the neo-liberal mood prevailing and fashionable in some countries will give rise to a reform movement aimed at restoring the vestiges of liberal local government. There is little evidence of this being the case, even if some attempt to restore the liberal 'separate capacity' can probably be discerned. On the other hand, the simple fact that the reform movement today is less active than in the past, and that some revisionist approach is gaining weight, suggests that such a possibility cannot be completely dismissed.

References

Ashford, Douglas E. (1982) *British Dogmatism and French Pragmatism*. London: George Allen & Unwin.

Ashford, Douglas E. and Thoenig, Jean-Claude (1981) *Les Aides financières de l'Etat aux collectivités locales en France et à l'etranger*. Paris: LITEC.

Belloni, Frank, Caciagli, Mario and Mattina, Liborio (1979) 'The Mass Clientelism Party: the Christian Democratic Party in Catania and in Southern Italy', *European Journal of Political Research* 7: 253–75.

Brand, Jack (1976) 'Reforming Local Government', in R. Rose (ed.), *The Dynamics of Public Policy*. London/Beverly Hills: Sage.

Castells, Manuel (1976) 'La Crise urbaine aux Etats Unis: vers la barbarie?' *Les Temps Modernes* 3: 1177–240.

Dente, Bruno (1985a) 'Centre–local Relations in Italy: the Impact of the Legal and Political Structures', in Y. Mény and V. Wright (eds), *Centre–periphery Relations in Western Europe*. London: George Allen & Unwin.

Dente, Bruno (1985b) 'Intergovernmental Relations as Central Control Policies: the Case of Italian Local Finance', *Environmental and Planning C: Government and Policy* 3: 383–402.

Dente, Bruno and Regonini, Gloria (1980) 'Urban Policy and Political Legitimation: the Case of Italian Neighbourhood Councils', *International Political Science Review* 1: 187–202.

Goldsmith, Michael (ed.) (1986) 'Essays on the Future of Local Government', mimeo.

Graziano, Luigi (1973) 'Patron–client Relationships in Southern Italy', *European Journal of Political Research* 1: 3–34.

Graziano, Luigi (1976) 'A Conceptual Framework for the Study of Clientelistic Behaviour', *European Journal of Political Research* 4: 149–74.

Grémion, Pierre (1976) *Le Pouvoir péripherique*. Paris: Editions du Seuil.

Hayward, Jack (1969) 'Presidential Suicide by Plebiscite: de Gaulle's Exit', *Parliamentary Affairs* 22: 289–319.

Karran, Terence (1986) 'Financing the System', in M. Goldsmith (ed.), 'Essays on the Future of Local Government', mimeo.

Kelley, Estel W. (1984) 'L'introduzione dei block grants negli Stati Uniti', in ISAP, *Le Relazioni centro–periferia*, pp. 2567–94. Milan: Giuffrè.

Kjellberg, Francesco (1979) 'A Comparative View of Municipal Decentralization: Neighbourhood Democracy in Oslo and Bologna', pp. 81–118, in L.J. Sharpe (ed.), *Decentralist Trends in Western Democracies*. London/Beverly Hills: Sage.

Lowi, Theodore J. (1972) 'Four Systems of Policy, Politics and Choice', *Public Administration Review* 32: 298–310.

Magnusson, Warren (1979) 'The New Neighbourhood Democracy: Anglo-American Experience in Historical Perspective', in L.J. Sharpe (ed.), *Decentralist Trends in Western Democracies*, pp. 119–56. London/Beverly Hills: Sage.

Mény, Yves (1983) 'Permanence and Change: the Relations between Central Government and Local Authorities in France', *Environment and Planning C: Government and Policy* 1: 17–28.

Newton, Kenneth (1980) *Balancing the Books*. London/Beverly Hills: Sage.

Ostrom, Vincent, Bish, Robert and Ostrom, Elinor (1984) *Il governo locale negli Stati Uniti*. Milan: Edizioni di Comunità.

Putnam, Robert D., Leonardi, Robert and Nanetti, Raffaella Y. (1985) *La pianta e le radici*. Bologna: Il Mulino.

Ronge, Volker (1974) 'The Politicization of Administration in Advanced Capitalist Societies', *Political Studies* 22: 86–93.

Rotelli, Ettore (ed.) (1974) *Regioni, forze politiche, forze sociali*. Rome: Officina.

Rotelli, Ettore (1981) *La non riforma: le autonomie nell'età dei partiti*. Rome: Edizioni Lavoro.

Sharpe, Laurence J. (ed.) (1981) *The Local Fiscal Crisis in Western Europe: Myths and Realities*. London/Beverly Hills: Sage.

Tarrow, Sidney (1977) *Between Center and Periphery: Grassroot Politicians in Italy and France*. New Haven, CT: Yale University Press.

Thoenig, Jean-Claude (1982) 'Les Politiques de réforme des collectivités locales en France', in J. Lagroye and V. Wright (eds), *Les Structures locales en Grande Bretagne et en France*, pp. 83–108. Paris: La Documentation Française.

Vandelli, Luciano (1984) 'Il controllo sugli enti locali dopo le Regioni: la Lombardia', in ISAP, *Le relazioni centro–periferia*, pp. 547–611. Milan: Giuffrè.

Weber, Max (1922) *Wirtschaft und Gesellschaft*. Tübingen: Mohr.

Wright, Vincent (1979) 'Regionalization under the French Fifth Republic: the Triumph of the Functional Approach', in L.J. Sharpe (ed.), *Decentralist Trends in Western Democracies*, pp. 193–234. London/Beverly Hills: Sage.

Index

access to services 122–4
Aid for Dependent Children (ADC) (USA) 25, 30
Aid to Families with Dependent Children (AFDC) (USA) 158
amalgamation reforms 48–51, 57, 59–60; *see also* boundary reforms
Anton, Thomas J. 156, 160
Ashford, D.E. 2, 8
Association of Finnish Cities 79
Austria 93
autonomous model of local authorities 40–1
autonomy of local government 152–3

Belgium 96
belief systems 150–1
Bentzon, K.H. 56
Bevan, Aneurin 20
Beveridge, William 21
Beveridge Plan 26
Bismarck, Count Otto von 22
block grants 55, 167, 182
Board for Municipal Economy (Finland) 79
Bonnet, Minister 144
boundary reforms 48–51, 57, 59–60, 89–91, 107–17, 119–20, 122–4, 178–9; *see also* structural reforms
boundary relationships 71–2
Bourjol, M. 6
Brand, J. 5, 66
Britain 5–6, 7, 8, 12, 13, 20, 21–2, 23, 24, 25–7, 30–5, 41, 47, 89–125, 180, 181
  and public choice theory 120–2
  functional capacity in 115–17
  obsession with large scale in 111–15
  population mobility in 117–20
  SDI density in 122–4
  sociogeographic factors in 103–5
  special character of 101–3

structural reforms in 101; *see also* boundary reforms
British Association of Social Workers 30
'bumping' of local governments 153–4
bureaucracy 172
  local 29–35
Burns, John 20

Caisse Nationale des Allocations Familiales (CNAF) (France) 24–5
Castle, Barbara 33
central business district (CBD) 106
centralization 173
central–local relations 95–100, 175, 177
  in Finland 78–81
  in France 132–6, 145–7
  in Napoleonic v. non-Napoleonic states 95–100
  in Scandinavia 48–56
  in USA 159–63
  'innovatory' model of 135
  integrational model of 41–3, 48–56
  traditional model of 134–5
  changes, macro-level 73–8
  eras of 154–63
  intended/unintended consequences of 70–1
  model of 72
  sources of 163–7
  v. reforms 70–2
Child Poverty Action Group (CPAG) 24
citizen participation 151
classifications 9
clientelism 174–6, 180, 183
Cockburn, C. 7
'commune blocks' 52, 53
communes 60, 96, 97, 113, 114, 140–1
Communist Party (France) 28, 132
Community Development Block Grants (CDBG) (USA) 159, 166, 167
Community Development Programme (CDP) 26

Contributors

Douglas E. Ashford is Andrew W. Mellon Professor of Comparative Politics, University of Pittsburgh, Pittsburgh, Pennsylvania, USA

Thomas J. Anton is A.A. Taubman Professor of Public Policy and American Institutions, Brown University, Providence, Rhode Island, USA

Bruno Dente is Associate Professor of Public Administration, University of Bologna, Italy, and Vice-Chairman of the IPSA Research Committee on Local Government and Politics

Markku Kiviniemi is researcher and teacher, Department of Political Science, University of Helsinki, Finland, and Research Manager, Administrative Development Agency of State, Helsinki, Finland

Francesco Kjellberg is Professor of Political Science, University of Oslo, Norway, and former Chairman of the IPSA Research Committee on Local Government and Politics

Yves Mény is Professor of Political Science, University of Paris II, France

L.J. Sharpe is University Lecturer in Public Administration and Fellow of Nuffield College, Oxford, UK